THE BOOK

OF

COMMON WORSHIP

PUBLISHED BY AUTHORITY OF THE GENERAL
ASSEMBLY OF THE PRESBYTERIAN
CHURCH IN THE UNITED
STATES OF AMERICA

For Voluntary Use in the Churches

PHILADELPHIA
THE PRESBYTERIAN BOARD OF PUBLICATION
AND SABBATH-SCHOOL WORK
1906

PREFACE

AMONG those Churches of the Lord Jesus Christ which follow the Presbyterian rule and order, Liberty of Worship has been esteemed a most precious privilege and inheritance; and while they have been both fearless and faithful to uphold it, against the intrusion of superstitious and burdensome ceremonies, they have also been diligent to seek, in the Public Services of Religion, the golden mean between a too great laxity and a tyrannical uniformity. Such things as are of Divine Institution they have observed in every Ordinance; and other things they have endeavoured to set forth " according to the Rules of Christian Prudence, agreeable to the general Rules of the Word of God "

Although the Books of Common Order, which were prepared for the Reformed Churches, at the beginning, in all countries, contained both prayers and other forms, yet were those books not so much imposed by way of inflexible regulation, as they were offered and accepted as profitable Aids to Worship; and they not only permitted but encouraged the exercise of Free Prayer. In a like spirit the Directory for Worship, adopted at a later time by the Church of Scotland, for the sake of unity with their brethren in the Church of England, so far from establishing an invariable form of Public Worship, expressly provided for a liberty of variation; and it did not in any way prohibit the use of prepared orders and prayers, conformable to the general directions given therein.

The same wise and blessed liberty is maintained in the Presbyterian Church in the United States of America even to this day. Accordingly it seemed good to the General

Assembly of 1903, hearkening to the desire of many pastors and churches, to appoint a Committee of Ministers and Ruling Elders who should prepare, " in harmony with the Directory for Worship, a Book of Simple Forms and Services, proper and helpful for voluntary use in Presbyterian churches, in the celebration of the Sacraments, in Marriages and Funerals, and in the Conduct of Public Worship." This work has been continued, in faithful obedience, and in humble reliance on the Holy Spirit, through nearly three years of patient labour, and has been submitted, in its progress, to two successive Assemblies. The principles by which the work has been guided were approved, and its completion was ordered. This having been done, so far as God enabled us, in the Book herewith presented, its publication is now " Authorized by the General Assembly, for Voluntary Use in the Churches."

This Book of Common Worship is, therefore, not to be taken in any wise as a liturgy imposed by authority. Nor is it a substitute for the Directory for Worship, but rather a supplement to it, wherein the instructions of the Standards are followed on all essential points, and aid is offered, to those who desire it, for the conduct of the Public Services of Religion with reverence and propriety. We have studied earnestly to embody the truths of our Holy Religion in the language of orderly devotion, to the end that by the Sacraments, the stated Ordinances of the Lord's Day, and all the ordinary and occasional offices of the Church, men may be both instructed and confirmed in the faith of Jesus Christ. We have searched the Holy Scriptures, the usage of the Reformed Churches, and the devotional treasures of early Christianity, for the most noble, clear, and moving expressions of the Spirit of Praise and Prayer ; and we have added to these ancient and venerable forms and models, such others as might serve, under the guidance of the same Spirit, to give a voice to the present needs, the urgent desires, and the vital hopes of the Church living in these latter days and in the freedom of this Republic.

Concerning the manner in which the different Services are ordered and arranged, and the best way in which they may be used to edification, a few suggestions are offered in the pages immediately following this Preface ; and throughout the Book, the careful reader will find that the words of guidance which precede the various parts of the services are designed, not only to mark their spiritual significance, but also to enable all the People to join in the Acts of Worship, that all things may be done decently and in order. The longer and more important rubrics are transcribed from the Directory for Worship of this Church, which disapproves alike of "confining Ministers to set or fixed forms of prayer for public Worship," and of permitting that important service to be disgraced "by mean, irregular, or extravagant effusions." It is to be remembered, therefore, that the forms here offered are to be used only "if the Minister so please," as a help in Common Worship, and not without a constant care and diligence, by "acquaintance with the Holy Scriptures, by meditation, by reading the best writers on the subject, and by a life of communion with God in secret, to endeavour to acquire both the spirit and the gift of Prayer."

In the Treasury of Prayers many things have been gathered together which may be not only useful, from time to time, in the conduct of Public Services, but also profitable for reading and study, for use in private devotion, and in that revival of Family Worship which is greatly needed in all our Churches. It is hoped, therefore. that the whole Book, having been prepared with a sincere wish to advance saving knowledge and true piety, may be received, studied, and used, by earnest members of this Church and by faithful Christians elsewhere, in the spirit of candour, simplicity, and brotherly love; devoutly meditating

upon the real meaning of the Christian faith, and endeavouring to adorn the Gospel of God our Saviour in all things.
And to this end we pray that the Holy Spirit will accom-
pany and bless this Book with His ever-present Grace;
that wherever it is used the hearts of men may be truly
drawn and led to the Throne of the Divine Mercy; and
that all the people may find comfort, joy, and strength as
they unite in the Common Worship of God who is revealed
in Jesus Christ our adorable Redeemer.

THE ASSEMBLY'S COMMITTEE:

HENRY VAN DYKE, *Chairman.*

LOUIS F. BENSON,   NOLAN R. BEST,
JOHN DE WITT,   JOHN H. CONVERSE,
CHARLES CUTHBERT HALL,   HOMER LEE,
JOHN CLARK HILL,   JOHN E. PARSONS,
W. BEATTY JENNINGS,   ROBERT N. WILLSON,
JAMES D. MOFFAT,   *Ruling Elders.*
W. ROBSON NOTMAN,
WILLIAM R. RICHARDS,
JAMES H. SNOWDEN,
WILLIAM R. TAYLOR,
            Ministers.

CONCERNING THE USE OF THIS BOOK.

¶ *None of the Forms of Service in this Book are intended to be in any sense obligatory ; but where a given Order is voluntarily used it will promote unity and the general convenience if the parts are followed as here arranged.*

¶ *In order that all the People should take their part in the Public Worship of God, it is most earnestly recommended that, in those churches which choose to make use of the following Orders and Forms of Service, every member of the Congregation should be supplied with a copy of this Book ; and, also, that the directions which precede each part of the different services should be studied beforehand both by Minister and People, so that confusion or uncertainty in the conduct of Worship may be avoided.*

¶ *The playing of a voluntary on the organ while the Congregation are assembling, the singing of a Psalm instead of the responsive reading from the* Psalter, *or of an* Anthem *after the Scripture reading, and other like observances, are left to the choice and usage of each church. But it should always be remembered that the Organist and the Choir are members of the Congregation, and that their cooperation will be of the greatest help to the Minister in conducting all the parts of Worship.*

¶ *To attain the prompt and hearty participation of the People, it is necessary that they should know beforehand what is expected of them. Therefore, when any change is to be made in the order of a Service as given in the Book (as, for example, in the use of* The Commandments *at the Morning Service,* The Beatitudes *at the Evening Service, or in the time of making the* Offering *or of singing the last* Hymn), *the Minister should be careful that the Congregation are duly notified. It is also desirable, in places where it is con-venient, that the numbers of the Hymns and of the Selection from the Psalter be posted where they can be seen by the Congregation.*

¶ *In connection with the* General Prayer *in the Lord's Day Services it is recommended that the Minister make faith-ful preparation of his own heart and mind to lead the People in their* Adorations, Thanksgivings, Supplications, *and* Intercessions. *If he should make any use, in thus preparing himself, of those which are given in the* TREASURY OF PRAYERS, *this should be done with forethought and much care, in order not only to avoid injudicious length, but also that the prayer may be framed to express his own thought and feeling, and may also be suited to the occasion or the special need of the congregation.*

¶ *The use of this Book will be profitable only to those who are careful not to make it a means of formal or restricted worship, either public or private ; but who remember always their duty as Christians both to seek and to cherish the gift of Prayer, by which they shall be enabled to frame wise and earnest and reverent petitions, as well for others as for themselves. And in every service of the Church it is fitting that the Minister and every one of the People should pray in silence, at the beginning, for the guidance and help of the Holy Spirit, and at the close of the service, that all who have taken part in it may receive the blessing of God through Jesus Christ.*

TABLE OF CONTENTS.

THE ORDER OF

MORNING SERVICE

ON THE LORD'S DAY.

THE CALL TO WORSHIP.

¶ *Let the Minister and all the People stand up and sing the following, or some other Hymn or Psalm calling to Worship.*

Praise God, from whom all blessings flow ;
Praise Him, all creatures here below ;
Praise Him above, ye heavenly host :
Praise Father, Son, and Holy Ghost. Amen.

¶ *Let the Minister read one of the following* SENTENCES, *the People standing.*
¶ *If any church so desire the Service may begin with the* SENTENCES.

OUR help is in the Name of the Lord, who made heaven and earth. The Lord is nigh unto all them that call upon Him, to all that call upon Him in truth. He will fulfil the desire of them that fear Him: He also will hear their cry, and will save them. (*Psalm* cxxiv. 8: cxlv. 18, 19.)

O come, let us worship and bow down : let us kneel before the Lord our maker. Know ye that the Lord He is God : it is He that hath made us, and not we ourselves ; we are His people, and the sheep of His pasture. (*Psalm* xcv. 6: c. 3.)

Seek ye the Lord while He may be found, call ye upon Him while He is near : Let the wicked forsake his way, and the unrighteous man his thoughts : and let him return unto the Lord, and He will have mercy upon him ; and to our God, for He will abundantly pardon. (*Isaiah* lv. 6, 7.)

The Lord is merciful and gracious, slow to anger, and plenteous in mercy. He hath not dealt with us after our sins; nor rewarded us according to our iniquities. If we confess our sins, He is faithful and just to forgive us our sins, and to cleanse us from all unrighteousness. (*Psalm* ciii. 8, 10: 1 *St. John* i. 9.)

Seeing that we have a great High Priest, that is passed into the heavens, Jesus the Son of God: Let us therefore come boldly unto the throne of grace, that we may obtain mercy, and find grace to help in time of need. (*Hebrews* iv. 14, 16.)

¶ *Then shall the Minister say,*

Let us pray.

¶ *Let the People reverently bow down while the Minister leads them in the* INVOCATION, *using if he will one of the following Prayers:*

THE INVOCATION.

ALMIGHTY God, who of Thy great mercy hast gathered us into Thy visible Church; Grant that we may not swerve from the purity of Thy worship; but so honour Thee, both in spirit and in outward form, that Thy Name may be glorified in us, and we may be true members of Thine only-begotten Son, Jesus Christ our Lord. *Amen.*

ETERNAL God, our Maker and our Lord, Giver of all grace, from whom every good prayer cometh, and who pourest Thy Spirit upon all who seek Thee; Deliver us, when we draw nigh to Thee, from coldness of heart and wanderings of mind; that with steadfast thoughts and pure affections we may worship Thee in spirit and in truth; through Jesus Christ our Lord. *Amen.*

LORD God of heaven and earth, who hast made the Church Thy dwelling-place, and chosen it as Thy rest for ever, and hast taught us in Thy Word not to forsake the assembling of ourselves together; Regard us in Thy mercy, we beseech Thee, and send Thy Holy Spirit upon us; that our worship may prepare us both to serve

Thee now, and to glorify Thee hereafter in Thine eternal kingdom; through Jesus Christ our Lord. *Amen.*

O GOD, who hast promised that in all places where Thou dost record Thy Name, Thou wilt meet with Thy servants to bless them; Fulfil now Thy promise, and make us joyful in Thy house of prayer; that our worship, being offered in the Name of Thy Son and by the guidance of Thy Spirit, may be acceptable unto Thee, and profitable unto ourselves; through our only Mediator and Advocate, Jesus Christ our Lord. *Amen.*

ALMIGHTY Lord and everlasting God, whom the heaven of heavens cannot contain, much less the temples which our hands have builded, but who art ever nigh unto the humble and contrite; Shed down Thy Holy Spirit, we beseech Thee, on all here assembled; that, being cleansed and illumined by His grace, we may worthily show forth Thy praise, meekly learn Thy Word, render due thanks for Thy mercies, and obtain a gracious answer to our prayers; through the merits of Jesus Christ our Lord. *Amen.*

THE CONFESSION OF SINS.

¶ *The People may say this* CONFESSION *with the Minister*

MOST holy and merciful Father; We acknowledge and confess in Thy Presence: Our sinful nature prone to evil and slothful in good; And all our shortcomings and offenses against Thee. Thou alone knowest how often we have sinned: In wandering from Thy ways; In wasting Thy gifts; In forgetting Thy love. But Thou, O Lord, have pity upon us; Who are ashamed and sorry for all wherein we have displeased Thee. Teach us to hate our errors; Cleanse us from our secret faults; And forgive our sins; For the sake of Thy dear Son our Saviour. And O most holy and loving Father; Send Thy purifying grace into our hearts, we beseech Thee; That we may henceforth live in Thy light and walk in Thy ways; According to the commandments of Jesus Christ our Lord. *Amen*

THE ASSURANCE OF PARDON.

¶ To be said by the Minister, the People still bowing down.

ALMIGHTY God, who doth freely pardon all who re-pent and turn to Him; Now fulfil in every contrite heart the promise of redeeming grace; remitting all our sins, and cleansing us from an evil conscience; through the perfect sacrifice of Christ our Lord; And keep us ever-more in the peace and joy of a holy life; that we may love and serve Him always; In the Name of the Father, the Son, and the Holy Ghost. *Amen.*

¶ Or this:

GOD so loved the world, that He gave His only-begot-ten Son, that whosoever believeth in Him should not perish, but have everlasting life.

Hear the gracious words of our Lord Jesus Christ unto all that truly repent and turn to Him:

Come unto Me, all ye that labour and are heavy laden, and I will give you rest.

Him that cometh to Me I will in no wise cast out.

The grace of our Lord Jesus Christ be with you all. *Amen.*

¶ Then let the Minister and the People, standing, say,

Minister. Now bless the Lord our God:
Answer. *And praise His glorious Name.*
Minister. O give thanks unto the Lord, for He is good:
Answer. *For His mercy endureth for ever.*

THE PSALTER.

¶ Then let a portion of the PSALTER be chanted, or read respon-sively by the Minister and the People, all standing, and at the end may be said or sung,

Glory be to the Father, and to the Son . and to the Holy Ghost;

As it was in the beginning, is now, and ever shall be: world without end. Amen.

¶ The People being seated shall attend devoutly to

THE PUBLIC READING OF THE HOLY SCRIPTURES.

¶ Let the Minister read from the Word of God *as it is written in the* Old *and* New Testaments, *clearly and distinctly, that the People may understand the meaning. If a lesson from each Testament is read, as is most proper and profitable, that from the* Old Testament *may be followed, in places where there are choirs, by the singing of an* Anthem *or* Response.

¶ Before each reading let the Minister say, Hear the Holy Scrip ture as it is written in such a chapter of such a book : *and after the reading,* The Lord bless to us the reading of His Holy Word.

¶ If the Old Testament *reading be the* TEN COMMANDMENTS, *after them the Minister shall read St. Matthew xxii 37–40, saying before he reads,* Hear also the SUMMARY OF THE LAW by our Lord Jesus Christ.

A HYMN OF PRAISE.

¶ Here let the People stand up and praise God with the spirit and with the understanding, making melody with their voices as well as with their hearts, unto the Lord. And at the close of the Hymn let them remain standing and join with the Minister in their CONFESSION OF FAITH.

THE CREED.

I BELIEVE in God the Father Almighty, Maker of heaven and earth:

And in Jesus Christ His only Son, our Lord ; Who was conceived by the Holy Ghost, Born of the Virgin Mary, Suffered under Pontius Pilate, Was crucified, dead, and buried : [He descended into hell ; *] The third day He rose again from the dead , He ascended into heaven, And sitteth on the right hand of God the Father Almighty ; From thence He shall come to judge the quick and the dead.

I believe in the Holy Ghost ; The Holy Catholic Church ; The Communion of Saints ; The Forgiveness of sins ; The Resurrection of the body ; and the Life everlasting. Amen.

¶ Then shall the Minister say,

Let us pray.

---

* Or, *He continued in the state of the dead, and under the power of death, until the third day.*

¶ *And the People, reverently bowing down, shall follow in their hearts*

THE GENERAL PRAYER.

¶ *The Minister, leading the People in their Common Prayers, shall come with a heart prepared to offer unto God —*

ADORATIONS: *for His glorious perfection, and for the revelation of Himself in His works, in His Word, and in His Son, Jesus Christ*

THANKSGIVINGS: *for all mercies of every kind, general and particular, spiritual and temporal, common and special, above all, for Jesus Christ, His unspeakable gift, and the hope of eternal life through Him.*

SUPPLICATIONS: *for the supply of all our needs temporal and spiritual, and for the aid and comfort of the Holy Ghost in all our duties and trials ·*

INTERCESSIONS: *for the whole world of mankind ; remembering especially our country and all who are invested with civil authority; the Church Universal and that with which we are particularly connected ; all missionaries and ministers of the Gospel ; and all others who are seeking to do good on earth ; all poor and sick and sorrowful people, (especially those for whom our prayers are asked ;) all little children and the youth assembled in schools and colleges; those who are in the midst of great danger or temptation; and all who are bound to us by ties of kinship or affection:*

¶ *In any or all of these* Adorations, Thanksgivings, Supplications, *and* Intercessions, *the Minister, if he will, may use any of the* Prayers *given in this Book, under the title of* TREASURY OF PRAYERS. *Or he may carefully order his thoughts and compose his spirit to utter with propriety the desires and petitions of the People, remembering what is suitable and necessary for them in their Common Worship. At the end of the General Prayer the Minister and People shall say together the* LORD'S PRAYER.

THE LORD'S PRAYER.

OUR Father which art in heaven, Hallowed be Thy Name. Thy kingdom come   Thy will be done in earth, As it is in heaven.   Give us this day our daily bread.   And forgive us our debts, As we forgive our debtors.   And lead us not into temptation, But deliver us from evil : For Thine is the kingdom, and the power, and the glory, for ever.   Amen.

The Offering.

¶ *The bringing of offerings for the service of God is to be performed as an Act of Worship Let the Minister, having made such* Announcements *as are needful and fitting, then say,* Let us make our Offering to Almighty God for (naming the cause). *If the choir sing a* Canticle *or* Anthem *it should be one proper for the occasion.*

¶ *When the gifts are brought to the Table, the Minister shall dedicate them to God with a brief Prayer for His blessing; the church-officers who have gathered the gifts standing, and the congregation bowing down.*

¶ *On special occasions the Offering may be made after the Sermon.*

A Prayer of Dedication.

O GOD, most merciful and gracious, of whose bounty we have all received ; We beseech Thee to accept this Offering of Thy people. Remember in Thy love those who have brought it, and those for whom it is given ; and so follow it with Thy blessing that it may promote peace and good-will among men, and advance the kingdom of our Lord and Saviour Jesus Christ. *Amen.*

¶ *Then let the People stand up and sing*

A Hymn.

¶ *Then the Minister, taking his text from the* Word of God, *and remembering that it is his office to instruct men in divine Truth, to hold forth Christ crucified as their Saviour, and to incite them to Christian faith and duty, shall preach*

The Sermon.

¶ *The Sermon being ended, let the People stand up and sing*

A Hymn.

¶ *Then shall the Minister say,*

Let us pray

¶ *Then let the People reverently bow down while the Minister leads them in Prayer, using if he so desire one of the following as*

THE CLOSING PRAYER.

O GOD, the Protector of all that trust in Thee, without whom nothing is strong, nothing is holy ; Increase and multiply upon us Thy mercy, that, Thou being our ruler and guide, we may so pass through things temporal, that we finally lose not the things eternal. Grant this, O heavenly Father, for Jesus Christ's sake, our Lord. *Amen.*

O LORD, the Author of spiritual life, who hast given unto us the good seed of Thy Word ; Grant that we may receive it into honest hearts : and so guard it by Thy grace from the wiles of Satan and the cares of this life, that the faith and hope and love which Thou hast begotten, may be in us the beginning of life eternal; through Jesus Christ our Lord. *Amen.*

O GOD, who hast sounded in our ears Thy divine and saving oracles; Enlighten the souls of us sinners to the full understanding of what has been spoken, that we may be not only hearers of spiritual words, but also doers of good works, following after faith unfeigned, blameless life, and irreproachable conduct; through Jesus Christ our Lord. *Amen.*

MOST merciful God, we beseech Thee to grant unto us that we may earnestly desire, wisely search out, truly perceive, and perfectly fulfil those things which are well pleasing in Thy sight, to the praise and glory of Thy Name. *Amen.*

O GOD, who art the Author of peace and Lover of concord, in knowledge of whom standeth our eternal life, whose service is perfect freedom , Defend us Thy humble servants in all assaults of our enemies ; that we, surely trusting in Thy defense, may not fear the power of any adversaries; through the might of Jesus Christ our Lord. *Amen.*

A LMIGHTY God, who hast given us grace at this time with one accord to make our common supplications unto Thee : and dost promise that when two or three are gathered together in Thy Name Thou wilt grant their requests ; Fulfil now, O Lord, the desires and petitions of Thy servants, as may be most expedient for them ; granting us in this world knowledge of Thy truth, and in the world to come life everlasting. *Amen.*

¶ *The People remaining in the posture of prayer, the Minister shall pronounce*

THE BENEDICTION

T HE grace of the Lord Jesus Christ, and the love of God, and the communion of the Holy Ghost, be with you all. *Amen.*

¶ *Or this :*

T HE peace of God, which passeth all understanding, keep your hearts and minds in the knowledge and love of God, and of His Son Jesus Christ our Lord ; and the blessing of God Almighty, the Father, the Son, and the Holy Ghost, be amongst you, and remain with you always *Amen.*

¶ *After the Benediction it is fitting that the Minister and People remain in silent prayer, beseeching God that none may leave His House without a blessing.*

¶ Note *that the last Hymn may be sung after the Prayer if such be the wish and usage of any church*

THE ORDER OF

EVENING SERVICE

ON THE LORD'S DAY.

¶ *Let a Hymn be sung, all the People standing, and then let the Minister read one or more of the following* SENTENCES.

GRACE be unto you, and peace, from God our Father, and from the Lord Jesus Christ. (1 *Corinthians* i. 3.)

Thus saith the high and lofty One that inhabiteth eternity, whose name is Holy; I dwell in the high and holy place, with him also that is of a contrite and humble spirit, to revive the spirit of the humble, and to revive the heart of the contrite ones. (*Isaiah* lvii. 15.)

The hour cometh, and now is, when the true worshippers shall worship the Father in spirit and in truth: for the Father seeketh such to worship Him God is a Spirit. and they that worship Him must worship Him in spirit and in truth. (*St John* iv. 23, 24.)

Let my prayer be set forth before Thee as incense ; and the lifting up of my hands as the evening sacrifice. (*Psalm* cxli. 2.)

O worship the Lord in the beauty of holiness : fear before Him, all the earth. (*Psalm* xcvi. 9)

Let the words of my mouth, and the meditation of my heart, be acceptable in Thy sight, O Lord, my strength and my redeemer. (*Psalm* xix. 14.)

Ask, and it shall be given you ; seek, and ye shall find, knock, and it shall be opened unto you : for every one that asketh receiveth ; and he that seeketh findeth ; and to him that knocketh it shall be opened (*St. Matthew* vii. 7, 8)

The Lord is good unto them that wait for Him, to the soul that seeketh Him. (*Lamentations* iii. 25.)

And the Spirit and the bride say, Come. And let him that heareth say, Come. And let him that is athirst come. And whosoever will, let him take the water of life freely. (*Revelation* xxii. 17.)

I will arise and go to my father, and will say unto him, Father, I have sinned against heaven, and before thee, and am no more worthy to be called thy son. (*St. Luke* xv. 18, 19.)

¶ *Then let the Minister say,*

Let us pray.

¶ *Let the People reverently bow down while the Minister leads them in the* INVOCATION *and* CONFESSION, *using if he will one of the following Prayers:*

THE INVOCATION AND CONFESSION.

O GOD, the Father of lights, with whom is no variableness nor shadow of turning; We beseech Thee to look in mercy upon us, Thy sinful and wayward children: and so direct the eyes of our faith unto Thee, that at all times we may receive a heavenly illumination, through Thy Word and Spirit; and walk securely, in confidence and peace, amid the shadows of this mortal life. And more especially at this hour of the evening sacrifice, bestow upon us the pardon of our sins, and such a vision of the truth as it is in Jesus, that the darkness of evil may be driven from our hearts, and we may render unto Thee songs of praise; through Christ our Lord. *Amen.*

ETERNAL God, in whom we live and move and have our being, whose face is hidden from us by our sins, and whose mercy we forget in the blindness of our hearts; Cleanse us, we beseech Thee, from all the defilements of this day, and deliver us from all proud thoughts and vain desires; that with lowliness and meekness we may draw near to Thee in prayer, confessing our sins, confiding in Thy grace, and finding in Thee our refuge and our strength, our hope and our salvation; through Jesus Christ Thy Son. *Amen.*

ALMIGHTY and most merciful God, who hast appointed our portion of labour, that we may serve Thee while it is day; and by whose ordinance the weariness of night cometh, that we may seek our rest in Thee; We beseech Thee now to lead and draw our hearts unto Thy dear Son, that, confessing our sin and weakness, we may receive of Him the grace promised unto the heavy-laden; and, being forgiven by His mercy, comforted by His Word, refreshed by His Spirit, and lifted up by His fellowship, we may find in this hour of worship a blessing for our souls; through Jesus Christ our Lord. *Amen.*

O GOD, Light of the hearts that see Thee, and Life of the souls that love Thee, and Strength of the thoughts that seek Thee, from whom to be turned away is to fall, to whom to be turned is to rise, and in whom to abide is to stand fast for ever; Grant us now Thy forgiveness and blessing, as we are here assembled to offer up our confession and supplications, and though we are unworthy to approach Thee, or to ask anything of Thee at all, vouchsafe to hear and to answer us, for the sake of our great High Priest and Advocate, Jesus Christ, our Lord. *Amen.*

¶ *The Prayer may close with these Petitions of* HOLY SCRIPTURE. *to be said responsively by the Minister and People, still bowing down.*

Create in us a clean heart, O God:
And renew a right spirit within us.
Cast us not away from Thy presence:
And take not Thy Holy Spirit from us.
Restore unto us the joy of Thy salvation:
And uphold us with Thy free Spirit.
O Lord, open Thou our lips.
And our mouth shall show forth Thy praise. Amen.

THE PSALTER

¶ *Then let a portion of the* PSALTER *be chanted, or read responsively by the Minister and the People, all standing, and at the end let all say or sing,*

Glory be to the Father, and to the Son: and to the Holy Ghost;
As it was in the beginning, is now, and ever shall be: world without end. Amen.

¶ *Or else, the* Gloria in Excelsis *as follows:*

GLORY be to God on high: and on earth peace, good will towards men.

We praise Thee, we bless Thee, we worship Thee · we glorify Thee, we give thanks to Thee for Thy great glory.

O Lord God, heavenly King: God the Father Almighty.

O Lord, the only-begotten Son, Jesus Christ: O Lord God, Lamb of God, Son of the Father,

That takest away the sins of the world: have mercy upon us.

Thou that takest away the sins of the world: receive our prayer.

Thou that sittest at the right hand of God the Father: have mercy upon us.

For Thou only art holy: Thou only art the Lord.

Thou only, O Christ, with the Holy Ghost: art most high in the glory of God the Father. Amen.

¶ Note *that, if any church so desire, a Hymn may be sung in place of the* PSALTER.

THE PUBLIC READING OF THE HOLY SCRIPTURES.

¶ *The People being seated shall attend devoutly to the Minister as he reads clearly and distinctly from the* Word of God. *Before the reading let the Minister say,* Hear the Holy Scripture as it is written in such a chapter of such a book: *and after the reading he shall say,* The Lord bless to us the reading of His Holy Word.

¶ *After the reading of Scripture, an* Anthem *or* Hymn *may be sung.*

. ¶ *Then let the Minister say,*

Let us pray.

¶ *And the People, reverently bowing down, shall follow in their
hearts*

The General Prayer.

¶ *The Minister, leading the People in their Common Prayers, shall
offer unto God such* Adorations *and* Thanksgivings ; *such* Intercessions *for the Church, for the State, and for all men, especially for those who are out of Christ and those who are in
any peril or distress; and such* Supplications *for enlighten-
ment, protection, and guidance, as he may think fitting for
this Service And if he will, he may use any of the Prayers
given in this Book (under the title of* Treasury of Prayers),
or those here following .

O GOD, in glory exalted, and in mercy ever-blessed : We
magnify Thee, we praise Thee, we give thanks unto
Thee for Thy bountiful providence, for all the blessings of
this present life, and all the hopes of a better life to come.
Let the memory of Thy goodness, we beseech Thee, fill our
hearts with joy and thankfulness; and let no unworthiness of ours provoke Thee to withhold from us any needed
good, seeing that all Thy blessings come not by our desert,
but only through the merit and mediation of Jesus Christ
our Lord. *Amen.*

O LORD of heaven and earth, who hast promised to reveal Thy glory by Jesus Christ among all nations ; Remember, we beseech Thee, Thy holy Church throughout
all the world. Unite all who profess and call themselves
Christians in the bond of a living faith as the body of
Christ, and so replenish them and us with the grace of Thy
Holy Spirit, that we may bring forth abundantly the fruits
of peace and good works, and may turn many to righteousness through the preaching of the Gospel. And grant that,
having persevered in the way of godliness to the end, we
may, with prophets, apostles, martyrs, confessors, and
saints of all ages, come into full communion with Thee,
and with one another, in Thine eternal and glorious kingdom ; through our Lord and Saviour Jesus Christ. *Amen.*

A LMIGHTY God, who hast heard the prayer of our
fathers, and established our Nation in freedom according
to the people's will; We implore Thy blessing on the Republic ; that Thou wouldst grant us peaceful times and
fruitful seasons ; that Thou wouldst bless our homes, pros-

per our industries, and defend us from our enemies; that Thou wouldst govern and protect Thy servant the President of the United States, and all to whom authority is given; the Governor of the State, and all law-makers and judges : that Thou wouldst unite the hearts of the people to dwell together in concord : and that Thou wouldst enrich our land with liberty and order, godliness and power; for the good of the world and the glory of Thy Name; through Jesus Christ our Lord. *Amen.*

O GOD, Creator and Preserver of all mankind, we implore Thy mercy in behalf of all classes and conditions of men; that it may please Thee to visit them with Thy help, according to their manifold necessities. Have compassion upon all who are out of Christ, and draw them unto Him. Show Thy pity upon all prisoners and captives; upon all sick and dying persons; and upon all who are poor, desolate, or afflicted. Enable them to look unto Thee, O most merciful Father, and to find Thee a present Saviour in their time of trouble. And let it please Thee to deliver them, and raise them up in due time, giving them patience under all their sufferings, the rich comfort of Thy grace on earth, and eternal rest with Thee in heaven; through our Lord Jesus Christ. *Amen.*

O ALMIGHTY Lord, and everlasting God, vouchsafe, we beseech Thee, to direct, sanctify, and govern, both our hearts and bodies in the ways of Thy laws, and in the works of Thy commandments; that through Thy most mighty protection, both here and ever, we may be preserved in body and soul; through our Lord and Saviour Jesus Christ. *Amen.*

LIGHTEN our darkness, we beseech Thee, O Lord; and by Thy great mercy defend us from all perils and dangers of this night; for the love of Thy only Son, our Saviour, Jesus Christ. *Amen.*

And the Prayer may close with the following ASCRIPTION:

NOW unto Him that is able to keep you from falling, and to present you faultless before the presence of His glory with exceeding joy; to the only wise God our

Saviour, be glory and majesty, dominion and power, both now and ever. *Amen.*

THE OFFERING.

¶ *Let the Minister, having made such* ANNOUNCEMENTS *as are need-ful and fitting, then say,* Let us make our Offering to Almighty God for (naming the cause). *If the choir sing a* Canticle *or* Anthem *it should be one proper for the occasion. When the gifts are brought to the Table, the Minister shall dedicate them to God with a brief prayer for His blessing ; the church-officers who have gathered the gifts standing, and the congre-gation bowing down.*

¶ *On special occasions the Offering may be made after the Sermon.*

A PRAYER OF DEDICATION.

ALL gracious God, who of Thine infinite love didst give Thine only-begotten Son, Jesus Christ, to die for our sins and rise again for our justification, and hast made us partakers of the divine nature through the gift of the Holy Spirit ; Accept the Offering which we now present unto Thee : and grant that our bodies, souls, and spirits may be unto Thee a living sacrifice, holy and well-pleasing in Thy sight ; and that going forth in Thy strength, we may be able truly to serve Thee, and in all things to obey Thy will ; through Jesus Christ our Lord. *Amen.*

¶ *Then let the People stand up and sing*

A HYMN.

¶ *Then the Minister, taking his text from the* Word of God, *and remembering that it is his office to instruct men in divine Truth, to hold forth Christ crucified as their Saviour, and to incite them to Christian faith and duty, shall preach*

THE SERMON.

¶ *The Sermon being ended, let the People stand up and sing*

A HYMN.

¶ *Then shall the Minister say,*

Let us pray

¶ *The People reverently bowing down, the Minister shall lead them in their devotions, using if he so desire one or more of the following Prayers, ending with the LORD'S PRAYER :*

THE CLOSING PRAYER.

GRANT, we beseech Thee, Almighty God, that the words, which we have heard this day with our outward ears, may through Thy grace be so grafted inwardly in our hearts, that they may bring forth in us the fruit of good living, to the honour and praise of Thy Name; through Jesus Christ our Lord. *Amen.*

LET Thy Gospel, O Lord, come unto us not in word only but in power, and in much assurance, and in the Holy Ghost, that we may be guided into all truth, and strengthened unto all obedience and enduring of Thy will with joyfulness; that, abounding in the work of faith, and the labour of love, and the patience of hope, we may finally be made partakers of the inheritance of the saints in light; through Jesus Christ our Lord. *Amen.*

O LORD Jesus Christ, who hast died for us, that whether we wake or sleep, we should live together with Thee; Be Thou our strength every morning, and our rest when the shadows of the evening are stretched out, O Jesus Christ our Lord. *Amen.*

O GOD, from whom all holy desires, all good counsels, and all just works do proceed; Give unto Thy servants that peace which the world cannot give; that both our hearts may be set to obey Thy commandments, and also that by Thee, we, being defended from the fear of our enemies, may pass our time in rest and quietness; through the merits of Jesus Christ our Saviour. *Amen.*

ETERNAL and ever-blessed God, who art the Author of our life, and the End of our pilgrimage; We beseech Thee so to guide us by Thy Word and Spirit, amid all perils and temptations, that we may not wander from Thy way, nor stumble upon the dark mountains; but may finish our course in safety, and come to our eternal rest in Thee; through the saving grace of our Lord Jesus Christ. *Amen.*

O LORD God, the Light of the faithful, the Strength of those who labour, and the Repose of the blessed dead; We bless Thee for all Thy saints who have witnessed in their lives a good confession, and especially for those dear unto us who have fallen asleep in Jesus. Grant us grace, O Lord, so to follow their good example, that we may be one with them in spirit, and finally share in their eternal rest; through Jesus Christ our Lord. *Amen.*

The Lord's Prayer.

¶ To be said by Minister and People.

OUR Father which art in heaven, Hallowed be Thy Name. Thy kingdom come. Thy will be done in earth, As it is in heaven. Give us this day our daily bread. And forgive us our debts, As we forgive our debtors. And lead us not into temptation, But deliver us from evil: For Thine is the kingdom, and the power, and the glory, for ever Amen.

¶ The People remaining in the posture of prayer, the Minister shall pronounce

The Benediction.

THE grace of the Lord Jesus Christ, and the love of God, and the communion of the Holy Ghost, be with you all. *Amen.*

¶ Or this:

THE peace of God, which passeth all understanding, keep your hearts and minds in the knowledge and love of God, and of His son Jesus Christ our Lord; and the blessing of God Almighty, the Father, the Son, and the Holy Ghost, be amongst you, and remain with you always. *Amen.*

¶ After the Benediction it is fitting that the Minister and People remain in silent prayer, beseeching God that none may leave His House without a blessing.

¶ Note that the last Hymn may be omitted, or its place in the Service changed, according to the wish and usage of any church.

ORDER OF WORSHIP.

¶ *This Service is intended for the use of any company of Christians, gathered together to worship God, on land or at sea, where there are no regular Church Ordinances, or where a Minister of the Gospel is not present.*

¶ *If it be desired, the Service may begin with the Singing of a Hymn, after which the Leader, standing, may read one or more of the following* SENTENCES *taken from the* HOLY SCRIPTURES.

SENTENCES.

MORNING.

THE Lord is nigh unto all them that call upon Him, to all that call upon Him in truth. He will fulfil the desire of them that fear Him; He also will hear their cry, and will save them.

Our help is in the Name of the Lord, who made heaven and earth.

Where two or three are gathered together in My Name, saith the Lord Jesus, there am I in the midst of them.

This is the confidence that we have in Him, that, if we ask anything according to His will, He heareth us.
Having these promises, let us draw near to the throne of grace with true hearts, in full assurance of faith.

My voice shalt Thou hear in the morning, O Lord; in the morning will I direct my prayer unto Thee, and will look up.

EVENING.

HE that dwelleth in the secret place of the Most High shall abide under the shadow of the Almighty.

Lord, I cry unto Thee make haste unto me; give ear unto my voice, when I cry unto Thee
Let my prayer be set forth before Thee as incense; and the lifting up of my hands as the evening sacrifice.

I will say of the Lord, He is my refuge, and my fortress: my God; in Him will I trust.

Return unto thy rest, O my soul; for the Lord hath dealt bountifully with thee.
Abide with us: for it is toward evening, and the day is far spent.

¶ *Then shall he say,*

Let us pray.

¶ *Let all the company bow down, following the Prayer in their hearts, and, if they so desire, joining audibly in the* CONFESSION OF SINS *and the* LORD'S PRAYER.

PRAYERS.

ALMIGHTY God, unto whom all hearts are open, all desires known, and from whom no secrets are hid; Cleanse the thoughts of our hearts by the inspiration of Thy Holy Spirit, that we may perfectly love Thee, and worthily magnify Thy holy Name; through Christ our Lord. *Amen.*

MOST holy and merciful Father; We acknowledge and confess in Thy Presence: Our sinful nature prone to evil and slothful in good; And all our shortcomings and offenses against Thee Thou alone knowest how often we have sinned: In wandering from Thy ways; In wasting Thy gifts; In forgetting Thy love. But Thou, O Lord, have pity upon us; Who are ashamed and sorry for all wherein we have displeased Thee. Teach us to hate our errors; Cleanse us from our secret faults; And forgive our sins; For the sake of Thy dear Son our Saviour. And O most holy and loving Father: Send Thy purifying grace into our hearts, we beseech Thee; That we may henceforth live in Thy light and walk in Thy ways; According to the commandments of Jesus Christ our Lord. *Amen.*

OUR Father which art in heaven, Hallowed be Thy Name. Thy kingdom come. Thy will be done in earth, As it is in heaven. Give us this day our daily bread. And forgive us our debts, As we forgive our debtors. And lead us not into temptation, But deliver us from evil: For Thine is the kingdom, and the power, and the glory, for ever. Amen.

THE PSALTER.

¶ *A portion of the* PSALTER *may then be read by the Leader, or recited responsively, closing with this* ASCRIPTION:

GLORY be to the Father, and to the Son: and to the Holy Ghost;
As it was in the beginning, is now, and ever shall be: world without end. Amen.

¶ *Let all the company, standing, repeat together*

THE APOSTLES' CREED.

I BELIEVE in God the Father Almighty, Maker of heaven and earth:
And in Jesus Christ His only Son, our Lord; Who was conceived by the Holy Ghost, Born of the Virgin Mary; Suffered under Pontius Pilate, Was crucified, dead, and buried; [He descended into hell;*] The third day He rose again from the dead; He ascended into heaven, And sitteth on the right hand of God the Father Almighty; From thence He shall come to judge the quick and the dead.
I believe in the Holy Ghost; The Holy Catholic Church; The Communion of Saints; The Forgiveness of sins; The Resurrection of the body; and the Life everlasting. Amen.

* Or, *He continued in the state of the dead, and under the power of death, until the third day.*

The Reading of the Holy Scriptures.

¶ *The Leader shall choose and read an appropriate lesson, or lessons, from the Bible, saying before he reads,* Let us listen reverently to the Holy Scripture, as it is written in the ——— chapter of ———, *and after the reading he shall say,* May God bless, to all our hearts, the reading of His Word.

A Hymn.

¶ *If it be convenient the company may then sing a Hymn, and after this, if it be desired, the Leader may read a Sermon, or a brief passage from some Christian book; or a word of exhortation and counsel may be spoken by the Leader or some other member of the company. If this is done, let another Hymn be sung before the closing Prayers. The Leader may choose from the following such as are appropriate; and, the company bowing down, he shall say,*

Let us pray.

Prayers.

Thanksgiving.

O GOD, by whose hand all living things were made, and by whose blessing they are nourished and sustained; We give Thee hearty thanks for all the bounties of Thy providence, wherewith Thou hast enriched our life; and we humbly pray that, enjoying Thy gifts in contentment, we may be enabled by Thy grace to use them to Thy praise. Especially we thank Thee for Thy great love in sending Thy Son to be the Saviour of the world and in calling us out of our sins into fellowship with Him: and we beseech Thee to grant us always Thy Holy Spirit, through whom we may grow continually in thankfulness toward Thee, as also into the likeness of Thy Son Jesus Christ our Lord. *Amen.*

Supplication.

O GOD, most holy, wise, and powerful Preserver and Governor of all Thy creatures and all their actions; Keep us this day in health of body and soundness of mind,

in purity of heart and cheerfulness of spirit, in contentment with our lot and charity with our neighbour; and
further all our lawful undertakings with Thy blessing. In
our labour strengthen us : in our pleasure purify us : in
our difficulties direct us : in our perils defend us : in our
troubles comfort us. and supply all our needs, according to
the riches of Thy grace in Christ Jesus our Lord. *Amen.*

A Traveller's Prayer.

L ORD God omnipotent, who reignest in the heavens and
on the earth ; We implore Thy guidance and protection
for all our journeyings. Against all perils be Thou our
strong defense, and in far regions be Thou our faithful
friend ; keep us in health and heart ; prosper the ends of
our adventure, and make the way of our going and of our
returning both safe and happy ; and so direct the steps of
all Thy pilgrims through this world, that we shall finally
arrive in the better country, even the heavenly, with Jesus
Christ our Lord. *Amen.*

A Prayer at Sea.

O ETERNAL Lord God, who alone spreadest out the
heavens, and rulest the raging of the sea ; We commend ourselves to Thine almighty protection on the great
deep. Guard us, we beseech Thee, from the dangers of
the sea, from sickness, from the violence of enemies, from
every evil ; and conduct us in safety to our desired haven,
with a grateful sense of Thy mercies ; through Jesus Christ
our Lord. *Amen.*

A Prayer for Friends and Kindred.

O LORD, our heavenly Father, bless and keep, we pray
Thee, our kindred, friends, and benefactors, and graciously watch between them and us, while we are absent
one from another, that in due time we may meet again to
praise Thee, and hereafter dwell together in heavenly mansions ; through Christ our Lord. *Amen.*

A General Intercession.

O GOD, the Creator and Preserver of all mankind, we humbly beseech Thee for all sorts and conditions of men, that Thou wouldest be pleased to make Thy ways known unto them, Thy saving health unto all nations. More especially, we pray for Thy holy Church universal; that it may be so guided and governed by Thy good Spirit, that all who profess and call themselves Christians may be led into the way of truth, and hold the faith in unity of spirit, in the bond of peace, and in righteousness of life. Finally, we commend to Thy fatherly goodness all those who are any ways afflicted, or distressed, in mind, body, or estate; that it may please Thee to comfort and relieve them, according to their several necessities; giving them patience under their sufferings, and a happy issue out of all their afflictions. And this we beg for Jesus Christ's sake. *Amen.*

A General Prayer in the Morning.

A LMIGHTY God, our Father and Preserver; We give Thee thanks that of Thy goodness Thou hast watched over us the past night, and brought us to a new day· and we beseech Thee to strengthen and guard us by Thy Spirit, that we may spend it wholly in Thy service and to Thy glory, looking for all prosperity to Thy blessing, and seeking only those things which are well-pleasing in Thy sight. Enable us, O Lord, while we labour for the life that now is, ever to have regard unto that heavenly life which Thou hast promised Thy children. Defend us in soul and body from all harm. And seeing it is a small thing to have begun well, except we also persevere, take us, O Lord, into Thy good keeping this day and all our days: continue and increase Thy grace within us, until we shall be perfectly united in the glory of Thy Son. Show Thy loving-kindness unto all men and women and little children, according to the need of every living soul, especially unto those whom we love, and those who are in any kind of trouble or distress, whom we now remember silently before Thee : [*here let there be a moment of prayer in silence:*] Protect our country and prosper Thy Church : Bless all who do good in the world, and restrain and convert all who do evil. And finally, be pleased to cast out of Thy remembrance all our past offenses, forgiving them in Thy boundless mercy and purifying our hearts that we may lead a better life; through Jesus Christ our Lord. *Amen.*

A GENERAL PRAYER IN THE EVENING.

O GOD most merciful, Light eternal in the darkness shining, by whom the night of sin and the blindness of our hearts are driven away : Since Thou hast appointed the day for labour and the night for rest; grant unto us, we beseech Thee, that our bodies may repose in peace and quietness, that afterward they may be able to endure the toil which Thou hast laid upon us in Thy service: Temper our sleep that it be not disorderly, and keep us spotless both in body and in soul, that our very rest may be to Thy glory, renewing the strength of our hearts and our joy in Thee : Enlighten the eyes of our understanding that we may not sleep in death, but obtain deliverance, through faith and hope, from all fear of this misery : Defend us against all assaults of our enemies, and take us into Thy holy protection. And although we have not passed this day without greatly sinning against Thee, we beseech Thee to hide our sins with Thy mercy, as Thou coverest all things on earth with the darkness of the night, that they may be blotted out from Thy remembrance, and we may abide in Thy Presence and Thy favour, both now and for evermore. Relieve and comfort, with Thy fatherly goodness, all who are afflicted or distressed in mind, body, or estate : Protect and prosper, with Thine almighty power, our country and our rulers, the whole Church of Christ on earth, our home, and all that we hold dear and sacred: Be pleased to guard and help those whom we silently remember before Thee: [*here let there be a moment of prayer in silence:*] Bless us and keep us, watch over us and save us, O God in whom we trust ; through Jesus Christ our Lord. *Amen.*

LIGHTEN our darkness, we beseech Thee, O Lord ; and by Thy great mercy defend us from all perils and dangers of this night; for the love of Thy only Son, our Saviour, Jesus Christ. *Amen.*

A Prayer of St. Chrysostom.

ALMIGHTY God, who hast given us grace at this time with one accord to make our common supplications unto Thee ; and dost promise that when two or three are gathered together in Thy Name Thou wilt grant their requests : Fulfil now, O Lord, the desires and petitions of Thy servants, as may be most expedient for them; granting us in this world knowledge of Thy truth, and in the world to come life everlasting. *Amen.*

¶ *All the company still bowing down, the Leader may close the Service with this*

Ascription.

NOW unto Him that is able to keep us from falling, and to present us faultless before the presence of His glory with exceeding joy ; to the only wise God our Saviour, be glory and majesty, dominion and power, both now and ever. *Amen.*

THE COMMANDMENTS.

¶ *This Order may be used as a separate Service : or it may be said at the opening of Morning Service instead of the Order there appointed, down to the* Reading of the Holy Scriptures; *in which case it may be preceded by a suitable Hymn.*

¶ *Let all stand while the Minister reads the* SENTENCES, *the People answering him.*

Minister. Blessed are the undefiled in the way : who walk in the law of the Lord.

Answer. Order my steps in Thy Word : and let not any iniquity have dominion over me.

Minister. Blessed are they that keep His testimonies and that seek Him with the whole heart.

Answer. With my whole heart have I sought Thee : O let me not wander from Thy commandments.

¶ *Then the Minister shall say,*

Let us pray.

¶ *Let the People reverently bow down while he leads them in*

THE INVOCATION.

A LMIGHTY God, unto whom all hearts are open, all desires known, and from whom no secrets are hid ; Cleanse the thoughts of our hearts by the inspiration of Thy Holy Spirit, that we may perfectly love Thee, and worthily magnify Thy holy Name ; through Christ our Lord *Amen.*

¶ *Then the Minister shall read* THE TEN COMMANDMENTS, *and the People, still bowing down, shall, after every Commandment, ask God's mercy for their transgressions in time past, and grace to keep the Law in time to come.*

GOD spake all these words, saying,

I am the Lord thy God, which have brought thee out of the land of Egypt, out of the house of bondage.

Thou shalt have no other gods before Me.

Lord, have mercy upon us, and incline our hearts to keep this law.

Thou shalt not make unto thee any graven image, or any likeness of any thing that is in heaven above, or that is in the earth beneath, or that is in the water under the earth : thou shalt not bow down thyself to them, nor serve them : for I the Lord thy God am a jealous God, visiting the iniquity of the fathers upon the children unto the third and fourth generation of them that hate Me; and showing mercy unto thousands of them that love Me, and keep My commandments.

Lord, have mercy upon us, and incline our hearts to keep this law.

Thou shalt not take the Name of the Lord thy God in vain : for the Lord will not hold him guiltless that taketh His Name in vain.

Lord, have mercy upon us, and incline our hearts to keep this law.

Remember the Sabbath-day, to keep it holy. Six days shalt thou labour, and do all thy work : but the seventh day is the Sabbath of the Lord thy God ; in it thou shalt not do any work, thou, nor thy son, nor thy daughter, thy man-servant, nor thy maid-servant, nor thy cattle, nor thy stranger that is within thy gates : for in six days the Lord made heaven and earth, the sea, and all that in them is, and rested the seventh day ; wherefore the Lord blessed the Sabbath-day, and hallowed it.

Lord, have mercy upon us, and incline our hearts to keep this law.

Honour thy father and thy mother · that thy days may be long upon the land which the Lord thy God giveth thee.

Lord, have mercy upon us, and incline our hearts to keep this law

Thou shalt not kill.

Lord, have mercy upon us, and incline our hearts to keep this law.

Thou shalt not commit adultery.

Lord, have mercy upon us, and incline our hearts to keep this law.

Thou shalt not steal.

Lord, have mercy upon us, and incline our hearts to keep this law.

Thou shalt not bear false witness against thy neighbour.

Lord, have mercy upon us, and incline our hearts to keep this law.

Thou shalt not covet thy neighbour's house, thou shalt not covet thy neighbour's wife, nor his man-servant, nor his maid-servant, nor his ox, nor his ass, nor any thing that is thy neighbour's.

Lord, have mercy upon us, and write all these Thy laws in our hearts, we beseech Thee.

¶ *Then the Minister shall say,*

Hear also what our Lord Jesus Christ saith :
Thou shalt love the Lord thy God with all thy heart, and with all thy soul, and with all thy mind. This is the first and great commandment. And the second is like unto it; Thou shalt love thy neighbour as thyself. On these two commandments hang all the Law and the Prophets.

¶ *After a short pause let the Minister continue in Prayer, using, if he will, the following, or other fitting words.*

WE confess to Thee, Almighty God, Father, Son, and Holy Ghost, that we have grievously sinned in thought, word, and deed. Make us truly contrite. Fill us with holy fear, and give us grace to amend our lives according to Thy Word, for the glory of Thy holy Name ; through Jesus Christ our Lord. *Amen.*

ALMIGHTY God, our heavenly Father, who of His great mercy hath promised forgiveness of sins to all them that with hearty repentance and true faith turn to Him ; Have mercy upon you ; pardon and deliver you from all your sins ; confirm and strengthen you in all goodness ; and bring you to everlasting life ; through Jesus Christ our Lord *Amen.*

NOW unto Him that is able to do exceeding abundantly above all that we ask or think, according to the power that worketh in us; unto Him be glory and dominion in the Church by Christ Jesus, throughout all ages, world without end. *Amen.*

THE BEATITUDES.

¶ *This Order may be used as a separate Service: or it may be said at the opening of Evening Service, instead of the Order there appointed, down to the* Reading of the Holy Scriptures; *in which case it may be preceded by a suitable Hymn.*

¶ *Let all stand while the Minister reads the* SENTENCES, *the People answering him.*

Minister. Draw nigh to God, and He will draw nigh to you. Humble yourselves in the sight of the Lord, and He shall lift you up.

Answer. *Bow down Thine ear, O Lord, hear me: for I am poor and needy*

Minister. Therefore will the Lord wait, that He may be gracious unto you, and therefore will He be exalted that He may have mercy upon you.

Answer. *Let Thy mercy, O Lord, be upon us, according as we hope in Thee*

¶ *Then the Minister shall say,*

Let us pray.

¶ *Let the People reverently bow down while he leads them in*

THE INVOCATION.

MERCIFUL God, we beseech Thee to cast Thy bright beams of light into our hearts, that we may discern the spiritual laws of Thy kingdom, and graciously incline us to a true obedience that we may not only hear, but also receive, these heavenly blessings of our Lord Jesus Christ *Amen.*

¶ *Then the Minister shall read* THE BEATITUDES *of the Lord Jesus; and the People, still bowing down, shall, after every Beatitude, humbly ask God that it may be fulfilled in their hearts.*

BLESSED are the poor in spirit: for theirs is the kingdom of heaven.

Lord, be gracious unto us, and help us to obtain this blessing.

Blessed are they that mourn: for they shall be comforted.

Lord, be gracious unto us, and help us to obtain this blessing.

Blessed are the meek : for they shall inherit the earth.

Lord, be gracious unto us, and help us to obtain this blessing.

Blessed are they which do hunger and thirst after righteousness: for they shall be filled.

Lord, be gracious unto us, and help us to obtain this blessing.

Blessed are the merciful : for they shall obtain mercy.

Lord, be gracious unto us, and help us to obtain this blessing.

Blessed are the pure in heart : for they shall see God.

Lord, be gracious unto us, and help us to obtain this blessing.

Blessed are the peacemakers : for they shall be called the children of God.

Lord, be gracious unto us, and help us to obtain this blessing.

Blessed are they which are persecuted for righteousness' sake: for theirs is the kingdom of heaven.

Grant unto us Thy Holy Spirit, O God, and enable us to obtain all these blessings, through Jesus Christ our Lord.

¶ *After a short pause, let the Minister continue in Prayer, using, if he will, the following, or other fitting words.*

GLORY be to Thee, O Christ, who hast opened the kingdom of heaven unto the poor in spirit, and given power to them that believe in Thee to become the sons of God. Deliver us, O Lord, in Thy great mercy, from all the secret sins that hinder us from true blessedness. Strengthen us to keep Thy counsels of perfection, and to walk in the way of Thy commandments. And grant unto us that peace which the world can neither give nor take away, that at the last we may come unto Thee in glory, O Thou most blessed Lord Jesus, our only Saviour. *Amen.*

NOW unto Him that is able to do exceeding abundantly above all that we ask or think, according to the power that worketh in us; unto Him be glory and dominion in the Church by Christ Jesus, throughout all ages, world without end. *Amen.*

THE CELEBRATION OF THE COMMUNION OR SACRAMENT OF THE LORD'S SUPPER

¶ *The Communion, or Supper of the Lord, is to be celebrated frequently; but how often, may be determined by the Minister and Eldership of each congregation, as they may judge most for edification.* — Directory for Worship, Chap. IX, § 1.

¶ *It is proper that public notice should be given to the congregation, at least the Lord's Day before the administration of the ordinance, and that, either then or on some day of the week, the people be instructed in its nature, and a due preparation for it, that all may come in a suitable manner to this holy feast* — Directory for Worship, Chap. IX, § 3

¶ *When the time is come for administration, the Minister shall say,*

DEARLY beloved, as we draw near to the Lord's Supper to celebrate the Holy Communion of the Body and Blood of Christ, we are gratefully to remember that our Lord instituted this Sacrament to be observed in His Church unto the end of the world: for the perpetual remembrance of the sacrifice of Himself in His death, the sealing all benefits thereof unto true believers, their spiritual nourishment and growth in Him, their further engagement in and to all duties which they owe unto Him; and to be a bond and pledge of their union with Him and with each other as members of His mystical body.

Let us consider earnestly our great need of having our comfort and strength so renewed in this our earthly pilgrimage and warfare; and especially how necessary it is that we come unto the Lord's Table with knowledge, faith, repentance, love, and with hearts hungering and thirsting after Christ. Not unto those who live willingly in transgression and offenses, holding fellowship with hatred, malice, or impurity; nor unto those who cherish pride and self-righteousness in their hearts, trusting secretly in their own works and merits, are these benefits of Christ offered. But all that are truly sorry for their sins and would be delivered from the burden of them, all that humbly put their trust in Christ, and desire His grace that they may lead a holy life, are invited and encouraged in His Name to come to this Sacrament.   Let us therefore so come that we may find refreshing and rest unto our souls.

¶ *Then let the People stand up and sing*

A HYMN.

¶ *If it be more convenient in any church, this Hymn may be omitted.*

¶ *The Table, on which the elements are placed, being decently covered, the bread in convenient dishes, and the wine in cups, and the Communicants orderly and gravely sitting around the Table, (or in their seats before it) in the presence of the Minister, he shall say,*

BELOVED in the Lord, attend to the Words of the Institution of the Holy Supper of our Lord Jesus Christ, as they are delivered by the Apostle Paul: "I have received of the Lord that which also I delivered unto you, That the Lord Jesus the same night in which He was betrayed took bread; and when He had given thanks, He brake it, and said, Take, eat: this is My body, which is broken for you: this do in remembrance of Me.   After the same manner also He took the cup, when He had supped, saying, This cup is the New Testament in My blood: this do ye, as oft as ye drink it, in remembrance of Me.   For as often as ye eat this bread, and drink this cup, ye do show the Lord's death till He come "
And now, in His Name, I take these elements

(¶ *Here the Minister may lay his hand upon the plate and the cup*)

to be set apart by prayer and thanksgiving to the holy use for which He has appointed them.

¶ *Then the Minister shall say,*

Let us pray.

¶ *If so desired, these* PRAYERS *and* THANKSGIVINGS *may be offered in the form following ; the People reverently bowing down:*

O GOD, who by the blood of Thy dear Son hast consecrated for us a new and a living way into the holiest of all ; Cleanse our minds, we beseech Thee, by the inspiration of Thy Holy Spirit, that, drawing near unto Thee with a pure heart and undefiled conscience, we may receive these Thy gifts without sin, and worthily magnify Thy holy Name ; through Jesus Christ our Lord. *Amen.*

¶ *Then the People, still bowing down, shall make these responses :*

Minister.	The Lord be with you.
People.	*And with thy spirit.*
Minister.	Lift up your hearts.
People	*We lift them up unto the Lord.*
Minister.	Let us give thanks unto the Lord our God.
People.	*It is meet and right so to do.*

¶ *Then the Minister, proceeding, shall say,*

IT is very meet, right, and our bounden duty, that we should, at all times and in all places, give thanks unto Thee, O Lord, Holy Father, Almighty and Eternal God, for all Thy bounties known and unknown ; but chiefly are we bound to praise Thee that Thou hast ransomed us from eternal death, and given us the joyful hope of everlasting life through Jesus Christ Thy Son, whom Thou didst send into the world to suffer death upon the cross for our redemption Thee, God the Father Everlasting : Thee, Only Begotten Son : Thee, Holy Spirit, the Comforter : Holy, Blessed and Glorious Trinity : we confess and praise with heart and mouth ; saying, with angels and archangels, and all the company of Heaven,

¶ *Here let the People, still bowing down, join aloud, singing or saying,*

HOLY, HOLY, HOLY, Lord God of Hosts ; Heaven and earth are full of the majesty of Thy glory. Hosanna in the highest. Blessed is He that cometh in the Name of the Lord. Hosanna in the highest.

¶ Then the Minister shall proceed, saying,

ALMIGHTY God, the Father of our Lord Jesus Christ, whose once offering up of Himself, by Himself, upon the cross, once for all, we commemorate before Thee; We beseech Thee to accept this our spiritual oblation of all possible praise for the same. And here we offer and present, O Lord, ourselves, our souls and bodies, to be a reasonable, holy, and living sacrifice, acceptable unto Thee through Jesus Christ Thy Son:

And we most humbly beseech Thee, Father of all mercies and God of all comfort, to vouchsafe Thy gracious presence, and the effectual working of Thy Spirit in us, and so to sanctify these elements both of Bread and Wine, and to bless Thine own Ordinance; that we may receive by faith Christ crucified for us, and so feed upon Him, that He may be one with us and we with Him; that He may live in us, and we in Him who hath loved us, and given Himself for us:

Even Jesus Christ our Lord; to whom, with Thee and the Holy Ghost, be praise and power, might, majesty, and dominion, both now and evermore. *Amen.*

¶ The Bread and Wine being thus set apart by Prayer and Thanksgiving, the Minister is to take the Bread, and break it, in view of the People, saying,

OUR Lord Jesus Christ, on the same night in which He was betrayed, having taken Bread, and blessed and broken it, gave it to His disciples; as I, ministering in His Name, give this Bread unto you; saying, Take, eat: this is My Body, which is broken for you; this do in remembrance of Me.

¶ Then the Minister, who is also himself to communicate, is to give the Bread to the Elders to be distributed.

¶ After having given the Bread, he shall take the Cup and say,

AFTER the same manner our Saviour also took the Cup; and having given thanks, as hath been done in His Name, He gave it to His disciples, saying, This Cup is the New Testament in My Blood, which is shed for many for the remission of sins: drink ye all of it.

¶ Then the Minister, who is also to partake of the Cup, shall give it to the Elders to be administered.

¶ *After all have communicated, the Minister shall say,*

Let us pray.

ALMIGHTY and ever-living God, we most heartily thank Thee for Thy rich mercy and invaluable goodness, vouchsafed to us in this sacred Communion, wherein we have assurance that we are very members of the mystical body of Thy Son, and heirs through hope of Thine everlasting kingdom. And, as we have been made partakers of Christ, so enable us to hold fast that which we have received, that no man may take our crown. Help us, we beseech Thee, to bear about with us continually the dying of the Lord Jesus, that the life also of Jesus may be made manifest in our mortal body ; and grant that we may remain alway in the holy fellowship of all faithful people, with whom in the unity of the Spirit, we now make our intercessions unto Thee :

O Lord, save Thy people and bless Thine inheritance : feed them also, and lift them up for ever. Remember, O Lord, Thy congregation, which Thou hast purchased of old : pour out Thy Spirit as floods upon the dry ground, and refresh Thy waiting heritage. Let Thy priests be clothed with righteousness, and let Thy saints shout for joy. Show Thy mercy also unto them that are afar off, and gather all the lost sheep into Thy fold ; for the sake of Jesus Christ our Lord. *Amen.*

MOST merciful God, we bless Thy holy Name for all Thy servants who have kept the faith, and, having accomplished their warfare, are at rest with Thee. We pray Thee to enable us so to follow their good example, that we with them may finally be partakers of Thy heavenly kingdom, and, at the glorious appearing of our Saviour Jesus Christ, may behold Him with unveiled face, being changed into His likeness ; when He shall present us, with all His Church, faultless before the presence of His glory with exceeding joy. Hear us, O heavenly Father, for His sake : to whom, with Thee and the Holy Ghost, be glory for ever and ever. *Amen.*

¶ *Then the People shall rise and sing*

A HYMN.

¶ *Then, the People reverently bowing down, the Minister shall pro-nounce*

THE BENEDICTION.

NOW the God of peace, that brought again from the dead our Lord Jesus, that great Shepherd of the sheep, through the blood of the everlasting covenant, make you perfect in every good work to do His will, working in you that which is well-pleasing in His sight, through Jesus Christ; to whom be glory for ever and ever. *Amen.*

¶ *After the Benediction it is fitting that the Communicants remain in silent prayer, beseeching God that none may leave His Table without a blessing.*

THE ADMINISTRATION OF BAPTISM TO INFANTS.

¶ *Baptism is not to be unnecessarily delayed ; nor to be adminis-tered in any case by any private person ; but by a Minister of Christ, called to be the steward of the mysteries of God.* — Direc-tory for Worship, Chap. viii, § 1.

¶ *Although Baptism is usually to be administered in the church, in the presence of the congregation, yet there may be cases when it will be expedient to administer this Sacrament in pri-vate houses ; of which the Minister is to be the judge.* — Direc-tory for Worship, Chap. viii, § 5.

¶ *After previous notice is given to the Minister, the Child to be baptized is to be presented to him by one or both the parents, whom the Minister shall address in this wise :*

DEARLY beloved, Almighty God, who has called us into His Church, has promised to be our God, and also the God and Father of our children; which covenant He renews in this Sacrament of Baptism, given to us and to our children, as a sign and seal of the washing away of our sins and our ingrafting into Christ. St. Paul assures us that the children of the faithful are to be numbered among the holy people of God. Our Saviour also, in the Gospel, calls the children unto Him, and blesses them, say-ing : Suffer the little children to come unto Me, and forbid them not: for of such is the Kingdom of God.

Forasmuch as you desire and claim these blessings for your *Child*, you will now engage, on your part, to perform those things which God requires of you, that the good will and pleasure of your Heavenly Father may not be hidden from your *Child*

¶ *Here the Minister shall address the following* QUESTIONS *to the Parents ; and the Parents, each of them, shall make answer :*

Question. Do you accept, for yourself and for your *Child*, the covenant of God, and therein con-secrate your *Child* to Him ?

Answer. I do.

Question. Do you promise to instruct your *Child* in the principles of our holy religion, as contained in the Scriptures, to pray with *him* and for *him*, and to bring *him* up in the nurture and admonition of the Lord ?

Answer. I do.

¶ Then the Minister shall say,

GRANT, O Lord, to *these* Thy *servants* grace to perform the things which *they have* promised before Thee:
And sanctify with Thy Spirit *this Child* now to be baptized according to Thy Word; through Jesus Christ our Lord. *Amen.*

¶ Then, all present reverently standing, the Minister shall say to the Parents,

What is the name of this Child ?

¶ Then the Minister (taking the Child in his arms, or leaving it in the arms of the Parent), pronouncing the name of the Child, shall pour or sprinkle water upon it, saying,

N——, I baptize thee in the Name of the Father, and of the Son, and of the Holy Ghost. Amen.

¶ Then the Minister shall say,

Let us pray.

MOST holy and merciful Father, we give Thee hearty thanks that Thou hast numbered us amongst Thy people, and dost also call our children unto Thee, marking them with this Sacrament, as a singular token and badge of Thy love. Wherefore, we beseech Thee to confirm Thy favour more and more toward us, and to take into Thy tuition and defense *this Child*, whom we offer and present unto Thee with common supplications. Grant that *he* may know Thee *his* merciful Father, through Thy Holy Spirit working in *his heart*, and that *he* may not be ashamed to confess the faith of Christ crucified; but may continue His faithful soldier and servant, and so prevail against evil that in the end *he* may obtain the victory, and be exalted into the liberty of Thy kingdom; through Jesus Christ our Lord. *Amen.*

¶ *Then the Minister and People may say together the* LORD'S *PRAYER, if the same is not said in the Service immediately preceding or following.*

THE LORD'S PRAYER.

OUR Father which art in heaven, Hallowed be Thy Name. Thy kingdom come. Thy will be done in earth, As it is in heaven Give us this day our daily bread. And forgive us our debts, As we forgive our debtors. And lead us not into temptation, But deliver us from evil · For Thine is the kingdom, and the power, and the glory, for ever. Amen.

¶ *Then the Minister shall say,*

THE grace of the Lord Jesus Christ, and the love of God, and the communion of the Holy Ghost, be with you all. *Amen.*

¶ *Infants descending from parents, either both or but one of them professing faith in Christ and obedience to Him, are within the covenant of promise, and are to be baptized.* — Larger Catechism, 166

¶ *The efficacy of Baptism is not tied to that moment of time wherein it is administered; yet, notwithstanding, by the right use of this Sacrament the grace promised is not only offered, but really exhibited and conferred by the Holy Ghost, to such (whether of age or infants) as that grace belongeth unto, according to the counsel of God's own will, in His appointed time. Grace and salvation are, however, not so inseparably annexed unto Baptism as that none can be regenerated or saved without it, or that all that are baptized are undoubtedly regenerated.* — Confession of Faith, Chap. xxviii, §§ 5, 6.

¶ *When, by death of the parents or otherwise, children are removed from their custody, the guardian or other person who has undertaken to rear them may present them for Baptism, provided he possess the qualifications requisite for having his own children baptized, and is willing to assume the obligations made by parents in the foregoing service.* — Minutes of the Synod of 1786.

THE ADMINISTRATION OF BAPTISM TO ADULTS

AND THEIR RECEPTION TO THE LORD'S SUPPER.

¶ *When unbaptized persons apply for admission into the Church, they shall, in ordinary cases, after giving satisfaction with respect to their knowledge and piety, make a public profession of their faith in the presence of the congregation, and thereupon be baptized.* — Directory for Worship, Chap. x, § 4.

¶ *The* Candidates *appearing before the Minister, he shall say,*

HEAR the Words of the Institution of this holy Sacrament, as delivered by our Lord and Saviour to His disciples, before His ascension to the right hand of God:

"All power is given unto Me in heaven and in earth. Go ye, therefore, and teach all nations, baptizing them in the Name of the Father, and of the Son, and of the Holy Ghost: teaching them to observe all things whatsoever I have commanded you: and, lo, I am with you alway, even unto the end of the world."

Hence St. Peter, on the day of Pentecost, called upon the people, saying, "Repent, and be baptized, every one of you, in the Name of Jesus Christ, for the remission of sins, and ye shall receive the gift of the Holy Ghost For the promise is unto you, and to your children, and to all that are afar off, even as many as the Lord our God shall call."

Doubt ye not, therefore, but earnestly believe, that He will number among His people *these* present Persons, truly repenting and coming unto Him by faith, and that this Baptism with water in His Name shall be unto *them* the sign and seal of the washing away of their sins, their engrafting into Christ, their regeneration by His Holy Spirit, and their engagement to be the Lord's

¶ *The Minister shall then say to the* Persons *to be baptized, and each one shall answer, as follows :*

DEARLY beloved, who are come hither desiring to be baptized, you are now faithfully, for your part, in the presence of God and this congregation, to promise and answer to the following Questions.

> *Question.* Do you receive and profess the Christian faith, and in this faith do you desire to be baptized ?
> *Answer.* I do.
> *Question.* Do you confess your sins, and turn from them with godly sorrow, and put all your trust in the mercy of God, which is in Christ Jesus ; and do you promise in His strength to lead a sober, righteous, and godly life ?
> *Answer.* I do.

¶ *The Question here following is to be omitted at this point in case this* ORDER OF BAPTISM *is used in connection with that for the* CONFIRMATION *of Baptismal Vows.*

> *Question.* Now desiring to be received to the Lord's Supper, do you promise to make diligent use of the means of grace, submitting yourself to the lawful authority and guidance of the Church, and continuing in the peace and fellowship of the people of God ?
> *Answer.* I do.

¶ *Then the Minister shall say,*

Let us pray.

WE beseech Thee, O Lord, that it may please Thee to receive, and to sanctify with Thy Spirit, *these Persons* now to be baptized according to Thy Word ; that *they* may obtain the fulness of Thy grace, and ever remain in the number of Thy faithful children ; through Jesus Christ our Lord.   *Amen.*

¶ *Then, all present reverently standing, the Person to be baptized will kneel down, and the Minister, pronouncing his name, shall pour or sprinkle water upon his forehead, saying,*

N——, I baptize thee in the Name of the Father, and of the Son, and of the Holy Ghost Amen.

¶ *Then the Minister shall say,*

WE receive *this Person* into the congregation of Christ's flock; in the confidence that *he* shall never be ashamed to confess the faith of Christ crucified, and to continue Christ's faithful *soldier* and *servant* unto *his* life's end.

¶ *Here, if Persons who have been baptized in infancy are to be received to the Lord's Supper, they may be called to come forward, and the Minister, omitting the remainder of this Order, may proceed with the Order for the Confirmation of Baptismal Vows the newly baptized persons still standing in their places before him.*

¶ *Then the Minister (laying his hand, if such be his discretion, upon the head of every one in order kneeling before him) shall say,*

DEFEND, O Lord, *this* Thy *Child* with Thy heavenly grace; that *he* may continue Thine for ever; and daily increase in Thy Holy Spirit more and more, until *he* come unto Thy everlasting kingdom. Amen.

Let us pray.

ALMIGHTY God, our heavenly Father, we give Thee hearty thanks and praise that Thou hast not withheld Thy loving kindness from *these* Thy *servants*, but hast given *them* shelter within the covenant of Thy peace, and makest *them* to sit down at Thy Table. We entreat Thee of Thy great mercy to perfect in *them* the good work Thou hast begun; that *they*, being defended by Thy fatherly hand, and strengthened with power through Thy Spirit in the inward man, may be enabled to keep this covenant without spot, unrebukable, until the day of the appearing of our Lord Jesus Christ. *Amen.*

NOW unto Him that is able to keep you from falling, and to present you faultless before the presence of His glory with exceeding joy; to the only wise God our Saviour, be glory and majesty, dominion and power, both now and ever. *Amen.*

¶ *Baptism is not to be administered to any that are out of the visible Church, and so strangers from the covenant of promise, till they profess their faith in Christ and obedience to Him.* — Larger Catechism, 166.

THE CONFIRMATION OF BAPTISMAL VOWS

AND

RECEPTION TO THE LORD'S SUPPER.

¶ *At the time appointed, the Minister shall say,*

*T*HESE *Persons* now to be named, who *are* baptized *children* of the Church, *have* been examined, and approved by the Session as to *their* knowledge and piety, and now *present themselves* publicly to confirm the vows made for *them* in Baptism

¶ *The Minister shall then read* their names, *and* they *will come forward, and stand before him.*

¶ *Then addressing* them, *the Minister shall say,*

D EARLY beloved, in your Baptism you received the sign and seal of your engrafting into Christ, and were solemnly engaged to be the Lord's. And forasmuch as you now desire to confirm the covenant then made in your behalf, and to obey His commandment by confessing Him before men, you are to make answer faithfully to the following Questions.

Question. Do you here, in the presence of God and this congregation, confess Christ as your Lord, and adhere to that Christian faith wherein you were baptized ?

Answer. I do

Question. Do you ratify and confirm the vows of your Baptism, and promise with God's help to serve the Lord, and keep His commandments all the days of your life ?

Answer. I do

¶ *Here, if any* Adults *have been baptized at the same Service, the Minister shall address the following Question to* them *as well as to* those *who* were *baptized in infancy, and* they shall be *included in the following parts of this Order.*

Question.   Now desiring to be received to the Lord's Supper, do you promise to make diligent use of the means of grace, submitting yourself to the lawful authority and guidance of the Church, and continuing in the peace and fellowship of the people of God ?

Answer.   I do

¶ *Then the Minister (laying his hand, if such be his discretion, upon the head of every one in order kneeling before him) shall say,*

DEFEND, O Lord, *this* Thy *Child* with Thy heavenly grace ; that *he* may continue Thine for ever ; and daily increase in Thy Holy Spirit more and more, until *he* come unto Thy everlasting kingdom.   Amen.

Let us pray.

ALMIGHTY God, our heavenly Father, we give Thee hearty thanks and praise that Thou hast not withheld Thy loving kindness from *these* Thy *servants,* but hast given *them* shelter within the covenant of Thy peace, and makest *them* to sit down at Thy Table.   We entreat Thee of Thy great mercy to perfect in *them* the good work Thou hast begun ; that *they,* being defended by Thy fatherly hand, and strengthened with power through Thy Spirit in the inward man, may be enabled to keep this covenant without spot, unrebukable, until the day of the appearing of our Lord Jesus Christ.   *Amen.*

NOW unto Him that is able to keep you from falling, and to present you faultless before the presence of His glory with exceeding joy ; to the only wise God our Saviour, be glory and majesty, dominion and power, both now and ever.   *Amen.*

¶ *Children born within the pale of the visible Church, and dedicated to God in Baptism, are under the inspection and government of the Church; and are to be taught to read and repeat the Catechism, the Apostles' Creed, and the Lord's Prayer. They are to be taught to pray, to abhor sin, to fear God, and to obey the Lord Jesus Christ. And when they come to years of discretion, if they be free from scandal, appear sober and steady, and to have sufficient knowledge to discern the Lord's body, they ought to be informed it is their duty and privilege to come to the Lord's Supper.* — Directory for Worship, Chap. x, § 1.

¶ *The years of discretion in young Christians cannot be precisely fixed. This must be left to the prudence of the eldership. The Officers of the church are the judges of the qualifications of those to be admitted to sealing ordinances, and of the time when it is proper to admit young Christians to them.* — Directory for Worship, Chap. x, § 2.

¶ *A public Service for the reception of baptized persons to the Communion is not to be regarded as a part of either Sacrament, nor as an invariable condition of their admission to the Lord's Supper, but simply as a method advisable in ordinary cases; the occasions when it may be necessary or proper to use some other method being left to the prudence and judgment of the Officers of the church.*

THE RECEPTION OF COMMUNICANTS FROM OTHER CHURCHES.

¶ *This Order may be used after the close of the two Services immediately preceding, or at a Service preparatory to the Communion.*

¶ *If Communicants are received from other Churches, the Minister may read their names, and, bidding them rise, may address them, saying*

DEARLY beloved, Having before made public confession of your faith in Christ, and having voluntarily transferred to this church your covenant relation of membership ; you now promise to wait diligently upon its ordinances, to study its peace and prosperity, and to yield becoming submission to its government and discipline.

¶ *Then the Minister may bid all the Members of the church to rise, and speaking for them, he shall say,*

IN the Name of the Lord Jesus, we, the Officers and Members of this church, bid you welcome to its fellowship and to its covenant privileges. We promise to watch over you and seek your welfare in the Lord. And we pray God that all of us, being united in the faith, may be preserved blameless unto the coming of our Lord Jesus Christ. *Amen.*

THE ORDER FOR

THE SOLEMNIZATION OF MARRIAGE.

¶ *Forasmuch as Marriage is a sacred relation, the ground of
human fellowship and society, and most precious to mankind;
although it be not a Sacrament nor peculiar to the Church of
Christ, it is proper that it be solemnized by a lawful Minister,
that he may give counsel from the Word of God to those enter-
ing holy wedlock, and invoke the Divine blessing upon them.*

¶ *The Persons to be married shall present themselves before the
Minister, the Woman standing at the left hand of the Man.
Then, all present reverently standing, the Minister shall say,*

DEARLY beloved, we are assembled here in the presence
of God, to join this Man and this Woman in holy Marriage; which is instituted of God, regulated by His commandments, blessed by our Lord Jesus Christ, and to be
held in honour among all men. Let us therefore reverently
remember that God has established and sanctified Marriage, for the welfare and happiness of mankind. Our Saviour has declared that a man shall forsake his father and
mother and cleave unto his wife. By His apostles, He has
instructed those who enter into this relation to cherish a
mutual esteem and love; to bear with each other's infirmities and weaknesses; to comfort each other in sickness,
trouble, and sorrow ; in honesty and industry to provide
for each other, and for their household, in temporal things ;
to pray for and encourage each other in the things which
pertain to God ; and to live together as the heirs of the
grace of life.
Forasmuch as these two Persons have come hither to be
made one in this holy estate, if there be any here present
who knows any just cause why they may not lawfully be
joined in Marriage, I require him now to make it known,
or ever after to hold his peace.

¶ *Then, speaking unto the Persons who are to be married, he shall say,*

I CHARGE you both, before the great God the Searcher of all hearts, that if either of you know any impediment, why ye may not lawfully be joined together in Marriage, ye do now confess it.   For be ye well assured that if any persons are joined together otherwise than as God's Word allows, their union is not blessed by Him.

¶ *Then, if no impediment appear, the Minister shall say,*

Let us pray.

ALMIGHTY and ever blessed God, whose Presence is the happiness of every condition, and whose favour sweetens every relation ; We beseech Thee to be present and favourable unto these Thy servants, that they may be truly joined in the honourable estate of Marriage, in the covenant of their God.   As Thou hast brought them together by Thy providence, sanctify them by Thy Spirit, giving them a new frame of heart fit for their new estate ; and enrich them with all grace, whereby they may enjoy the comforts, undergo the cares, endure the trials, and perform the duties of life together as becometh Christians, under Thy heavenly guidance and protection ; through our Lord Jesus Christ.   *Amen.*

¶ *Then the Minister shall say to the Man,*

M——, wilt thou have this Woman to be thy wife, and wilt thou pledge thy troth to her, in all love and honour, in all duty and service, in all faith and tenderness, to live with her, and cherish her, according to the ordinance of God, in the holy bond of Marriage ?

The Man shall answer,

I will.

¶ Then the Minister shall say to the Woman,

N——, wilt thou have this Man to be thy husband, and wilt thou pledge thy troth to him, in all love and honour, in all duty and service, in all faith and tenderness, to live with him, and cherish him, according to the ordinance of God, in the holy bond of Marriage ?

The Woman shall answer,

I will.

¶ Then the Minister may say,

WHO giveth this Woman to be married to this Man ?

¶ Then the father, (or guardian or any friend,) of the Woman shall put her right hand into the hand of the Minister, who shall cause the Man with his right hand to take the Woman by her right hand and to say after him as follows ·

I, M., take thee N., To be my wedded wife ; And I do promise and covenant, Before God and these witnesses, To be thy loving and faithful husband, In plenty and in want, In joy and in sorrow, In sickness and in health, As long as we both shall live.

¶ Then shall they loose their hands ; and the Woman with her right hand taking the Man by his right hand, shall likewise say after the Minister

I, N., take thee M., To be my wedded husband , And I do promise and covenant, Before God and these witnesses, To be thy loving and faithful wife, In plenty and in want, In joy and in sorrow, In sickness and in health, As long as we both shall live.

¶ Then, if a Ring be provided, it shall be given to the Minister, who shall return it to the Man, who shall then put it upon the fourth finger of the Woman's left hand, saying after the Minister,

THIS Ring I give thee, In token and pledge, Of our constant faith, And abiding love.

¶ Then the Minister shall say,

Let us pray.

MOST merciful and gracious God, of whom the whole family in heaven and earth is named; Bestow upon these Thy servants the seal of Thine approval, and Thy fatherly benediction· granting unto them grace to fulfil, with pure and steadfast affection, the vow and covenant between them made. Guide them together, we beseech Thee, in the way of righteousness and peace, that loving and serving Thee, with one heart and mind, all the days of their life, they may be abundantly enriched with the tokens of Thine everlasting favour, in Jesus Christ our Lord   *Amen*

OUR Father which art in heaven, Hallowed be Thy Name. Thy kingdom come   Thy will be done in earth, As it is in heaven Give us this day our daily bread   And forgive us our debts, As we forgive our debtors. And lead us not into temptation, But deliver us from evil: For Thine is the kingdom, and the power, and the glory, for ever. Amen

¶ Then shall the Minister say unto all who are present,

BY the authority committed unto me as a Minister of the Church of Christ, I declare that *M.* and *N.* are now Husband and Wife, according to the ordinance of God, and the law of the State: in the Name of the Father, and of the Son and of the Holy Ghost   Amen.

¶ Then, causing the Husband and Wife to join their right hands, the Minister shall say,

WHOM therefore God hath joined together, let no man put asunder.

¶ And the Minister shall pronounce this BLESSING

The Lord bless you and keep you : The Lord make His face to shine upon you and be gracious unto you :
The Lord lift up His countenance upon you and give you peace ·
Both now and in the life everlasting.   *Amen*

THE BURIAL OF THE DEAD.

¶ *When all are assembled in the house or in the church, the Minister shall begin the Service with one or more of these* SENTENCES *from the Holy Scriptures.*

OUR help is in the Name of the Lord, who made heaven and earth. (*Psalm* cxxiv. 8.)

FOR we are strangers before Thee and sojourners, as were all our fathers: our days on the earth are as a shadow, and there is none abiding. (1 *Chronicles* xxix. 15.)

ALL flesh is grass, and all the goodliness thereof is as the flower of the field : the grass withereth, the flower fadeth : but the word of our God shall stand for ever. (*Isaiah* xl. 6–8)

LIKE as a father pitieth his children, so the Lord pitieth them that fear Him. For He knoweth our frame ; He remembereth that we are dust. (*Psalm* ciii. 13, 14)

I AM the Resurrection, and the Life : he that believeth in Me, though he were dead, yet shall he live : and whosoever liveth and believeth in Me shall never die. (*St. John* xi. 25, 26.)

¶ *Then let the Minister say,*

Let us pray.

¶ *Then shall he lead the People in the* INVOCATION, *using if he will one of the following Prayers, and ending with the* LORD'S PRAYER.

ALMIGHTY God, the Fountain of all wisdom, who knowest our necessities before we ask and our ignorance in asking ; We beseech Thee to have compassion upon our infirmities ; and those things, which for our unworthiness we dare not and for our blindness we cannot ask, vouchsafe to give us, for the worthiness of Thy Son, Jesus Christ our Lord. *Amen.*

ALMIGHTY God, our heavenly Father, who art our Refuge and Strength, and a very present Help in time of trouble; Enable us, we pray Thee, to put our trust in Thee, and seeing that we have an High Priest who is touched with the feeling of our infirmities, may we come boldly unto the throne of grace, that we may obtain mercy, and find grace to help in this time of need, through Jesus Christ our Lord. *Amen.*

OUR Father in heaven, whose pity is infinite and whose will is sovereign; Be pleased to look down upon our sorrow, and for the sake of Thy dear Son, enable us so to hear Thy holy Word, that through patience and comfort of the Scriptures we may have hope; and grant us the consolation of Thy Holy Spirit, that we, humbly acknowledging our many sins, may nevertheless hold fast the assurance of Thy mercy and the blessed hope of everlasting life, through Him who died and rose again and ever liveth with Thee, even Jesus Christ our Lord. *Amen.*

OUR Father which art in heaven, Hallowed be Thy Name. Thy kingdom come. Thy will be done in earth, As it is in heaven. Give us this day our daily bread. And forgive us our debts, As we forgive our debtors. And lead us not into temptation, But deliver us from evil. For Thine is the kingdom, and the power, and the glory, for ever. Amen.

¶ *Then let one or more of the following* PSALMS *be chanted or read, closing with the* Gloria Patri :

PSALM XXXIX. 4-13.

LORD, make me to know mine end, and the measure of my days, what it is: that I may know how frail I am.
　Behold, thou hast made my days as a handbreadth; and mine age is as nothing before thee: verily every man at his best state is altogether vanity.
　Surely every man walketh in a vain show; surely they are disquieted in vain: he heapeth up riches, and knoweth not who shall gather them.
　And now, Lord, what wait I for : my hope is in thee.

Deliver me from all my transgressions. make me not the reproach of the foolish

I was dumb, I opened not my mouth : because thou didst it

Remove thy stroke away from me : I am consumed by the blow of thine hand

When thou with rebukes dost correct man for iniquity, thou makest his beauty to consume away like a moth: surely every man is vanity.

Hear my prayer, O Lord, and give ear unto my cry ; hold not thy peace at my tears : for I am a stranger with thee, and a sojourner, as all my fathers were.

O spare me, that I may recover strength : before I go hence, and be no more.

PSALM XC.

LORD, thou hast been our dwelling place : in all generations.

Before the mountains were brought forth, or ever thou hadst formed the earth and the world : even from everlasting to everlasting, thou art God.

Thou turnest man to destruction : and sayest, Return, ye children of men.

For a thousand years in thy sight are but as yesterday when it is past: and as a watch in the night

Thou carriest them away as with a flood; they are as a sleep : in the morning they are like grass which groweth up.

In the morning it flourisheth, and groweth up · in the evening it is cut down, and withereth.

For we are consumed by thine anger. and by thy wrath are we troubled.

Thou hast set our iniquities before thee· our secret sins in the light of thy countenance

For all our days are passed away in thy wrath: we spend our years as a tale that is told

The days of our years are threescore years and ten ; and if by reason of strength they be fourscore years yet is their strength labour and sorrow; for it is soon cut off, and we fly away.

Who knoweth the power of thine anger : even according to thy fear, so is thy wrath.

So teach us to number our days : that we may apply our hearts unto wisdom.

Return, O Lord, how long and let it repent thee concerning thy servants.

O satisfy us early with thy mercy . that we may rejoice and be glad all our days

Make us glad according to the days wherein thou hast afflicted us and the years wherein we have seen evil

Let thy work appear unto thy servants : and thy glory unto their children.

And let the beauty of the Lord our God be upon us : and establish thou the work of our hands upon us ; yea, the work of our hands establish thou it.

Glory be to the Father, and to the Son : and to the Holy Ghost ;

As it was in the beginning, is now, and ever shall be : world without end. Amen.

AT THE BURIAL OF A CHILD.

PSALM CIII. 13–18.

LIKE as a father pitieth his children · so the Lord pitieth them that fear him.

For he knoweth our frame : he remembereth that we are dust.

As for man, his days are as grass as a flower of the field, so he flourisheth.

For the wind passeth over it, and it is gone. and the place thereof shall know it no more.

But the mercy of the Lord is from everlasting to everlasting upon them that fear him : and his righteousness unto children's children ;

To such as keep his covenant : and to those that remember his commandments to do them.

PSALM CXXX.

OUT of the depths have I cried unto thee, O Lord

Lord, hear my voice : let Thine ears be attentive to the voice of my supplications.

If Thou, Lord, shouldest mark iniquities : O Lord, who shall stand ?

But there is forgiveness with thee : that thou mayest be feared.

I wait for the Lord, my soul doth wait: and in his word do I hope.

My soul waiteth for the Lord more than they that watch for the morning : I say, more than they that watch for the morning.

Let Israel hope in the Lord : for with the Lord there is mercy, and with him is plenteous redemption.

And he shall redeem Israel . from all his iniquities.

PSALM XXIII.

THE Lord is my shepherd : I shall not want.

He maketh me to lie down in green pastures : he leadeth me beside the still waters.

He restoreth my soul : he leadeth me in the paths of righteousness for his name's sake.

Yea, though I walk through the valley of the shadow of death, I will fear no evil : for thou art with me ; thy rod and thy staff they comfort me.

Thou preparest a table before me in the presence of mine enemies . thou anointest my head with oil ; my cup runneth over.

Surely goodness and mercy shall follow me all the days of my life : and I will dwell in the house of the Lord for ever.

Glory be to the Father, and to the Son : and to the Holy Ghost ;

As it was in the beginning, is now, and ever shall be: world without end. Amen

¶ *If so desired, a Hymn or Anthem may here be sung.*

¶ *Then let the Minister read one of the following* Lessons *from the* HOLY SCRIPTURES, *and before the reading let him say,* Hear the Word of God as written for our admonition and comfort.

1 CORINTHIANS XV. 20–28 ; 35–58.

NOW is Christ risen from the dead, and become the first-fruits of them that slept For since by man came death, by man came also the resurrection of the dead. For as in Adam all die, even so in Christ shall all be made alive.

But every man in his own order. Christ the first-fruits, afterward they that are Christ's at his coming.

Then cometh the end, when he shall have delivered up the kingdom to God, even the Father; when he shall have put down all rule, and all authority and power. For he must reign, till he hath put all enemies under his feet. The last enemy that shall be destroyed is death. For he hath put all things under his feet. But when he saith, All things are put under him, it is manifest that he is excepted, which did put all things under him. And when all things shall be subdued unto him, then shall the Son also himself be subject unto him that put all things under him, that God may be all in all.

But some man will say, How are the dead raised up? and with what body do they come? Thou fool, that which thou sowest is not quickened, except it die. And that which thou sowest, thou sowest not that body that shall be, but bare grain, it may chance of wheat, or of some other grain: but God giveth it a body as it hath pleased him, and to every seed his own body. All flesh is not the same flesh: but there is one kind of flesh of men, another flesh of beasts, another of fishes, and another of birds. There are also celestial bodies, and bodies terrestrial: but the glory of the celestial is one, and the glory of the terrestrial is another. There is one glory of the sun, and another glory of the moon, and another glory of the stars: for one star differeth from another star in glory. So also is the resurrection of the dead. It is sown in corruption, it is raised in incorruption: it is sown in dishonour, it is raised in glory: it is sown in weakness, it is raised in power: it is sown a natural body, it is raised a spiritual body. There is a natural body, and there is a spiritual body. And so it is written, The first man Adam was made a living soul; the last Adam was made a quickening spirit. Howbeit that was not first which is spiritual, but that which is natural, and afterward that which is spiritual. The first man is of the earth, earthy; the second man is the Lord from heaven. As is the earthy, such are they also that are earthy; and as is the heavenly, such are they also that are heavenly. And as we have borne the image of the earthy, we shall also bear the image of the heavenly. Now this I say, brethren, that flesh and blood cannot inherit the kingdom of God: neither doth corruption inherit incorruption. Behold, I show you a mystery, We shall not all sleep, but we shall all be changed, in a moment, in the twinkling of an eye, at the last trump: for the trumpet shall sound, and the dead shall be raised incorruptible, and we shall be changed. For this corruptible must put on incorruption, and this mortal must put on immortality. So when this corruptible shall have put on incorruption, and this mortal shall have put on immortality, then shall be brought to pass the saying that is written, Death is swallowed up in victory. O death, where is thy sting? O grave, where is thy victory? The sting of death is sin; and the strength of sin is the law. But thanks be to God, which giveth us the victory through our Lord Jesus Christ. Therefore, my beloved brethren, be ye steadfast, unmovable, always abounding in the work of the Lord, forasmuch as ye know that your labour is not in vain in the Lord.

¶ *Or this:*

St. John xiv. 1–3, 15–20, 25–27; 1 Thessalonians iv. 13, and v. 1–11

LET not your heart be troubled: ye believe in God, believe also in me. In my Father's house are many mansions; if it were not so, I would have told you. I go to prepare a place for you. And if I go and prepare a place for you, I will come again, and receive you unto myself; that where I am, there ye may be also

If ye love me, keep my commandments. And I will pray the Father, and he shall give you another Comforter, that he may abide with you for ever; even the Spirit of truth; whom the world cannot receive, because it seeth him not, neither knoweth him: but ye know him; for he dwelleth with you, and shall be in you. I will not leave you comfortless: I will come to you. Yet a little while, and the world seeth me no more; but ye see me; because I live, ye shall live also. At that day ye shall know that I am in my Father, and ye in me, and I in you.

These things have I spoken unto you, being yet present with you. But the Comforter, which is the Holy Ghost, whom the Father will send in my name, he shall teach you all things, and bring all things to your remembrance, whatsoever I have said unto you. Peace I leave with you, my peace I give unto you : not as the world giveth, give I unto you. Let not your heart be troubled, neither let it be afraid.

I WOULD not have you to be ignorant, brethren, concerning them which are asleep, that ye sorrow not, even as others which have no hope. For if we believe that Jesus died and rose again, even so them also which sleep in Jesus will God bring with him. For this we say unto you by the word of the Lord, that we which are alive and remain unto the coming of the Lord shall not prevent them which are asleep. For the Lord himself shall descend from heaven with a shout, with the voice of the archangel, and with the trump of God ; and the dead in Christ shall rise first : then we which are alive and remain shall be caught up together with them in the clouds, to meet the Lord in the air : and so shall we ever be with the Lord. Wherefore comfort one another with these words.

But of the times and the seasons, brethren, ye have no need that I write unto you. For yourselves know perfectly, that the day of the Lord so cometh as a thief in the night. For when they shall say, Peace and safety ; then sudden destruction cometh upon them, as travail upon a woman with child ; and they shall not escape. But ye, brethren, are not in darkness, that that day should overtake you as a thief. Ye are all the children of light, and the children of the day : we are not of the night, nor of darkness. Therefore let us not sleep, as do others ; but let us watch and be sober. For they that sleep sleep in the night ; and they that be drunken are drunken in the night. But let us, who are of the day, be sober, putting on the breastplate of faith and love ; and for an helmet, the hope of salvation. For God hath not appointed us to wrath, but to obtain salvation by our Lord Jesus Christ, who died for us, that, whether we wake or sleep, we should live together with him. Wherefore comfort yourselves together, and edify one another, even as also ye do.

¶ *Or this:*

REVELATION XXI. 1–4, 22–27, XXII. 1–7.

AND I saw a new heaven and a new earth: for the first heaven and the first earth were passed away; and there was no more sea

And I John saw the holy city, new Jerusalem, coming down from God out of heaven, prepared as a bride adorned for her husband. And I heard a great voice out of heaven, saying, Behold, the tabernacle of God is with men, and he will dwell with them, and they shall be his people, and God himself shall be with them, and be their God. And God shall wipe away all tears from their eyes; and there shall be no more death, neither sorrow, nor crying, neither shall there be any more pain: for the former things are passed away

And I saw no temple therein: for the Lord God Almighty and the Lamb are the temple of it. And the city had no need of the sun, neither of the moon, to shine in it: for the glory of God did lighten it, and the Lamb is the light thereof. And the nations of them which are saved shall walk in the light of it: and the kings of the earth do bring their glory and honour into it. And the gates of it shall not be shut at all by day: for there shall be no night there. And they shall bring the glory and honour of the nations into it And there shall in no wise enter into it anything that defileth, neither whatsoever worketh abomination, or maketh a lie; but they which are written in the Lamb's book of life.

And he shewed me a pure river of water of life, clear as crystal, proceeding out of the throne of God and of the Lamb. In the midst of the street of it, and on either side of the river, was there the tree of life, which bare twelve manner of fruits, and yielded her fruit every month: and the leaves of the tree were for the healing of the nations. And there shall be no more curse: but the throne of God and of the Lamb shall be in it, and his servants shall serve him: And they shall see his face, and his name shall be in their foreheads And there shall be no night there; and they need no candle, neither light of the sun; for the Lord God giveth them light: and they shall reign for ever and ever. And he said unto me, These sayings are faithful and true: and the Lord God of the holy prophets sent his angel to shew unto his servants the things which must shortly be done.

Behold, I come quickly: blessed is he that keepeth the sayings of the prophecy of this book.

At the Burial of a Child.

2 Samuel xii. 16–23.

DAVID therefore besought God for the child ; and David fasted, and went in, and lay all night upon the earth. And the elders of his house arose, and went to him, to raise him up from the earth : but he would not, neither did he eat bread with them.

And it came to pass on the seventh day, that the child died. And the servants of David feared to tell him that the child was dead: for they said, Behold, while the child was yet alive, we spake unto him, and he would not hearken unto our voice: how will he then vex himself, if we tell him that the child is dead ? But when David saw that his servants whispered, David perceived that the child was dead : therefore David said unto his servants, Is the child dead ? and they said, He is dead. Then David arose from the earth, and washed, and anointed himself, and changed his apparel, and came into the house of the Lord, and worshipped: then he came to his own house ; and when he required, they set bread before him, and he did eat. Then said his servants unto him, What thing is this that thou hast done ? thou didst fast and weep for the child, while it was alive; but when the child was dead, thou didst rise and eat bread. And he said, While the child was yet alive, I fasted and wept. for I said, Who can tell whether God will be gracious to me, that the child may live ? But now he is dead, wherefore should I fast? can I bring him back again? I shall go to him, but he shall not return to me.

St. Mark x. 13–16.

AND they brought young children to him, that he should touch them: and his disciples rebuked those that brought them. But when Jesus saw it, he was much displeased, and said unto them, Suffer the little children to come unto me, and forbid them not: for of such is the kingdom of God. Verily I say unto you, Whosoever shall not receive the kingdom of God as a little child, he shall not enter therein. And he took them up in his arms, put his hands upon them, and blessed them.

REVELATION XXII. 4, VII 16–17.

AND they shall see his face, and his name shall be in their foreheads.

They shall hunger no more, neither thirst any more; neither shall the sun light on them, nor any heat. For the Lamb which is in the midst of the throne shall feed them, and shall lead them unto living fountains of waters: and God shall wipe away all tears from their eyes.

¶ *And at the close of the reading from the* HOLY SCRIPTURES *the Minister may say,*

THE Lord gave, and the Lord hath taken away: blessed be the Name of the Lord.

¶ *If it be thought desirable, an Address may here be made.*

¶ *Then a Hymn may be sung, or may be read by the Minister.*

¶ *Then the People, standing, may join with the Minister in their* CONFESSION OF FAITH

I BELIEVE in God the Father Almighty, Maker of heaven and earth:

And in Jesus Christ His only Son, our Lord; Who was conceived by the Holy Ghost, Born of the Virgin Mary, Suffered under Pontius Pilate, Was crucified, dead, and buried; [He descended into hell;*] The third day He rose again from the dead; He ascended into heaven, And sitteth on the right hand of God the Father Almighty; From thence He shall come to judge the quick and the dead.

I believe in the Holy Ghost; The Holy Catholic Church; The Communion of Saints, The Forgiveness of sins, The Resurrection of the body; and the Life everlasting. Amen.

---

* Or, *He continued in the state of the dead, and under the power of death, until the third day.*

¶ *Then let the Minister say,*

Let us pray.

¶ *The Minister may, if he so desire, use any of the following Prayers, ordering the same with discretion, and having regard unto the present circumstances.*

FOR RESIGNATION.

O LORD God, our heavenly Father, who alone art the Author and the Disposer of our life, from whom our spirits have come, and to whom they shall return; We acknowledge Thy sovereign power and right both to give and to take away, as seemeth good in Thy sight; and we most humbly beseech Thee, that unto all Thy righteous dealings we may yield ourselves with due resignation and patience; being assured that though we understand not the mystery of Thy ways, yet always in faithfulness, O Lord, dost Thou afflict us, and for Thy mercy's sake; through Jesus Christ our Lord. *Amen.*

FOR THOSE BEREAVED.

A LMIGHTY and most merciful God, the Consolation of the sorrowful, and the Support of the weary, who dost not willingly grieve or afflict the children of men; Look down in tender love and pity, we beseech Thee, upon Thy bereaved servants, whose joy is turned into mourning; so that, while they mourn, they may not murmur, or faint under Thy rod; but, remembering all Thy mercies, Thy promises, and Thy love in Christ, may resign themselves meekly into Thy hands, to be taught and disciplined by Thee. Convert them wholly to Thyself, and fill their desolate hearts with Thy love, that they may cleave more closely to Thee, who bringest life out of death, and who canst turn their grief into eternal joy; through Jesus Christ our Lord. *Amen.*

FOR THE RIGHT USE OF AFFLICTION.

O GOD, whose days are without end, and whose mercies cannot be numbered; Make us, we beseech Thee, deeply sensible of the shortness and uncertainty of human life, and let Thy Holy Spirit lead us through this present world in holiness and righteousness all the days of our

lives; that, when we shall have served Thee in our generation, we may be gathered unto our fathers, having the
testimony of a good conscience ; in the communion of Thy
holy Church ; in the confidence of a certain faith ; in the
comfort of a reasonable, religious and holy hope , in favour
with Thee, our God; and in perfect charity with the
world.   All which we ask through Jesus Christ our Lord.
Amen.

For Comfort.

O LORD Jesus Christ, we beseech Thee to comfort these
Thy servants in their present sorrow ; and as Thou
didst send the Holy Ghost to be the Comforter of Thy
people; strengthen them by the manifestation of His gracious indwelling, that they may be enabled to contemplate
the joy of that better home, where Thou art ever seen and
worshipped as the Light and Satisfaction of Thine elect,
who dwellest with the Father, in the unity of the same
Spirit, one God, world without end   *Amen.*

For the Comfort of Christ's Presence

O LORD Jesus Christ, who Thyself didst weep beside the
grave, and art touched with the feeling of our sorrows;
Fulfil now Thy promise that Thou wilt not leave Thy
people comfortless, but wilt come to them   Reveal Thyself unto Thine afflicted servants, and cause them to hear
Thee saying, "I am the Resurrection and the Life " Help
them, O Lord, to turn to Thee with true discernment, and
to abide in Thee through living faith; that, finding now
the comfort of Thy presence, they may have also a sure
confidence in Thee for all that is to come; until the day
break, and these shadows flee away.   Hear us for Thy
great mercy's sake, O Jesus Christ our Lord.   *Amen.*

At the Burial of a Child.

MOST merciful Father, who hast hastened to take unto
Thyself the soul of this child ; Grant to us who are
still in our pilgrimage, and who walk as yet by faith, that
having served Thee with constancy on earth, we may be
joined hereafter with Thy blessed children in glory everlasting ; through Jesus Christ our Lord.   *Amen.*

In Remembrance of God's Grace to the Departed.

O GOD, who art the Strength of Thy saints and who redeemest the souls of Thy servants; We bless Thy Name for all those who have died in the Lord, and who now rest from their labours, having received the end of their faith, even the salvation of their souls. Especially we call to remembrance Thy loving-kindness and Thy tender mercies to this Thy servant. For all Thy goodness that withheld not *his* portion in the joys of this earthly life, and for Thy guiding hand along the way of *his* pilgrimage; we give Thee thanks and praise. Especially we bless Thee for Thy grace that kindled in *his* heart the love of Thy dear Name; that enabled *him* to fight the good fight, to endure unto the end, and to obtain the victory; yea, to become more than conqueror, through Him that loveth us We magnify Thy holy Name that *his* trials and temptations being ended, sickness and death being passed, with all the dangers and difficulties of this mortal life, *his* spirit is at home in Thy presence, at whose right hand dwelleth eternal peace And grant, O Lord, we beseech Thee, that we who rejoice in the triumph of Thy saints may profit by their example, that becoming followers of their faith and patience we also may enter with them into an inheritance incorruptible and undefiled, and that fadeth not away; through Jesus Christ our Lord. *Amen*

For Grace to Imitate the Righteous Dead.

ALMIGHTY and ever-living God, we yield unto Thee most high praise and hearty thanks for the wonderful grace and virtue declared in all Thy saints, who have been the choice vessels of Thy favour, and the lights of the world in their several generations; most humbly beseeching Thee to give us grace so to follow the example of their steadfastness in Thy faith, and obedience to Thy holy commandments, that at the day of the general resurrection, we, with all those who are of the mystical body of Thy Son, may be set on His right hand, and hear His most joyful voice saying: Come, ye blessed of My Father, inherit the kingdom prepared for you from the foundation of the world Grant this, O Father, for Jesus Christ's sake, our only Mediator and Advocate *Amen.*

¶ Or this:

ALMIGHTY God, who hast knit together Thine elect in one communion and fellowship, in the mystical body of Thy Son Christ our Lord; Grant us grace so to follow Thy blessed saints in all virtuous and godly living, that we may come to those unspeakable joys which Thou hast prepared for them that unfeignedly love Thee ; through Jesus Christ our Lord. *Amen.*

For Grace to Follow Christ.

O LORD Jesus Christ, who by Thy death didst take away the sting of death ; Grant unto us Thy servants so to follow in faith where Thou hast led the way, that we may at length fall asleep peacefully in Thee, and awake after Thy likeness; through Thy mercy, who livest with the Father and the Holy Ghost, one God, world without end. *Amen.*

For Endurance unto the End.

O GOD, Thou King eternal, immortal, and invisible, the blessed and only Potentate; May we, who cannot see Thee with the eye of flesh, behold Thee steadfastly with the eye of faith, that we may not faint under the manifold trials and temptations of this mortal life, but endure as seeing Thee who art invisible; and grant that having fulfilled Thy will upon earth, we may behold Thy face in heaven, and be made partakers of those unspeakable joys which Thou hast promised to them who love Thy Son Jesus Christ our Lord, and wait His appearing; for whose sake, we beseech Thee to hear us; and unto whom, with Thee the Father and the Holy Ghost, we ascribe all glory and praise, for ever and ever. *Amen.*

The Benediction.

NOW the God of peace, that brought again from the dead our Lord Jesus, that great Shepherd of the sheep, through the blood of the everlasting covenant, make you perfect in every good work to do His will, working in you

that which is well-pleasing in His sight, through Jesus
Christ, to whom be glory for ever and ever. *Amen.*

¶ *Or this·*

THE peace of God, which passeth all understanding, keep
your hearts and minds in the knowledge and love of
God, and of His Son Jesus Christ our Lord, and the bless-
ing of God Almighty, the Father, the Son, and the Holy
Ghost, be amongst you, and remain with you always.
Amen.

¶ *When they are come to the grave, while the Body of the Dead is
made ready to be laid therein, let the Minister say,*

MAN that is born of a woman hath but a short time to
live, and is full of misery. He cometh up, and is cut
down like a flower; he fleeth as it were a shadow, and
never continueth in one stay.

In the midst of life we are in death: of whom may we
seek for succour, but of Thee, O Lord, who for our sins art
justly displeased?

Yet, O Lord God most holy, O Lord most mighty, O holy
and most merciful Saviour, deliver us not into the bitter
pains of eternal death.

Thou knowest, Lord, the secrets of our hearts; shut not
Thy merciful ears to our prayer; but spare us, Lord most
holy, O God most mighty, O holy and merciful Saviour,
Thou most worthy Judge eternal, suffer us not at our last
hour, for any pains of death, to fall from Thee.

¶ *Or this·*

I AM the Resurrection and the Life, saith the Lord; He
that believeth in Me, though he were dead, yet shall he
live: and whosoever liveth and believeth in Me, shall never
die.

For we know that if our earthly house of this tabernacle
were dissolved, we have a building of God, an house not
made with hands, eternal in the heavens

¶ *Then, while earth is cast upon the Body by some standing by, the Minister shall say,*

FORASMUCH as it hath pleased Almighty God to take out of this world the soul of our *brother* departed (*or*, this child), we therefore commit *his* body to the ground, earth to earth, ashes to ashes, dust to dust; looking for the Resurrection of the dead, and the life of the world to come, through our Lord Jesus Christ; at whose coming in glorious majesty the earth and the sea shall give up their dead; and the mortal bodies of those who sleep in Him shall be changed, and made like unto His own glorious body; according to the mighty working whereby He is able to subdue all things unto Himself.

¶ *Then may be said or sung·*

I HEARD a voice from heaven saying unto me, Write, Blessed are the dead which die in the Lord from henceforth: Yea, saith the Spirit, that they may rest from their labours; and their works do follow them.

¶ *Then the Minister shall offer one of the following* Prayers, *or some other, and shall follow it with the* BENEDICTION.

O MERCIFUL God, the Father of our Lord Jesus Christ, who is the Resurrection and the Life; in whom whosoever believeth shall live, though he die; and whosoever liveth and believeth in Him shall not die eternally; We humbly beseech Thee, O Father, to raise us from the death of sin unto the life of righteousness; that, when we shall depart this life, we may rest in Him; and that at the Resurrection we may be found acceptable in Thy sight, and receive that blessing which Thy well-beloved Son shall then pronounce to all that love and serve Thee, saying, Come, ye blessed children of My Father, receive the kingdom prepared for you from the beginning of the world: grant this, we beseech Thee, O merciful Father, through Jesus Christ, our Mediator and Redeemer. *Amen.*

ALMIGHTY God, with whom do live the spirits of them that depart hence in the Lord, and with whom the souls of the faithful, after they are delivered from the burden of the flesh, are in joy and felicity; We give Thee hearty thanks for that it hath pleased Thee to deliver them out of the miseries of this sinful world; beseeching Thee, that it may please Thee, of Thy gracious goodness, shortly to accomplish the number of Thine elect, and to hasten Thy kingdom; that we, with all those that are departed in the true faith of Thy holy Name, may have our perfect consummation and bliss, both in body and soul, in Thy eternal and everlasting glory; through Jesus Christ our Lord. *Amen.*

THE BENEDICTION.

THE grace of the Lord Jesus Christ, and the love of God, and the communion of the Holy Ghost, be with you all. *Amen.*

AT THE BURIAL OF THE DEAD AT SEA.

¶ *The same Order may be used; but the* WORDS OF COMMITTAL *shall be as follows.*

FORASMUCH as it hath pleased Almighty God to take out of this world the soul of our *brother* departed (*or*, this child), we therefore commit *his* body to the deep; looking for the Resurrection of the dead, and the life of the world to come, through our Lord Jesus Christ; at whose coming in glorious majesty the sea shall give up her dead; and the mortal bodies of those who sleep in Him shall be changed, and made like unto His own glorious body; according to the mighty working whereby He is able to subdue all things unto Himself.

THE LICENSING OF CANDIDATES TO PREACH THE GOSPEL.

¶ *Men who are seeking an entrance to the Christian Ministry, having been taken under the care of Presbytery, and having fulfilled the requirements of the Form of Government (Chap. xiv). are then to be licensed by Presbytery to preach the Gospel and so to make a competent trial of their gifts for the sacred office.*

¶ *At the discretion of Presbytery, the Licensing of Candidates may follow a specially appointed Service of praise, prayer, and the preaching of the Word ; or it may be done, after the examination of Candidates, at a regular session of Presbytery   The appointed hour being come, the Moderator shall call the Presbytery and all present to attend with reverence the Licensure of Candidates for the Christian Ministry.*

¶ *Let all stand while the Moderator, or the Minister appointed, reads the following* SENTENCES.

PRAISE waiteth for Thee, O God, in Zion : and unto Thee shall the vow be performed.

Blessed is the man whom Thou choosest, and causest to approach unto Thee, that he may dwell in Thy courts , we shall be satisfied with the goodness of Thy house, even of Thy holy temple

The harvest truly is plenteous, but the labourers are few ; Pray ye therefore the Lord of the harvest, that He will send forth labourers into His harvest.

¶ *Let all bow down while the Moderator, or some other Presbyter appointed, leads in Prayer, saying :*

LET us pray for the increase of the Ministry, the welfare of the Church, and the conversion of the world to Christ.

¶ *Here shall follow the* PRAYER, *which, if so desired, may be in form as found in the* TREASURY OF PRAYERS, *pp.* 130–133

¶ *Then the Moderator shall say*

BRETHREN in Christ: God by His Holy Spirit calls men to serve Him according to the gifts bestowed upon them: and to chosen servants He grants this grace that they should make known the riches of Christ by the preaching of the Gospel. Unto His Church He has given commandment not only to pray for the increase of the Ministry, but also to prove and try those who seek the sacred office, that no man be ordained suddenly, but that men of pure heart and good conduct, able to speak to edification, be found for the service of the sanctuary. Therefore it is proper that those who desire to give themselves to this Ministry should not only prepare themselves by study, prayer, and good works, but should also have opportunity to make trial of their gifts by the experience of preaching, and to approve themselves to the churches as workmen fitted rightly to divide the Word of Truth. According to the Form of Government of this Church the oversight of these matters is committed to the Presbytery, which is to examine every Candidate for the sacred office in regard to his religious experience, his motives in seeking the Ministry, and his proficiency in that knowledge which is necessary for a teacher of men. Having made this examination, and being satisfied with its result, this Presbytery of —— is ready to license and approve, as *Probationers* for the Ministry, the following *Persons*, [*here let the Candidates be named*,] who will now present *themselves* before *their* brethren

¶ *Let the* Candidates *stand before the Moderator while he asks the following* QUESTIONS, *to each of which* they *shall answer, saying*, I do.

DO you believe the Scriptures of the Old and New Testaments to be the Word of God, the only infallible rule of faith and practice ?

Do you sincerely receive and adopt the Confession of Faith of this Church, as containing the system of doctrine taught in the Holy Scriptures ?

Do you promise to study the peace, unity, and purity of the Church ?

Do you promise to submit yourself, in the Lord, to the government of this Presbytery, or of any other Presbytery in the bounds of which you may be called ?

¶ *The* Candidates *shall remain standing, and the Moderator, calling upon all the Members of the Presbytery to rise, shall say ·*

IN the Name of the Lord Jesus Christ, and by that authority which He hath given to the Church for its edification, we do license you to preach the Gospel, wherever God in His providence may call you : and for this purpose, [*here the Moderator may take each of the Candidates by the hand, saying to each,*] may the blessing of God rest upon you, and the Spirit of Christ fill your heart. *Amen.*

¶ *Then may be sung the following or some other Hymn*

O WORD of God Incarnate,
　 O Wisdom from on high,
O Truth unchanged, unchanging,
　 O Light of our dark sky ;
We praise Thee for the radiance
　 That from the hallowed page,
A lantern to our footsteps,
　 Shines on from age to age.

The Church from her dear Master
　 Received the gift divine,
And still that light she lifteth
　 O'er all the earth to shine.
It is the golden casket
　 Where gems of truth are stored ;
It is the heaven-drawn picture
　 Of Christ, the living Word.

It floateth like a banner
　 Before God's host unfurled ;
It shineth like a beacon
　 Above the darkling world.
It is the chart and compass
　 That o'er life's surging sea,
'Mid mists, and rocks, and quicksands,
　 Still guides, O Christ, to Thee.

O make Thy Church, dear Saviour,
   A lamp of purest gold,
To bear before the nations
   Thy true light as of old
O teach Thy wandering pilgrims
   By this their path to trace,
Till, clouds and darkness ended,
   They see Thee face to face. Amen.

¶ *Then the Moderator, or the Minister appointed, shall say,*

Let us pray.

¶ *The* PRAYER *may be offered in these or other fitting words·*

O GOD, the Father eternal, who hast made Thy risen
and ever-glorious Son, Jesus Christ, Head over all
things to Thy Church. Bestow upon *these* Thy *servants*,
whom we bless in Thy Name, the sevenfold gifts of Thy
Holy Spirit, that *they* may be endowed with power to
preach Thy Gospel, and may prove *their* fitness to serve
Thee in the Ministry of the Word.   Grant unto *them* riches
of heavenly wisdom, and guidance of divine love, that *they*
may live near to God and near to man, in fellowship with
Thy Son.   Strengthen *their* faith, confirm *their* courage,
and deepen *their* joy in work for Thee, renewing in *their*
hearts and on *their* lips the glad tidings of salvation, and
giving unto *them* the great reward of those that turn many
to righteousness.   So may the time of *their* probation bear
fruit unto everlasting life, and lead *them* into the full assurance that Thou hast called and blessed *them* for the
ministry of the Gospel.

Lord, hasten the coming of Thy kingdom; build up Thy
holy Church throughout the world, hear the prayers and
prosper the labours of all Thy good and faithful servants;
and Thine shall be the glory for ever and ever.   *Amen.*

THE grace of the Lord Jesus Christ, and the love of God,
and the communion of the Holy Ghost, be with you all
Amen.

THE ORDINATION OF MINISTERS.

¶ *A Candidate for the Holy Ministry, having made proof, as required by the Form of Government, of his fitness to preach the Gospel, and having received a duly attested call to the Pastorate of a congregation, and having fully satisfied the Presbytery that he is qualified for the sacred office, shall be presented for Ordination.*

¶ *When the Presbytery shall approve a Candidate who has fulfilled all the other requirements of the Form of Government, but has not received a call to the Pastorate of a particular congregation, he may be ordained to the work of the Ministry as an Evangelist, and the necessary changes shall be made in the following Order.*

¶ *The day appointed for Ordination being come, and the Presbytery convened, a Minister previously designated shall conduct Divine Service according to the usual Order, or such special Order as the Presbytery may deem proper, and the same, or another appointed to preside, shall conduct the* ORDINATION, *saying as follows:*

THE Presbytery of —— —— is here assembled to ordain to the sacred office of the Ministry, A. B., [whom you have called to be your Pastor. We have duly considered the call which you have presented to him through us.] We have diligently inquired into *his* soundness of doctrine and holiness of life, and are certified of *his* meetness in respect to gifts and learning for this excellent work, as required in God's holy Word. We, therefore, present *him* before you to receive ordination with the laying on of the hands of the Presbytery.

The words in brackets throughout this Order are to be omitted at the ordination of an Evangelist.

¶ *Then the* Candidate *shall stand before the Presiding Minister, who shall say*·

DEARLY beloved in the Lord, you have heard both in your examination by the Presbytery, and in the words already spoken in this place, and in the lessons taken out of Holy Scripture, of what dignity and of how great importance is this Ministry whereunto you are called. And now again we exhort you, in the Name of our Lord Jesus Christ, that you have in remembrance unto how high and weighty an office you are to be ordained ; that is to say, to be a messenger, watchman, and steward of the Lord, to teach and admonish, to feed and provide for, the Lord's family ; and to look for the sheep of Christ that are dispersed abroad in the midst of this evil world, that they may be saved through Him for ever.

We have good hope that you have well weighed these things before this time, and that you have clearly determined by God's grace to give *yourself* wholly to this office, whereunto it hath pleased God to call you ; so that you may daily grow stronger in your Ministry, and may be *a* wholesome and godly *example* and *pattern* for the people to follow.

And now that this present congregation of Christ may also understand your mind and will in these things, and that this your promise may the more move you to do your duty, you shall answer plainly to all these things which we, in the Name of God, and of His Church, demand of you.

Do you believe the Scriptures of the Old and New Testaments to be the Word of God, the only infallible rule of faith and practice ?
Answer : I do so believe.

Do you sincerely receive and adopt the Confession of Faith of this Church, as containing the system of doctrine taught in the Holy Scriptures?
Answer : I do so receive it.

Do you approve of the government and discipline of the Presbyterian Church in these United States ?
Answer : I do.

Do you promise subjection to your brethren in the Lord ?
Answer : I do.

Have you been induced, as far as you know your own heart, to seek the office of the Holy Ministry from love to God and a sincere desire to promote His glory in the Gospel of His Son?
Answer : I have been thus induced.

Do you promise to be zealous and faithful in maintaining the truths of the Gospel and the purity and peace of the Church ; whatever persecution or opposition may arise to you on that account ?
Answer : I do so promise.

Do you engage to be faithful and diligent in the exercise of all private and personal duties, which become you as a Christian and a Minister of the Gospel; as well as in all relative duties, and the public duties of your office ; endeavouring to adorn the profession of the Gospel by your conversation ; and walking with exemplary piety before the flock over which God shall make you overseer ?
Answer : I do so engage, relying on God's grace.

At the Ordination of a Pastor :

ARE you now willing to take the charge of this congregation, agreeably to your declaration at accepting their call ? And do you promise to discharge the duties of a Pastor to them, as God shall give you strength?
Answer : I am willing, and I do so promise, the Lord being my Helper.

Or,

At the Ordination of an Evangelist :

ARE you now willing to undertake the work of an Evangelist; and do you promise to discharge the duties which may be incumbent on you in this character as God shall give you strength ?
Answer : I am willing, and I do so promise, the Lord being my Helper.

¶ *The* Candidate, *having answered these Questions in the affirmative*

The Presiding Minister shall propose to the People the following Questions, requesting that they answer them in the affirmative by holding up their right hands·

DO you, the People of this congregation, continue to profess your readiness to receive *A. B.*, whom you have called to be your Minister?

Do you promise to receive the Word of Truth from his mouth, with meekness and love; and to submit to him in the due exercise of discipline?

Do you promise to encourage him in his arduous labour, and to assist his endeavours for your instruction and spiritual edification?

Do you engage to continue to him, while he is your Pastor, that competent worldly maintenance which you have promised; and whatever else you may see needful for the honour of religion and his comfort among you?

¶ *The People having answered these Questions in the affirmative*

¶ *The* Candidate *shall then kneel, and the Presiding Minister shall by Prayer, and with the Laying on of the Hands of the Presbytery, according to the Apostolic example, solemnly Ordain him to the holy office of the Gospel Ministry, using if he will one of the following Prayers:*

Let us pray.

ALMIGHTY God and everlasting Father, who dost govern all things in heaven and earth by Thy wisdom, and hast from the beginning ordained for Thy Church the Ministry of Reconciliation, giving some apostles, and some prophets, and some evangelists, and some pastors and teachers, for the perfecting of the saints, for the work of the Ministry, and for the edifying of the body of Christ; Look in mercy, we beseech Thee, on *this* Thy *servant*, upon whom we lay our hands in Thy Name [*here the Presiding Minister and the other Ministers shall lay their hands upon the head of the* Candidate], and whom we thus ordain and set apart to the holy office of the Ministry. Pour down upon *him* the grace of Thy Holy Spirit, confirming in heaven what we do in Thy Church on earth, and owning *him* as *a* true *Minister* of the Gospel of Thy Son. Vouchsafe to *him* that authority and gentleness, that purity and spiritual discernment, that zeal and meekness, which shall make *him an example* and *guide* to the flock; that so making full proof of *his* Ministry, and continuing in the same, *he* may both save himself and those that hear *him*. Grant this, O heavenly Father, for the love of Thy dear Son Jesus Christ our Lord. *Amen.*

¶ *Or this·*

O LORD, to whom all power is given in heaven and in earth; who hast so loved the world, that to redeem and purify sinners Thou didst humble Thyself to the death of the cross, and there shed Thy most innocent blood; Look upon us mercifully, O Lord, Thou only Prophet, Priest, and King to Thine own flock; and grant unto *this* Thy *servant*, upon whom we lay our hands in Thy Name [*here the Presiding Minister and the other Ministers shall lay their hands upon the head of the* Candidate], and whom we thus ordain and set apart to the work of the Ministry, such endowment of Thy Holy Spirit, that *he* may rightly divide Thy Word, to the conversion of sinners, the instruction of Thy flock, and the overthrow of error and vice. Give unto *him*, good Lord, Thy grace and wisdom, whereby the enemies of Thy truth may be confounded, the ignorant enlightened, and Thy sheep fed in the wholesome pastures of Thy holy Word. Multiply Thy graces upon *him*. Comfort and strengthen *him* in all virtue Govern and guide *his* Ministry to the praise of Thy holy Name, the promotion of Thy kingdom, the comfort of Thy Church, and to the spread of Thy blessed Gospel throughout the whole world; and unto Thee, with the Father, and with the Holy Ghost, be all honour, praise, and glory, now and ever. *Amen*

¶ *Prayer being ended, the newly ordained Minister shall rise, and the Presiding Minister, addressing him, shall say*

IN the Name of the Lord Jesus Christ, and by that authority which He has given to His Church, I do hereby declare you to be ordained to the office of the Holy Ministry [and duly inducted to the pastoral charge of this congregation].

¶ *Then the Presiding Minister, and afterward all the Members of the Presbytery, shall take him by the right hand, saying in words to this purpose:*

WE give you the right hand of fellowship, to take part of this Ministry with us.

¶ *After which the Minister presiding, or some other appointed for the purpose, shall give a solemn* CHARGE *to him [and to the People].*

¶ *Then a Hymn may be sung.*

¶ *Then shall the following or some other* PRAYER *be offered by the Minister appointed; the People reverently bowing down.*

Let us pray.

EVER living God, our heavenly Father, who didst of old time call those whom Thou wouldst for Thy service in the Ministry, and who by Thy providence dost continue to raise up evangelists, pastors, and teachers for Thy Church ; Bless, we entreat Thee, Thy *servant* here set apart to be *a Minister* [and a Pastor, and the congregation committed to his care]. Endue *them* with spiritual grace; help *them* to perform the vows that *they have* made; and continuing faithful unto death, may *they* at length receive the crown of life which the Lord, the righteous Judge, will give *them* in that day. Grant this, O Lord, for the sake of Thy dear Son Jesus Christ our Lord, who, with Thee and the Holy Spirit, liveth and reigneth, one God, world without end. *Amen.*

¶ *Then the Congregation shall be dismissed with this or some other* BENEDICTION, *the People still bowing down:*

THE peace of God, which passeth all understanding, keep your hearts and minds in the knowledge and love of God, and of His Son Jesus Christ our Lord ; and the blessing of God Almighty, the Father, the Son, and the Holy Ghost, be amongst you, and remain with you always. *Amen.*

THE INSTALLATION OF A PASTOR WHO HAS BEEN PREVIOUSLY ORDAINED.

¶ *When any Minister is to be settled in a congregation, the install-ment, which consists in constituting a pastoral relation be-tween him and the people of that particular church, may be performed either by the Presbytery, or by a Committee ap-pointed for that purpose, as may appear most expedient.* —Form of Government, Chap. XVI, § 4.

¶ *On the day appointed, the Presbytery or Committee having been duly constituted, a Minister previously designated shall conduct Divine Service according to the usual Order, or such special Order as the Presbytery may deem proper; and a SER-MON shall be delivered by the Minister thereto appointed.*

¶ *The Sermon being ended, the Presiding Minister shall state to the congregation the design of their meeting, and recite the proceedings of the Presbytery in relation thereto, in the follow-ing words, or such other as may be applicable to the circum-stances.*

DEARLY beloved: The call of this congregation to the Reverend *A. B.* to become your Pastor, has been duly presented to the Presbytery of ——, and by them carefully considered. After inquiring into all the circumstances, it has been placed in his hands, and he has signified to the Presbytery his willingness to accept thereof. We are here at this present time by appointment and order of the said Presbytery; and by its authority do now proceed to consti-tute and install him, in the Name of the Lord Jesus Christ, as the Pastor of this congregation

¶ *Then the Minister to be installed shall stand before the Presiding Minister, who shall propose to him the following* QUESTIONS.

ARE you now willing to take the charge of this congre-gation, as their Pastor, agreeably to your declaration at accepting their call?
Answer. I am now willing.

Do you conscientiously believe and declare, as far as you know your own heart, that, in taking upon you this charge, you are influenced by a sincere desire to promote the glory of God, and the good of His Church?

Answer. I so believe and declare

Do you solemnly promise, that, by the assistance of the grace of God, you will endeavour faithfully to discharge all the duties of a Pastor to this congregation; and will be careful to maintain a deportment in all respects becoming a Minister of the Gospel of Christ, agreeably to your ordination engagements?

Answer. I do.

¶ *Having received satisfactory answers to all these Questions, the Presiding Minister shall propose to the People the following* QUESTIONS, *requesting that they answer them in the affirmative by holding up their right hands*

DO you, the People of this congregation, continue to profess your readiness to receive *A. B.*, whom you have called to be your Minister?

Do you promise to receive the Word of Truth from his mouth, with meekness and love; and to submit to him in the due exercise of discipline?

Do you promise to encourage him in his arduous labour, and to assist his endeavours for your instruction and spiritual edification?

Do you engage to continue to him, while he is your Pastor, that competent worldly maintenance which you have promised; and whatever else you may see needful for the honour of religion and his comfort among you?

¶ *The People having answered these Questions in the affirmative, the Presiding Minister shall say:*

IN the Name of the Lord Jesus Christ, the great Head of the Church, and by authority of this Presbytery, I do pronounce and declare that the Reverend *A. B.*, is duly constituted the Pastor of this congregation. Let us therefore pray, dearly beloved, unto God, the Fountain of all grace and glory, that He may be pleased to sanctify with His heavenly blessing this relation of Pastor and People which has now in His Name been established

Let us pray.

ALMIGHTY God and everlasting Father, who dost govern all things in heaven and earth by Thy wisdom, and
hast from the beginning ordained for Thy Church the Ministry of Reconciliation; We thank Thee for Thy goodness
to us this day in Thy House and we beseech Thee to continue Thy loving-kindness to this congregation, and to Thy
servant who has now been set over them in holy things.
Send down upon him the gifts of Thy Holy Spirit, and
so replenish him from above that he may rightly divide
the Word of Truth; so endue him with purity of life that
he may be an example to this flock: and grant that in all
things he may faithfully serve before Thee, to the glory of
Thy great Name, in the conversion of sinners unto Thee,
and the upbuilding of Thy people in holiness and in all
Christian service unto salvation.

O Lord God, the Sanctifier of the faithful, visit, we pray
Thee, this congregation with Thy love and favour; prepare their hearts to receive Thy Word; enlighten their
minds more and more with the light of the everlasting
Gospel, increase in them true religion; nourish them with
all goodness; and of Thy great mercy keep them in the
unity of the Spirit and in the bonds of love; through
Jesus Christ our Lord; whom with Thee and the Holy
Ghost, we worship and glorify as one God, world without
end. *Amen.*

¶ *Prayer being ended, the Presiding Minister, or some other appointed for the purpose, shall give a solemn* CHARGE *to the Pastor, and to the People.*

¶ *A Hymn appropriate to the occasion may then be sung.*

¶ *Then shall the following or some other* PRAYER *be offered by the
Minister appointed, the People reverently bowing down.*

Let us pray.

O LORD, our heavenly Father, we beseech Thee not only
for Thy favour upon this Pastor and People, but also
that Thou wilt bless Thy whole Church in this land, and
throughout the world. Gather Thy true people into the

unity of the faith, and take from them all bitterness and unkindness, all needless divisions and misunderstandings. May grace, mercy, and peace be multiplied to all who love our Lord Jesus Christ in sincerity   Pour out Thy Holy Spirit upon all men, and hasten the time when every people shall be blessed in the knowledge of Thee, and of Thy Son Jesus Christ our Lord.   *Amen.*

¶ *Then the congregation shall be dismissed with this or some other* BENEDICTION, *the People still bowing down.*

THE peace of God, which passeth all understanding, keep your hearts and minds in the knowledge and love of God, and of His Son Jesus Christ our Lord ; and the blessing of God Almighty, the Father, the Son, and the Holy Ghost, be amongst you, and remain with you always. *Amen.*

¶ *It is becoming, that, after the close of the Service, the Members of the congregation, especially the Elders and other Officers, should come forward and express to their Pastor their welcome and affectionate regard.*

THE ORDINATION OF RULING ELDERS.

¶ *Ruling Elders are properly the representatives of the people, chosen by them for the purpose of exercising government and discipline, in conjunction with pastors or ministers* (Form of Government, Chap. v). *When any person shall have been elected to the office of Ruling Elder, and shall have declared his willingness to accept thereof, he shall be set apart to his office in the manner prescribed by the Form of Government* (Chap. xiii).

¶ *Divine Service having been celebrated according to the usual Order, the* Persons *to be ordained shall, after the Sermon, present* themselves *before the pulpit at the call of the Minister, who shall thus address the congregation:*

DEARLY Beloved : As in the Old Testament the Elders exercised an honourable office of government among the people of God, so also in the New Testament the Apostle ordained Elders in every church; commanding that they that rule well be counted worthy of double honour, especially they who labour in the Word and doctrine.

Therefore, this Church has from the beginning included in her government not only Ministers and Pastors, who are to preach the Gospel and administer the Sacraments in the Name of Christ and as His representatives: but also Ruling Elders chosen by the people to represent them, and to be joined with Pastors and Ministers in the exercise of government and discipline in the Church.

These Ruling Elders in each congregation, together with the Pastor, constitute the Session, to whom it is committed to admit and exclude members, to regulate the worship, guard the doctrine, direct the activity, and conserve the interests of the congregation. The Elders are also to represent their brethren in Presbyteries, Synods, and General Assemblies, when commissioned thereto. And it is the duty of the Elders severally to set the example of a godly walk and conversation, and to assist the Pastor in the visitation of the people, and in their spiritual guidance and comfort *These brethren* here present [*here the Minister shall mention the* names *of the* Persons *chosen*] having been chosen, in the mode most approved and in use in this congregation, to the office of Ruling Elder, and having signified *their* willingness to serve, we do therefore, in the Name of the Lord Jesus Christ, now proceed to *their* ordination.

¶ *Then the Minister, addressing the* Elders-elect, *shall say,*

FORASMUCH as you have declared your willingness to take this office upon you, I now require you to answer the following Questions, appointed by the Church to be put to those who are to be ordained as Elders.

Do you believe the Scriptures of the Old and New Testaments to be the Word of God, the only infallible rule of faith and practice ?

Do you sincerely receive and adopt the Confession of Faith of this Church, as containing the system of doctrine taught in the Holy Scriptures ?

Do you approve of the government and discipline of the Presbyterian Church in these United States ?

Do you accept the office of Ruling Elder in this congregation, and promise faithfully to perform all the duties thereof ?

Do you promise to study the peace, unity, and purity of the Church ?

¶ *The* Elders-*elect having answered these Questions in the affirmative, the Minister shall address to the Members of the church the following* QUESTION :

DO you, the Members of this church, acknowledge and receive *these brethren* as *Ruling Elders*, and do you promise to yield *them* all that honour, encouragement, and obedience in the Lord, to which *their* office, according to the Word of God, and the constitution of this Church, entitles *them?*

¶ *The Members of the church having answered this Question in the affirmative, by holding up their right hands, the Minister shall proceed to set apart the* Candidates *to their office, by Prayer, (and if desired, the Laying on of Hands,) the* Elders-elect *devoutly kneeling.*

Let us pray.

SET apart, we beseech Thee, O Lord, *these Thy servants* to the work whereunto Thou hast called *them* by the voice of this people. Endue *them* plenteously with heavenly wisdom. Grant *them* Thy grace, that *they* may be *good men*, full of the Holy Ghost and of faith, ruling in the fear of God. Give *them* favour and influence with the people. Make *them* faithful unto death, and when the Chief Shepherd shall appear, may *they* receive a crown of glory that fadeth not away. *Amen.*

¶ *Then the Minister shall say.*

IN the Name of the Lord Jesus Christ, and by the authority committed to me in His Church, I hereby declare you duly constituted and set apart to the office of Ruling Elder.

I now charge you, in the Name of the Lord Jesus, to be faithful in this your office.

I also charge you, Christian people, to be faithful to *these Elders* whom you have chosen to rule over you in the Lord ; and that you render them all due obedience, co-operation and support, and follow *them* so far as ye see *them* follow Christ.

¶ *Where there is an existing Session, it is proper that the Members of that body should here take the newly ordained* Elders *by the hand, saying in words to this purpose:*

WE give you the right hand of fellowship, to take part of this Office with us.

¶ *If Elders who have been already ordained are to be installed at the same Service, the* Order *for their* Installation *may be here introduced.*

¶ *Then the Minister shall say.*

MAY the great Head of the Church so enrich us with His heavenly grace, that at the last we shall hear Him saying unto us Well done, good and faithful servant ; enter thou into the joy of thy Lord.

THE INSTALLATION OF RULING ELDERS WHO HAVE BEEN PREVIOUSLY ORDAINED

¶ *When an Elder has terminated his connection with his Session by removal to another church, or by resignation, or when he is re-elected under the rotary system, he is to be reinstalled before he can regularly exercise the duties of his office.* — Minutes of the General Assembly, 1878, 1882.

¶ *When Elders are to be newly ordained at the same Service with the installation of those who have been previously ordained, the following Order may be introduced in* The Order for the Ordination of Ruling Elders, *immediately before the Benediction.*

BELOVED *Brethren:* Having already been solemnly ordained to the office of Ruling Elder, you do now present *yourselves* in response to the voice of this congregation, to be installed again for the discharge of the active duties of your office

You will therefore now give answer to the following Questions

Do you accept the office of Ruling *Elder* in this congregation, and promise faithfully to perform all the duties thereof ?

Do you promise to study the peace, unity, and purity of the Church ?

¶ *The* Elders-*elect having answered these Questions in the affirmative, the Minister shall address to the Members of the church the following* QUESTION:

DO you, the Members of this church, acknowledge and receive *these Brethren* as *Ruling Elders*, and do you promise to yield *them* all that honour, encouragement, and obedience in the Lord, to which *their* office, according to the Word of God, and the constitution of the Church, entitles *them ?*

¶ *The Members of the church shall answer in the affirmative by holding up their right hands.*

¶ *Then the Minister shall say,*

I HEREBY declare you to be invested with the Office of Ruling Elder in this congregation.

¶ *Then the Minister shall say,*

MAY the great Head of the Church so enrich us with His heavenly grace, that at the last we shall hear Him saying unto us: Well done, good and faithful servant; enter thou into the joy of thy Lord.

THE ORDER FOR

THE ORDINATION OF DEACONS.

¶ *Deacons are distinct officers in the Church, whose business it is to take care of the poor, and to distribute among them the collections raised for their use. To them also may be properly committed the management of the temporal affairs of the church* (Form of Government, Chap. vi). *When any person shall have been elected to the office of Deacon, and shall have declared his willingness to accept thereof, he shall be set apart to his office in the manner prescribed by the Form of Government* (Chap. xiii).

¶ *Divine Service having been celebrated according to the usual Order, the* Persons *to be ordained shall, after the Sermon, present* themselves *before the pulpit at the call of the Minister, who shall thus address the congregation:*

DEARLY Beloved: Concerning the institution of the office of Deacon we read in the sixth chapter of the Book of the Acts, that in the beginning the Apostles themselves ministered to the poor; but afterwards, being overburdened with these ministrations, they advised that certain men be chosen by the Church, to whom the service of the poor was committed as their peculiar care; therefore this Church has recognized the work and office of these men, to whom in the New Testament is given the title of Deacons, as of Apostolic institution, and needful for the welfare of the whole Body of Christ, to the end that the Ministers might continually give themselves to prayer and to the ministry of the Word.

Of this office St. Paul requires that the Deacons must be grave, not double-tongued, not given to much wine, not greedy of filthy lucre, holding the mystery of the faith in a pure conscience; ruling their children and their own houses well. And of them that have used this office well he declares that they purchase to themselves a good degree, and great boldness in the faith, which is in Christ Jesus.

These brethren here present (*here the Minister shall mention the* names *of the* Persons *chosen*) having been chosen, in the mode most approved and in use in this congregation, to the office of Deacon, and having signified *their* willingness to serve. we do therefore, in the Name of the Lord Jesus Christ, now proceed to *their* ordination.

¶ *Then the Minister addressing the* Deacons-*elect shall say,*

FORASMUCH as you have declared your willingness to take this office upon you, I now require you to answer the following Questions, appointed by the Church to be put to those who are to be ordained as Deacons.

Do you believe the Scriptures of the Old and New Testaments to be the Word of God, the only infallible rule of faith and practice?

Do you sincerely receive and adopt the Confession of Faith of this Church, as containing the system of doctrine taught in the Holy Scriptures?

Do you approve of the government and discipline of the Presbyterian Church in these United States?

Do you accept the office of Deacon in this congregation, and promise faithfully to perform all the duties thereof?

Do you promise to study the peace, unity, and purity of the Church?

¶ *The* Deacons-*elect having answered these Questions in the affirmative, the Minister shall address to the Members of the church the following* QUESTION:

DO you, the Members of this church, acknowledge and receive *these brethren* as *Deacons,* and do you promise to yield *them* all that honour, encouragement, and obedience in the Lord, to which *their* office, according to the Word of God, and the constitution of this Church, entitles *them?*

¶ *The Members of the church having answered this Question in the affirmative, by holding up their right hands, the Minister shall proceed to set apart the* Candidates *to* their *office, by Prayer, (and if desired, the Laying on of Hands,) the* Deacons-*elect devoutly kneeling.*

Let us pray.

O LORD JESUS, who, being rich, for our sakes became poor, that we through Thy poverty might be rich; Set apart and consecrate *these* Thy *servants* to the office of Deacon. Give *them* Thine own spirit of sympathy with all human sorrow and distress, and of holy, self-denying service in behalf of those who are in want and suffering. Guide and sustain *them* in *their* ministry of love until *their* work on earth is done; and bestow upon *them* the great rewards of Thy heavenly kingdom. *Amen.*

¶ Then the Minister shall say,

IN the Name of the Lord Jesus Christ, and by the authority committed to me in His Church, I hereby declare you duly set apart and ordained to the office of Deacon.

I now charge you, in the Name of the Lord Jesus, to be faithful in this your office.

I also charge you, Christian people, to be faithful to *these Deacons*, baptizing *their* ministry to the poor with your daily prayers, supplying it constantly and cheerfully with your liberal gifts, and remembering that Christ has appointed the poor to represent Himself in our offices of sympathy and benevolent service on earth.

Then shall the King say unto them on the right hand, Come, ye blessed of My Father, inherit the kingdom prepared for you from the foundation of the world; for I was a hungered, and ye gave Me meat; I was thirsty, and ye gave Me drink; I was a stranger, and ye took Me in; naked, and ye clothed Me; I was sick, and ye visited Me; I was in prison, and ye came unto Me Verily, I say unto you, Inasmuch as ye have done it unto one of the least of these My brethren, ye have done it unto Me.

¶ Where there is an existing Board of Deacons it is proper that the Members of that body take the newly ordained Deacons by the hand, saying in words to this purpose:

WE give you the right hand of fellowship, to take part of this Office with us.

¶ Then the Minister shall say,

NOW unto Him that is able to do exceedingly abundantly above all that we ask or think, according to the power that worketh in us; unto Him be glory in the Church by Christ Jesus, throughout all ages, world without end. *Amen.*

¶ *Where Deacons who have already been ordained are to be installed in any congregation,* The Order for *their* Installation *may follow* The Order for the Installation of Ruling Elders who have been previously Ordained.

LAYING THE CORNER-STONE OF A CHURCH.

¶ *The People, being assembled at the place where the church is to be built, shall rise, and the Minister shall read the following* SENTENCES:

OUR help is in the Name of the Lord, who made heaven and earth.

Except the Lord build the house, they labour in vain that build it.

¶ *Then let the following* PSALM (1 Chronicles xxix. 10-18) *be read responsively by the Minister and People, all standing, ending with the* Gloria Patri :

BLESSED be thou, Lord God of Israel : our Father, for ever and ever.

Thine, O Lord, is the greatness, and the power, and the glory, and the victory, and the majesty : for all that is in the heaven and in the earth is thine.

Thine is the kingdom, O Lord : and thou art exalted as head over all.

Both riches and honour come of thee : and thou reignest over all.

And in thine hand is power and might : and in thine hand it is to make great, and to give strength unto all.

Now therefore, our God, we thank thee : and praise thy glorious name.

But who am I, and what is my people : that we should be able to offer so willingly after this sort?

For all things come of thee : and of thine own have we given thee.

For we are strangers before thee : and sojourners, as were all our fathers.

Our days on the earth are as a shadow : and there is none abiding.

O Lord, our God, all this store that we have prepared to build thee an house for thy holy name cometh of thine hand : and is all thine own

I know also, my God, that thou triest the heart · and hast pleasure in uprightness.

As for me, in the uprightness of mine heart I have willingly offered all these things: and now have I seen with joy thy people, which are present here, to offer willingly unto thee.

O Lord God of Abraham, Isaac, and of Israel, our fathers; keep this for ever in the imagination of the thoughts of the heart of thy people, and prepare their heart unto thee.

Glory be to the Father, and to the Son ; and to the Holy Ghost;

As it was in the beginning, is now, and ever shall be ; world without end. Amen.

¶ *Then shall the Minister say,*

Let us pray.

DIRECT us, O Lord, in all our doings, with Thy most gracious favour, and further us with Thy continual help; that in all our works begun, continued, and ended in Thee, we may glorify Thy holy Name, and finally, by Thy mercy, obtain everlasting life ; through Jesus Christ our Lord. *Amen*

¶ *Then shall an appropriate Hymn be sung, all standing, after which, all, still standing, shall join with the Minister in their* CONFESSION OF FAITH.

THE CREED.

I BELIEVE in God the Father Almighty, Maker of heaven and earth :

And in Jesus Christ His only Son, our Lord; Who was conceived by the Holy Ghost, Born of the Virgin Mary, Suffered under Pontius Pilate, Was crucified, dead, and buried ; [He descended into hell ;*] The third day He rose

* Or, *He continued in the state of the dead, and under the power of death, until the third day.*

again from the dead; He ascended into heaven, And sitteth on the right hand of God the Father Almighty; From thence He shall come to judge the quick and the dead.

I believe in the Holy Ghost; The Holy Catholic Church; The Communion of Saints, The Forgiveness of sins; The Resurrection of the body; and the Life everlasting. Amen.

¶ *Here shall follow the* Laying of the Stone. *After such documents and other articles as are to be preserved have been deposited in the cavity prepared for them, the Minister, or other Person appointed for the purpose, assisted by the builder, shall lay the Stone in its place. Then the Minister, placing his hand on it, shall say*

IN the Name of the Father, and of the Son, and of the Holy Ghost, we lay this Corner-Stone of a house to be erected here under the name of ——— Church, and devoted to the worship of Almighty God.

Behold, I lay in Zion a chief corner-stone, elect, precious: and he that believeth on Him shall not be confounded.

Other foundation can no man lay than that is laid : which is Jesus Christ.

¶ *Then shall he say,*

Let us pray.

LORD God, who art the Beginning and the End, by whom all things were created; Grant us the fulness of Thy mercy, and establish Thou this Stone which we plant in Thy Name

Accept, we beseech Thee, the humble service of all who contribute of their substance unto this building; let Thy blessing rest upon them, and also upon those who labour in erecting it, to shield them from all accidents and dangers ; and grant unto them, and all of us here present, Thy heavenly grace, that our gifts and all our service may be sanctified, and we may become in soul and body living temples of the Holy Ghost. All which we ask through the abundant merits of our Lord and Saviour, who liveth and reigneth with Thee and the Holy Ghost, ever one God, world without end. *Amen.*

OUR Father which art in heaven, Hallowed be Thy Name. Thy kingdom come. Thy will be done in earth, As it is in heaven Give us this day our daily bread. And forgive us our debts, As we forgive our debtors And lead us not into temptation, But deliver us from evil: For Thine is the kingdom, and the power, and the glory, forever. Amen.

¶ *Here may be given an* ADDRESS. *After which, if so approved, an* OFFERING *in aid of the building fund may be made.*

¶ *Then shall be sung a suitable Hymn, and the Minister shall pronounce*

THE BENEDICTION.

THE grace of the Lord Jesus Christ, and the love of God, and the communion of the Holy Ghost, be with you all. *Amen.*

THE DEDICATION OF A CHURCH.

¶ *The congregation being duly assembled shall rise, and the following* PSALM *shall be read responsively by the Minister and the People.*

¶ *Or, if so desired, the Ministers taking part in the Service shall enter at the door, where they shall be received by the Trustees and Elders, and proceed with them up the aisle, reciting responsively the following* PSALM, *the presiding Minister leading:*

THE earth is the Lord's, and the fulness thereof: the world, and they that dwell therein;

For he hath founded it upon the seas: and established it upon the floods.

Who shall ascend into the hill of the Lord: or who shall stand in his holy place?

He that hath clean hands and a pure heart: who hath not lifted up his soul unto vanity, nor sworn deceitfully;

He shall receive the blessing from the Lord: and righteousness from the God of his salvation;

This is the generation of them that seek him: that seek thy face, O Jacob:

Lift up your heads, O ye gates: and be ye lifted up, ye everlasting doors: and the King of glory shall come in;

Who is this King of glory?

The Lord strong and mighty: the Lord mighty in battle.

Lift up your heads, O ye gates: even lift them up, ye everlasting doors: and the King of glory shall come in;

Who is this King of glory?

The Lord of hosts: he is the King of glory.

Glory be to the Father, and to the Son: and to the Holy Ghost;

As it was in the beginning, is now, and ever shall be: world without end. Amen.

¶ Then shall be sung the following or some other suitable Hymn:

ALL people that on earth do dwell,
  Sing to the Lord with cheerful voice;
Him serve with fear, His praise forth tell;
  Come ye before Him and rejoice.

The Lord ye know is God indeed,
  Without our aid He did us make;
We are His folk, He doth us feed,
  And for His sheep He doth us take.

O enter then His gates with praise,
  Approach with joy His courts unto;
Praise, laud, and bless His Name always,
  For it is seemly so to do.

For why? The Lord our God is good
  His mercy is for ever sure;
His truth at all times firmly stood,
  And shall from age to age endure. Amen.

¶ Then shall the Minister and People make their CONFESSION OF
  FAITH, *saying*

I BELIEVE in God the Father Almighty, Maker of heaven
  and earth:
And in Jesus Christ His only Son, our Lord; Who was
conceived by the Holy Ghost, Born of the Virgin Mary;
Suffered under Pontius Pilate, Was crucified, dead, and
buried; [He descended into hell; *] The third day He rose
again from the dead; He ascended into heaven, And sitteth
on the right hand of God the Father Almighty; From
thence He shall come to judge the quick and the dead.
  I believe in the Holy Ghost; The Holy Catholic Church;
The Communion of Saints; The Forgiveness of sins; The
Resurrection of the body; and the Life everlasting. Amen.

  * Or, *He continued in the state of the dead, and under the power
of death, until the third day.*

¶ *The People being seated, the presiding Minister shall say,*

DEARLY beloved in the Lord : God our Heavenly Father, having in His grace, which is in Jesus Christ our Lord, brought to its consummation, our work of preparing for the honour of His holy Name, a house within whose walls His Gospel is to be truly preached, His Sacraments are to be faithfully administered, and prayer and praise are to be offered unto Him, we are now gathered in His Presence for the purpose of devoting this house, by a solemn act of worship, to its proper and sacred use. Let us therefore seek His blessing on this Service.

¶ *Then shall the Minister say,*

Let us pray.

¶ *If so desired, the* PRAYER *may be in the form following.*

O LORD God, almighty and most merciful, whom the heaven, even the heaven of heavens cannot contain, much less temples built with hands, but who also dwellest with men, and delightest Thyself in the assemblage of Thy people ; Cleanse our hearts, we beseech Thee, from all evil thought and desire, and vouchsafe Thy divine Presence and blessing, that both those things may please Thee which we do at this present, and also that we may at length obtain Thy favour with life everlasting in Thy heavenly kingdom ; through Jesus Christ our Lord. *Amen.*

¶ *Here let the Minister and the People say together the* LORD'S PRAYER:

OUR Father which art in heaven, Hallowed be Thy Name. Thy kingdom come. Thy will be done in earth, As it is in heaven. Give us this day our daily bread. And forgive us our debts, As we forgive our debtors. And lead us not into temptation, But deliver us from evil: For Thine is the kingdom, and the power, and the glory, forever. Amen.

¶ *The Scripture shall then be read. Proper lessons are from the* OLD TESTAMENT, 1 Kings viii. 22-53, *and from the* NEW TESTAMENT, 1 Corinthians iii., Ephesians ii , or Revelation xxi

¶ Then shall the Minister speak these WORDS OF DEDICATION, *the People standing, and joining in the words printed in Capitals*

HOLY, Blessed, and Glorious Trinity . three Persons and one God :

TO THEE WE DEDICATE THIS HOUSE.

Father of our Lord Jesus Christ: Our Father which art in heaven :

TO THEE WE DEDICATE THIS HOUSE.

Son of God, the Only Begotten of the Father, Head of the Body, which is the Church : Head over all things to the Church ; Prophet, Priest, and King of Thy people :

TO THEE WE DEDICATE THIS HOUSE.

God the Holy Ghost, proceeding from the Father and the Son · given to be our abiding Teacher, Sanctifier, and Comforter ; Lord and Giver of Life :

TO THEE WE DEDICATE THIS HOUSE.

¶ Then shall the Minister say,

ARISE, O Lord, into Thy rest, Thou and the ark of Thy strength   Let Thy priests be clothed with righteousness, and let Thy people shout for joy. Put Thy Name in this place. Let Thine eyes be opened toward it ; and hearken unto the supplications of Thy people when they pray in this place, and hear Thou in heaven Thy dwelling place, and when thou hearest, forgive   *Amen.*

¶ Then shall the appointed Minister say,

Let us pray

¶ And the Congregation, reverently bowing down, shall follow in their hearts

THE PRAYER OF CONSECRATION.

O ALMIGHTY and everlasting God, Thou dwellest not in temples made with hands, neither art Thou worshipped with men's hands, as though Thou neededst anything, seeing that Thou givest to all life and breath and all things ; when we bring Thee our best, we serve Thee only with what is Thine own ; and when we have done all, we are but unprofitable servants. Yet do Thou, O Lord, who delightest Thyself in the praises of the Sanctuary, accept

the offering of this house which Thy people have builded
to the glory of Thy holy Name. We consecrate it to Thee,
the Father, the Son, and the Holy Ghost, to be henceforth
the House of God, and a gate of heaven; we set it apart
from all common and worldly uses, for a temple and a sanctuary, where Thy holy Gospel shall be preached; where
the prayers of the Church shall be made unto Thee without
ceasing; where Thy high praises shall be devoutly sung;
where the ordinances of Thy Word shall be duly administered; to which Thy people shall throng with cheerful
steps.   How amiable are Thy tabernacles, O Lord of Hosts !
I was glad when they said unto me, let us go into the
House of the Lord.

When Thy holy Word is preached in this place may it
be spoken in the demonstration of the Spirit and with
power; speak Thou comfortably to Thy people, O Lord,
through the lips of Thine ambassadors, and let Thy Word
be as the fire, and as the hammer to hardened hearts.
When Thy holy Sacraments are here administered, may
those spiritual graces which the outward signs do represent and signify, flow into the hearts of Thy servants; so
that receiving the seal of Baptism, they shall indeed receive the renewing of the Holy Ghost; and partaking of
the Lord's Table, they shall indeed feed by faith on the
Body and Blood of Christ.   Here let God be worshipped in
spirit and in truth, and let not our Father's house be made
a place of merchandise.   Here when Thy people come to
offer their gifts upon Thine altar, let them consider Him,
who though He was rich for our sakes became poor, that
we through His poverty might be made rich.   Let the
glory of the Lord fill this house, and the Spirit of God descend and dwell in His Church.   *Amen.*

A LMIGHTY and everlasting God, who hast declared Thy
love for the world by giving Thine only begotten
Son, that whosoever believeth in Him should not perish
but have everlasting life ; Vouchsafe to Thy Church gifts
of spiritual power, to the hastening in all the world of Thy
Kingdom which is righteousness and peace and joy in the
Holy Ghost.

Now unto the King eternal, immortal, invisible, the only
wise God, be honour and glory for ever and ever.   *Amen.*

¶ *If it be the will of the congregation to make an Offering, it may be received here, and consecrated with Prayer.*

¶ *Then a Hymn shall be sung.*

¶ *Then shall follow*

THE SERMON

¶ *A Hymn may be sung after the Sermon.*

¶ *Then the Minister shall say,*

Let us pray.

¶ *If so desired, the* PRAYER *may be offered in the form following ·*

MOST glorious God ; Accept through Thy beloved Son, our thanksgivings for Thine unspeakable love and goodness.   Thou art the Father of mercies, and God of all consolation, full of compassion, forgiving iniquity, transgression, and sin.   We thank Thee that Thou hast founded Thy Church upon the Apostles and Prophets, Jesus Christ Himself being the chief Corner Stone.   We thank Thee that Thou hast committed to Thy ministers the Word of reconciliation   Continue Thy loving-kindness unto us, that we may rejoice and be glad in Thee all our days.   Guide us by Thy counsel, and afterward receive us to Thy glory ; where, with all the blessed host of heaven, we may behold, adore, and perfectly and joyfully praise Thee, our most glorious Creator, Redeemer, and Sanctifier, for ever and ever.   *Amen.*

¶ *Or this*

O GOD, whose glory is great in all Thy churches, and the praises of whose Name resound in the assemblies of Thy saints ; We, Thy servants, would humble ourselves before Thee, and worship Thine infinite Majesty.   We celebrate Thy wisdom, power, and goodness, that shine forth in the works of creation and redemption through Jesus Christ our Lord   We bless Thee for all temporal and spiritual good that we continually receive at Thy bountiful hands.   But more especially, with all Thy people assembled this day, we praise Thee that Thou didst send into the world Thy Son to save us ; and having delivered Him up for our offenses, didst raise Him again for our justification ; and through His glorious resurrection hast given us the blessed hope of everlasting life. O Lord, may these our thanksgivings come up with acceptance before Thy throne. Make us worthy to have part in the resurrection of the just, and the glory of Thine eternal kingdom: whither Jesus the Forerunner hath for us entered, where now He lives and reigns, and is worshipped and glorified, with Thee and the Holy Ghost, One God, blessed for evermore. *Amen*

¶ *The People remaining in the posture of prayer, the Minister shall pronounce*

THE BENEDICTION.

THE grace of the Lord Jesus Christ, and the love of God, and the communion of the Holy Ghost, be with you all. *Amen*

THE TREASURY OF PRAYERS.

¶ *These Prayers may be used, if the Minister so desires, in connec-*
tion with the MORNING SERVICE, *and the* EVENING SERVICE.
They are also commended to Christians, at other times, for
guidance and help in their devotions; being gathered and com-
piled from the Holy Scriptures, from the records of the early
Church, and from the fathers of the Reformed Faith, with such
additions as have been made in our own time by those who have
prayed and laboured in the same Spirit.

I. GENERAL PRAYERS FOR COMMON WORSHIP.

II. PRAYERS FOR CERTAIN TIMES AND SEASONS.

III. INTERCESSIONS FOR SPECIAL OBJECTS AND PERSONS.

IV. BRIEF PETITIONS.

V. ASCRIPTIONS OF PRAISE . . . 151

GENERAL PRAYERS FOR COMMON WORSHIP.

ADORATIONS.

I.

ETERNAL and ever-blessed God, we bow down before Thy divine majesty, adoring Thee, the Lord of heaven and earth, of whom and through whom and to whom are all things; unto whom be glory for ever and ever. *Amen.*

II.

LORD God eternal; sovereign and immutable; holy, just, and merciful; Maker of all things by Thy power; Ruler of all things in Thy wisdom; We adore Thee for the wonders of the heavens and the earth; for the goodness of Thy dealings and the perfection of Thy secret counsels; for Thy saving love revealed in Jesus Christ, and Thy living presence made known by the Holy Spirit. By day and night, with voice and heart, praise and adoration shall be given unto Thee, O Lord most mighty and most merciful, from generation unto generation, for ever and ever. *Amen.*

III.

HOLY, Holy, Holy! Lord God almighty; There is none like unto Thee, who hast set Thy glory above the heavens. Praise waiteth for Thee in Zion, and unto Thee shall the vow be performed. Hearken to the adoration of Thy people, we beseech Thee, and let the words of our mouths and the meditations of our hearts be acceptable in Thy sight, O Lord our Strength and our Redeemer. *Amen.*

IV.

O GOD, whose being and perfections are infinite, eternal, and unchangeable, the same yesterday, to-day, and for ever: Thou art glorious in holiness, full of love and compassion, abundant in grace and truth. All Thy works praise Thee in all places of Thy dominion: and Thy Son hath glorified Thee upon earth. Therefore we bow down and adore Thee, Father, Son, and Holy Ghost, one God, blessed for evermore. *Amen.*

V.

O LORD, Thou art our God, we will exalt Thee, we will praise Thy Name: for Thou hast done wonderful things. By the stars of heaven Thou hast spoken: and in the heart of man Thy voice is heard. Through Thy Word Thou hast given light; and in Thy Son the brightness of Thy glory is revealed. Lift up our hearts unto Thee, O God, and receive our adoration; through Jesus Christ. *Amen.*

THANKSGIVINGS.

I.

ALMIGHTY God, Father of all mercies, we, Thine unworthy servants, do give Thee most humble and hearty thanks for all Thy goodness and loving-kindness to us, and to all men. We bless Thee for our creation, preservation, and all the blessings of this life; but above all, for Thine inestimable love in the redemption of the world by our Lord Jesus Christ; for the means of grace, and for the hope of glory. And, we beseech Thee, give us that due sense of all Thy mercies, that our hearts may be unfeignedly thankful, and that we show forth Thy praise, not only with our lips, but in our lives; by giving up ourselves to Thy service, and by walking before Thee in holiness and righteousness all our days; through Jesus Christ our Lord, to whom, with Thee and the Holy Ghost, be all honour and glory, world without end. *Amen.*

II.

O GOD, by whose hand all living things were made, and by whose blessing they are nourished and sustained, We give Thee hearty thanks for all the bounties of Thy providence, wherewith Thou hast enriched our life; and we humbly pray that, enjoying Thy gifts in contentment, we may be enabled by Thy grace to use them to Thy praise. Especially we thank Thee for Thy great love in sending Thy Son to be the Saviour of the world, and in calling us out of our sins into fellowship with Him: and we beseech Thee to grant us always Thy Holy Spirit, through whom we may grow continually in thankfulness toward Thee, as also into the likeness of Thy Son Jesus Christ our Lord. *Amen.*

III.

ALMIGHTY and most merciful Father, from whom cometh every good and perfect gift; We give Thee praise and hearty thanks for all Thy mercies:

For Thy goodness that hath created us; Thy bounty that hath sustained us; Thy fatherly discipline that hath chastened and corrected us; Thy patience that hath borne with us; Thy love that hath redeemed us. [*Here any special mercy may be named.*]

Grant unto us with Thy gifts a heart to love Thee, and enable us to show our thankfulness for all Thy benefits by giving up ourselves to Thy service, and cheerfully submitting in all things to Thy blessed will; through Jesus Christ our Lord. *Amen.*

IV.

MOST heartily do we thank Thee, O Lord, for all Thy mercies of every kind, and for Thy loving care over all Thy creatures. We bless Thee for the gift of life, for Thy protection round about us, for Thy guiding hand upon us, and for the many tokens of Thy love within us; especially for the saving knowledge of Thy dear Son, our Redeemer; and for the living presence of Thy Spirit, our Comforter. We thank Thee for friendship and duty, for good hopes and precious memories, for the joys that cheer us and for the trials that teach us to trust in Thee. In all these things, our heavenly Father, make us wise unto a right use of Thy great benefits; and so direct us that in word and deed we may render an acceptable thanksgiving unto Thee, in Jesus Christ our Saviour. *Amen.*

V.

MOST gracious God, the Fountain of all blessing; Thou hast opened Thy hand to fill us with all good things: Thou dost govern us as a King, Thou feedest us like a shepherd, Thou keepest us beneath the shadow of Thy wings in safety, Thou providest for us as a father, Thou lovest us as a friend and thinkest on us perpetually, and art exceeding merciful to all that fear Thee; and unto Thee, O Lord, we ascribe the praise and honour of our redemption:

As Thou hast opened Thy hand upon us for a covering, so also enlarge our hearts with thankfulness and fill our mouths with praise. And grant that what Thou hast sown in loving-kindness may spring up in duty, and let Thy grace so strengthen our purposes that we may sin no more, but walk in the paths of Thy commandments; that we, living here in the light of Thy favour, may at last enter into the glory of our Lord, and give eternal praise to Thy exalted and ever blessed Name. *Amen.*

SUPPLICATIONS.

I.

O GOD, most holy, wise, and powerful Preserver and Governor of all Thy creatures and all their actions; Keep us, we beseech Thee, in health of body and soundness of mind, in purity of heart and cheerfulness of spirit, in contentment with our lot and charity with our neighbour; and further all our lawful undertakings with Thy blessing. In our labour strengthen us: in our pleasure purify us: in our difficulties direct us: in our perils defend us: in our troubles comfort us: and supply all our needs according to the riches of Thy grace in Christ Jesus our Lord. *Amen.*

II.

PROVIDE for us, O most merciful Father, both now and in the days to come, those things which are needful for our welfare in soul and body, and guide us by Thy Word and Spirit, in the way of a willing obedience to Thee. Teach us ever to look unto Thee as our Master and Rewarder, that all our work may be done in Thy service; replenish us with Thy daily gifts, that we may not lack any good thing; and keep us ever in a humble and grateful mind, that we may live peaceably with all men, and praise Thee by well-doing, according to the commandment of our Lord Jesus Christ. *Amen.*

III.

O LORD, our heavenly Father, who art ever ready to give good things to them that ask Thee; Hear the supplications of Thy children, in our weakness and ignorance, and supply all our needs, in body and in soul, according to Thy knowledge of our necessities and the fulness of Thy love. Strengthen us to keep Thy commandments; deliver us from our infirmities; and uphold us with Thy free Spirit. Enable us for those duties which Thou hast laid upon us, that our work being well done, we may enjoy the fruit of our labour, in a good conscience and a contented mind. And so direct us in all our ways, that we may have the light of Thy Word upon our path, and the fellowship of Thy Spirit in our hearts, and may ever continue among the faithful followers of Thy Son Jesus Christ our Lord. *Amen.*

IV.

O THOU most wise and ever-gracious Lord, the Framer of our bodies and the Father of our spirits, who hast kept our souls in life and guided our feet into Thy House of Prayer: We pray for each other, all for each, that Thou wouldest bless us outwardly in our bodies, and inwardly in our souls: grant us good success in all our labours, and bring us to Thine everlasting kingdom; through Jesus Christ our Lord. *Amen.*

V.

O LORD, our heavenly Father, almighty and everlasting God, who hast safely brought us to the beginning of this day; Defend us in the same with Thy mighty power, and grant that this day we fall into no sin, neither run into any kind of danger; but that all our doings, being ordered by Thy governance, may be righteous in Thy sight; through Jesus Christ our Lord. *Amen.*

INTERCESSIONS.

I.

A LMIGHTY God, who hast taught us to make intercession for all men; We pray not only for ourselves here present, but we beseech Thee also to bring all such as are yet ignorant, from the miserable captivity of error to the pure understanding of Thy heavenly truth: that we all, with one consent and unity of mind, may worship Thee, our only God and Saviour · that all Thy ministers and people may both in their life and doctrine be found faithful : and that, by them, all poor sheep which wander and go astray, may be gathered and brought home to Thy fold.

Moreover, because the reins of government are in Thy hands, we beseech Thee to direct and bless all who are in lawful authority ; especially Thy servant, the President of the United States, and all others to whom the people have entrusted power, together with the whole body of the Commonwealth: let Thy fatherly favour so preserve them, and Thy Holy Spirit so govern their hearts, that religion may be purely maintained, and our land may abide in righteousness and peace.

Finally we beseech Thee, for all those who are called to bear any cross or tribulation ; that it may please Thee to sustain them with the sweet comfort of Thy Holy Spirit, until Thou send a full deliverance out of all their troubles ; so that through their patience and constancy Thy kingdom may increase and shine through all the world.   And these, with all other mercies, we humbly beg of Thee, in the Name of Jesus Christ, Thy Son, our Lord. *Amen.*

II.

O GOD, the Creator and Preserver of all mankind, we humbly beseech Thee for all sorts and conditions of men ; that Thou wouldest be pleased to make Thy ways known unto them, Thy saving health unto all nations. More especially, we pray for Thy holy Church universal ; that it may be so guided and governed by Thy good Spirit, that all who profess and call themselves Christians may be led into the way of truth, and hold the faith in unity of spirit, in the bond of peace, and in righteousness of life. Finally, we commend to Thy fatherly goodness all those who are any ways afflicted, or distressed, in mind, body, or estate [and especially those for whom our prayers are asked at this time] : that it may please Thee to comfort and relieve them, according to their several necessities ; giving them patience under their sufferings, and a happy issue out of all their afflictions. And this we beg for Jesus Christ's sake. *Amen.*

III.

O GOD, who art the Hope of all the ends of the earth; Remember the whole creation, pity our race, and save the world from sin. Protect our land from whatever threatens her welfare, so that religion and virtue may flourish more and more. Give the spirit of wisdom and godly fear to Thy servant, the President of the United States, and all who are in authority over us. Give humility to the rich and grace to use their riches to Thy glory: bless the people in their callings and families, and be Thou a refuge to the poor in their distress. Make every home a shelter from temptation and a nursery of noble youth; take also the homeless beneath Thy protection. Cleanse and sanctify the Church which Thou hast loved; and reveal the Spirit of Thy Son through the life and service of Thy people. Enlighten all who are perplexed in faith, support those who are tempted, awaken those who sleep, comfort the afflicted, and encourage such as are ready to faint. Encompass with Thy favour all whose lives Thou hast bound up with our own, and, if there be any who do us wrong, remove all bitterness from our hearts while we pray for Thy blessing upon them. Give peace, O Lord, in our time, and unite all hearts in the love of Thy dear Son, Jesus Christ our Lord. *Amen.*

IV.

O GOD, who art mindful of Thy children everywhere; Reveal Thy mercy unto all men, and remember, in Thy great good-will, those for whom we now make intercession.

Remember Thy Church which Thou hast purchased of old. Peace be within her walls, and prosperity within her palaces.

Remember Thy mercy and Thy truth toward the house of Israel; and let all the ends of the earth see the salvation of our God.

Remember our Nation which Thou hast established; give wisdom and power from above to Thy servants on whom Thou hast laid the burden of authority, especially the President of the United States; and bind together the whole body of the Commonwealth in the unity of brotherhood.

Remember all the persecuted and afflicted; speak peace

to troubled hearts; strengthen the weak, confirm the strong; instruct the ignorant, deliver the oppressed, relieve the needy that hath no helper; and lead us all by the waters of comfort, and in the ways of righteousness, to Thine everlasting rest; through Jesus Christ our Lord. *Amen.*

v.

ALMIGHTY God, who lovest all that Thou hast made; Show Thy mercy unto the whole world, we beseech Thee; and bless all the children of men according to their manifold necessities. Enlighten and guide the ignorant; spare the wayward and rebellious, and restrain them from their evil ways; strengthen the sons of labour for their toil, and help the sons of consolation in their ministry; deliver the captives and all folk that are brought low; and make the nations of the earth to dwell together in peace and brotherhood.

Endue Thy servant our Chief Magistrate, the Governor of this State, and all who bear authority in our land, with wisdom and ability, and enrich the whole people with the spirit of justice and kindness, that our country may be a refuge for the oppressed and a fountain of good for all mankind.

Purify and exalt Thy Church throughout the world, filling all who call upon the Lord Jesus Christ with His Spirit, and enabling them for mightier works of mercy in His Name; that the power of faith and love may be manifested in the Christian life, and the hearts of all men everywhere may be drawn to Thy dear Son, the Light of the World. And grant, O most merciful Father, for His sake, that in the branch of Thy Church wherein Thou hast joined us unto Him, we may evermore know Him truly, love Him entirely, and serve Him faithfully.

Finally we beseech Thee, O God, be very gracious unto all who stand in urgent need of Thy mercy, [especially unto those for whom our prayers are asked] Be Thou the Strength of the weary, the Comfort of the sorrowful, the Friend of the desolate, the Light of the wandering, the Hope of the dying, and the Saviour of the lost, for Jesus' sake. *Amen.*

A General Confession of Sins.

ALMIGHTY and most merciful Father; We have erred, and strayed from Thy ways like lost sheep. We have followed too much the devices and desires of our own hearts. We have offended against Thy holy laws. We have left undone those things which we ought to have done; And we have done those things which we ought not to have done; And there is no health in us. But Thou, O Lord, have mercy upon us, miserable offenders. Spare thou those, O God, who confess their faults. Restore Thou those who are penitent; According to Thy promises declared unto mankind in Christ Jesus our Lord. And grant, O most merciful Father, for His sake; That we may hereafter live a godly, righteous, and sober life, To the glory of Thy holy Name. Amen.

PRAYERS FOR CERTAIN TIMES AND SEASONS.

New Year's Day

ALMIGHTY and most merciful Father, who hast continued our life from year to year; Grant that by longer life we may become less desirous of temporal pleasures and more careful of eternal happiness. So teach us to number our days that our minds may be more withdrawn from vanity and folly, more enlightened with the knowledge of Thy will, and more invigorated with power to obey it. O Lord, calm our thoughts, direct our desires, and fortify our purposes, that we may walk with cheerful confidence in the path which Thou hast appointed for us, growing wiser and stronger in spirit as we advance in years ; and so support us by Thy grace that we may live in Thy favour and die in Thy peace ; for the sake of Jesus Christ our Lord. *Amen.*

O THOU who art from everlasting to everlasting, without beginning or end of days; Replenish us with heavenly grace, at the beginning of this year, that we may be enabled to accept all its duties, to perform all its labours, to welcome all its mercies, to meet all its trials, and to advance through all it holds in store for us, with cheerful courage and a constant mind. O Lord, suffer us not to be separated from Thee, either by joy or sorrow, or any sin or weakness of our own; but have compassion upon us, and forgive us, and keep us in the strong confidence of Thine eternal love in Jesus Christ: that as Thou hast called us to immortality through Him, so we may pass the residue of our years in the power of an endless life; and to Thy Name shall be all the praise. *Amen.*

EVER-LIVING God, by whose mercy we have come to the gateway of another year; Grant that we may enter it with humble and grateful hearts; and confirm our resolution, we beseech Thee, to walk more closely in Thy way, and labour more faithfully in Thy service, according to the teaching and example of Thy Son our Lord. Let not the errors and offenses of the past cling to us, but pardon us and set us free, that with a purer purpose and a better hope, we may renew our vows in Thy Presence, and set forth under the guidance of Thy Spirit, to travel in that path which shineth more and more unto the perfect day of Thy heavenly kingdom. *Amen.*

GOOD FRIDAY.

ALMIGHTY and everlasting God, who of Thy tender love toward mankind hast sent Thy Son, our Saviour Jesus Christ, to take upon Him our flesh, and that in the form of a servant, and to suffer death, even the death of the cross, for our redemption; Mercifully grant that this mind may be in us which was also in Christ Jesus, that we may both follow the example of His humble obedience and patient suffering, and also be made partakers of His glorious resurrection, to live with Thee for ever. Grant this for the sake of Thy Son, our Saviour, Jesus Christ. *Amen.*

O MOST merciful Father, who of Thy tender compassion toward us guilty sinners didst give Thine only-begotten Son to be an offering for our sins; Grant us grace, we humbly beseech Thee, that being united unto Him by Thy Spirit, and made partakers of His sufferings and His death, we may crucify the corrupt inclinations of the flesh, die daily unto the world, and lead holy and unblamable lives. Cleaving unto His cross in all the temptations of life, may we hold fast the profession of our faith without wavering, and finally attain unto the resurrection of the just; through the merits of this same once crucified but now risen and exalted Saviour. *Amen.*

LORD Jesus Christ, Thou holy and spotless Lamb of God, who didst take upon Thyself our sins, and bear them in Thy body on the cross; We bless Thee for all the burdens Thou hast borne, for all the tears Thou hast wept, for all the pains Thou hast suffered, for all the words of comfort Thou hast spoken from the cross, for all Thy conflicts with the powers of darkness, and for Thine eternal victory over death and hell. With the host of the redeemed, we ascribe unto Thee power and riches and wisdom and strength and honour and glory and blessing, for ever and ever. *Amen.*

EASTER DAY.

ALMIGHTY God, who hast brought again from the dead our Lord Jesus, the glorious Prince of salvation, with everlasting victory over hell and the grave ; Grant us power, we beseech Thee, to rise with Him to newness of life, that we may overcome the world with the victory of faith, and have part at last in the resurrection of the just; through the merits of the same risen Saviour, who liveth and reigneth with Thee and the Holy Ghost, ever one God, world without end *Amen.*

ALMIGHTY God, who through Thine only-begotten Son Jesus Christ hast overcome death, and opened unto us the gate of everlasting life; We humbly beseech Thee, that, as by Thy special grace preparing us Thou dost put into our minds good desires, so by Thy continual help we may bring the same to good effect ; through Jesus Christ our Lord, who liveth and reigneth with Thee and the Holy Ghost, ever one God, world without end. *Amen.*

O THOU Son of God and Son of man, who by Thy victory over death hast brought life and immortality to light; Raise us, by faith in Thee, from the grave of sin, and deliver us from the mortal darkness of unbelief: that our hearts may be fortified with an eternal hope, and our affections set upon the things which are above, and our spirits clothed at last with a celestial body : in the likeness of that glory wherein Thou art exalted for evermore at the right hand of the Father. *Amen*

O THOU God and Father of our Lord Jesus Christ, we render Thee most humble and hearty thanks, that when He had descended into the grave, Thou didst not suffer Thy Holy One to see corruption, but didst show unto Him the path of life, and raise Him from the dead, and set Him at Thine own right hand in the heavenly places. Grant us grace, we beseech Thee, to apprehend with true faith the glorious mystery of our Saviour's resurrection, and fill our hearts with joy and a lively hope, that amid all the sorrows, trials, and temptations of our mortal state, and in the hour of death, we may derive strength and comfort from this sure pledge of an inheritance incorruptible and undefiled, and that fadeth not away. *Amen.*

THANKSGIVING DAY.

ALMIGHTY God, our heavenly Father, whose mercies are without number, and the treasure of whose goodness is infinite ; We render Thee thanks for all the gifts Thou hast bestowed upon us; evermore beseeching Thy compassion ; that as Thou grantest the petitions of them that faithfully ask Thee, Thou wilt never forsake them, but prepare them for the rewards to come, in Thy everlasting kingdom; through Jesus Christ our Lord *Amen.*

O ALMIGHTY and everlasting God, who hast blessed the labours of the husbandman, and given unto us the fruits of the earth in their season ; Grant us grace to use the same to Thy glory, to the relief of those that are needy, and to our own comfort ; through Jesus Christ, who is the Living Bread which cometh down from heaven and giveth life unto the world; to whom, with Thee and the Holy Spirit, be all honour and glory, now and for ever. *Amen.*

MOST high and mighty Ruler of the universe, by whom our Nation hath been established in freedom and preserved in union; We praise Thee for Thy favour shown unto our fatheis, and Thy faithfulness continued unto their children: for the rich land given us for an inheritance, and the great power entrusted to the people: for the fidelity of men set in authority, and the peace maintained by righteous laws: for protection against our enemies, and deliverance from inward strife: for an honourable place among the nations, and the promise of increasing strength. Lord, Thou hast not dealt so with any people: Keep Thou the Commonwealth beneath Thy care, and guide the State according to Thy will: and Thine shall be the glory and the praise and the thanksgiving, from generation to generation. *Amen.*

ADVENT.

ALMIGHTY God, give us grace that we may cast away the works of darkness, and put upon us the armour of light, now in the time of this mortal life, in which Thy Son Jesus Christ came to visit us in great humility; that in the last day, when He shall come again in His glorious majesty to judge both the quick and dead, we may rise to the life immortal, through Him who liveth and reigneth with Thee and the Holy Ghost, now and ever.   *Amen.*

O LORD Jesus Christ, who at Thy first coming didst send Thy messenger to prepare Thy way before Thee; Grant that the ministers and stewards of Thy mysteries may likewise so prepare and make ready Thy way, by turning the hearts of the disobedient to the wisdom of the just, that at Thy second coming to judge the world we may be found an acceptable people in Thy sight, who livest and reignest with the Father and the Holy Spirit, ever one God, world without end.   *Amen.*

O GOD, who dost gladden us with the continual looking for of our redemption; Grant that Thy only-begotten Son our Lord Jesus Christ, whom we now receive as our Redeemer, we may one day in safety behold coming as our Judge, who liveth and reigneth with Thee, in the unity of the Godhead, world without end.   *Amen.*

ALMIGHTY God, we beseech Thee, grant unto Thy people grace that they may wait with vigilance for the advent of Thy Son our Lord, that when He shall arise from Thy right hand to visit the earth in righteousness and Thy people with salvation, He may not find us sleeping in sin, but diligent in Thy service, and rejoicing in Thy praises, that so we may enter in with Him unto the marriage of the Lamb; through His merits, who liveth and reigneth with Thee and the Holy Ghost, ever one God, world without end. *Amen.*

CHRISTMAS DAY.

FATHER in heaven, whose mercy we praise in the yearly remembrance of the birth of Thy beloved Son, Jesus Christ our Lord; Grant that as we welcome our Redeemer, His presence may shed abroad, in our hearts and in our homes, the light of heavenly peace and joy. Make known unto all men, by Thy Word and Spirit, the Gospel of His blessed incarnation, whereby Thou hast clearly revealed Thy love for the world. And help us so to celebrate this day, in humility and gratitude, in unselfish love and cheerful service, that our keeping of Christmas may be a blessing to our souls, a memorial of Christ, a benefit to our fellowmen, and a thanksgiving unto Thee for Thine unspeakable gift of the Saviour. *Amen.*

O ALMIGHTY God, who by the birth of Thy Holy One into the world didst give Thy true light to dawn upon our darkness; Grant that as Thou hast given us to believe in the mystery of His incarnation, and hast made us partakers of the divine nature, so in the world to come we may ever abide with Him, in the glory of His kingdom; through the same Jesus Christ our Lord. *Amen.*

ALMIGHTY God, who hast given us Thy only-begotten Son to take our nature upon Him, and as at this time to be born of a pure virgin; Grant that we, being regenerate, and made Thy children by adoption and grace, may daily be renewed by Thy Holy Spirit; through the same our Lord Jesus Christ, who liveth and reigneth with Thee and the Spirit, ever one God, world without end. *Amen.*

A Day of Humiliation.

O ALMIGHTY God, who desirest not the death but the life of sinners, Despise not Thy people returning unto Thee in their affliction, but for the glory of Thy Name be pleased to hear and succour us; that the hearts of men may know that these scourges proceed from Thy justice and cease by Thy mercy; through Christ our Lord. *Amen.*

O MOST mighty God, King of kings and Lord of lords, without whose care the watchman waketh but in vain; We implore, in this our time of need, Thy succour and blessing in behalf of our rulers and magistrates, and of all the people of this land. Remember not our many and great transgressions ; turn from us the judgments which we feel, and the yet greater judgments which we fear; and give us wisdom to discern, and faithfulness to do, and patience to endure, whatsoever shall be well-pleasing in Thy sight; that so Thy chastenings may yield the peaceful fruits of righteousness, and that at the last, we may rejoice in Thy salvation; through Jesus Christ our Lord. *Amen.*

A LMIGHTY God, who forgivest the iniquities of Thy people, and healest all their diseases ; who hast promised to heal us in Thy Son's Name, and hast sent Him to bear our burdens ; Look down upon us, Thine unworthy servants, who humble ourselves before Thee and acknowledge that we have justly provoked Thine anger. We beseech Thee to have mercy upon us, and to forgive us; and of Thy loving-kindness to remove this [*here let the national affliction be named*], the judgment of Thy hand, with which Thou hast visited us; and this we ask for the honour of Thy great Name ; through Jesus Christ our Lord. *Amen.*

A Session of the General Assembly.

A LMIGHTY God, who by Thy Holy Spirit dost inhabit the whole company of the faithful; Graciously regard, we beseech Thee, Thy servants gathered before Thee at this time, in the General Assembly and chief council of this Church. Shed down upon *them* heavenly wisdom and grace; enlighten *them* with true knowledge of Thy Word; inspire *them* with a pure zeal for Thy glory; and so order all *their* doings through Thy good Spirit that unity and peace may prevail among *them;* that truth and righteousness may flow forth from *them;* and that, by *their* endeavours, all Thy ministers and congregations may be established and comforted, Thy Gospel everywhere purely preached and truly followed, Thy kingdom among men extended and strengthened, and the whole body of Thine elect people grow up into Him who is Head over all things to the Church, Jesus Christ our Lord. *Amen.*

ALMIGHTY and everlasting God, who by Thy Holy Spirit didst enlighten the minds of Thy servants the Apostles and Elders, met together at Jerusalem to take counsel for the peace and unity of Thy Church, and hast promised by Thy Son Jesus Christ to be with Thy faithful ministers to the end of the world; Grant us, we beseech Thee, the same enlightening and life-giving Spirit, that those things which seem good unto the Holy Ghost may also seem good unto us. Let brotherly love continue, and in lowliness of mind let each esteem other better than himself, save us from all uncharitable judging and rash speaking. Let the peace of God rule in our hearts, and the law of kindness dwell upon our lips; and of Thy great mercy vouchsafe, we beseech Thee, so to direct, sanctify, and govern us in all our doings, by the indwelling of Thy good Spirit, that the Gospel of Christ may be truly preached, devoutly received, and heartily obeyed, in all places, to the breaking down of the kingdom of sin and Satan; till at length the whole flock of Thy dispersed sheep being gathered into Thy fold, under the one Bishop and Shepherd of our souls, shall become partakers of everlasting life, through the merits and mediation of Thy dear Son Jesus Christ our Lord; to whom be glory in the Church, world without end. *Amen.*

A MEETING OF SYNOD OR PRESBYTERY.

ALMIGHTY God, who through the Apostles of Thy Son Jesus Christ didst order the governance of Thy flock, causing Elders to be ordained in every church, both to teach and to rule, send now Thy blessing upon [the Synod, *or* Presbytery, of ——] assembled in Thy Name.   Grant unto Thy servants the spirit of power, and of love, and of a sound mind, that *we* may be wise in council and diligent in service, faithful stewards of the things belonging to Thy kingdom, and worthy successors of the Apostles whom our Lord sent forth to testify of Him.   Direct and govern *us* by Thy Holy Spirit, preserving *us* from hasty judgment and vain dispute, inspiring *us* with hearty love and true devotion, and guiding *us* both to devise and do those things which shall be for the glory of Christ's Name, for the welfare of His Church, for the peace of all believers, for the spread of the Gospel, and for the good of the whole world. *Amen.*

A SESSION OF CONGRESS.

MOST gracious God, we humbly beseech Thee, as for the people of this Nation in general, so especially for their Senate and Representatives in Congress assembled ; That Thou wouldest be pleased to direct and prosper all their consultations, to the advancement of Thy glory, the good of Thy Church, the safety, honour, and welfare of the people ; that all things may be so ordered and settled by their endeavours, upon the best and surest foundations, that peace and happiness, truth and justice, virtue and piety, may be established among us.   These and all other necessaries, for them, for us, and Thy whole Church, we humbly beg in the Name of Jesus Christ, our most blessed Lord and Saviour.   *Amen.*

A SESSION OF THE LEGISLATURE.

O THOU who rulest in equity and declarest righteous judgment; Send down upon the Legislature of this State, [here] lawfully convened, the spirit of concord, purity, and justice, that all false counsels and evil influences may be absent from the assembly, and that the servants of the people may be directed in wisdom and integrity, according to Thy laws.   So guide and prosper with Thy blessing whatsoever may be devised and enacted, that it may redound to the honour and welfare of this Commonwealth, to the peace and prosperity of the whole Union, and to the glory of Thy Name.   *Amen.*

A DAILY PRAYER FOR THE ARMY.

O LORD God, high and mighty, who doest Thy will in the army of heaven and amongst the inhabitants of the earth ; Stretch forth the shield of Thy most merciful protection over us Thy servants, and the Army [*or* Regiment] in which we serve. Lead and guide us evermore by the counsel of Thy goodness; strengthen and defend us with Thy might ; that we may steadfastly continue an honour and bulwark of our land, a terror to evil-doers, and a sure defense against every enemy ; and finally, having quitted ourselves like men, and as good soldiers of the Lord Jesus, may we enter into Thy eternal glory ; through Him who is our only Deliverer and the Captain of our salvation, Jesus Christ our Lord. *Amen.*

A DAILY PRAYER FOR THE NAVY.

O ETERNAL Lord God, who alone spreadest out the heavens and rulest the raging of the sea, and hast compassed the waters with bounds until day and night come to an end ; Be pleased to receive into Thy almighty and most gracious protection the persons of us Thy servants, and the Fleet [*or* Ship] in which we serve. Preserve us from the dangers of the deep and from the violence of enemies ; that we may be a safeguard unto our country, and a security for such as do business in the mighty waters : that the inhabitants of our land may have peace and freedom to serve Thee ; and that in due season we may return to our homes, with a thankful remembrance of Thy mercies ; and, finally, having passed the sea of this troublous life, may enter the haven of eternal rest; through Him, who is our only Refuge and Saviour, Jesus Christ our Lord. *Amen.*

IN TIME OF DEARTH AND FAMINE.

O GOD, heavenly Father, whose gift it is that the rain doth fall, and the earth bring forth her increase ; Behold, we beseech Thee, the afflictions of Thy people ; increase the fruits of the earth by Thy heavenly benediction ; and grant that the scarcity and dearth which we now suffer, may through Thy goodness be mercifully turned into plenty; that we, receiving Thy bountiful liberality, may use the same to Thy glory, the relief of those that are needy, and our own comfort; for the love of Jesus Christ our Lord, to whom, with Thee and the Holy Ghost, be all honour and glory, now and for ever. *Amen.*

In Time of Pestilence.

HOLY and mighty Lord, who didst turn back the angel of the plague from the dwellings of Thy people; We beseech Thee to hear our cry for those who are suffering and dying, [*here, if any place be specially afflicted, let it be named,*] under the visitation of disease. Mercifully bless the means which are used to stay the spread of sickness, strengthen those who labour to heal and comfort the afflicted, support those who are in pain and distress, speedily restore those who have been brought low, and unto all who are beyond healing, grant Thy heavenly consolation and Thy saving grace; through Jesus Christ our Lord. *Amen.*

After a Great Disaster.

ALMIGHTY God, who art a very present help in time of trouble; Let not the heart of Thy people fail when fear cometh, but do Thou sustain and comfort them until these calamities be overpast: and since Thou knowest the cause and reason why this grievous disaster, [of fire, flood, earthquake, shipwreck, or other trouble,] hath fallen upon men, so do Thou heal the hurt and wounded, console the bereaved and afflicted, protect the innocent and helpless, and deliver any who are still in peril, for Thy great mercy's sake. *Amen.*

In Time of Insurrections and Tumults.

O ALMIGHTY Lord God, who alone riddest away tyrants by Thine everlasting determination, and stillest the noise and tumult of the people; Stir up Thy great strength, we beseech Thee, and come and help us; scatter the counsels of them that secretly devise mischief, and bring the dealings of the violent to naught; cast down the unjust from high places, and cause the unruly to cease from troubling; allay all envious and malicious passions, and subdue the haters and the evil-doers; that our land may have rest before Thee, and that all the people may praise Thee, our Help and our Shield, both now and evermore. *Amen.*

In Time of War.

O ALMIGHTY God, supreme Ruler and Governor of all things, who art a strong tower of defense to them that fear Thee, and whose power no creature is able to resist; Unto Thee do we cry in the hour of our country's need. To Thee it belongeth justly to punish sinners and to be merciful to those who repent. Save and deliver us, we humbly beseech Thee, from the hands of our enemies; abate their pride, assuage their malice, and confound their devices; that we, being armed with Thy defense, may be preserved evermore from all perils, to glorify Thee, who art the only Giver of all victory; through the merits of Thy Son Jesus Christ our Lord. *Amen.*

O LORD God of infinite mercy, we humbly beseech Thee to look down upon the nations now engaged in war. Reckon not against Thy people their many iniquities, for from the lusts of our own hearts come wars and fightings amongst us. Look in mercy on those immediately exposed to peril, conflict, sickness, and death: comfort the prisoners, relieve the sufferings of the wounded, and show mercy to the dying. Remove in Thy good providence all causes and occasions of war; dispose the hearts of those engaged therein to moderation; and of Thy great goodness restore peace among the nations; through Jesus Christ our Lord. *Amen.*

In Time of Peace Restored.

O ETERNAL God, our heavenly Father, who alone makest men to be of one mind, and stillest the outrage of a violent and unruly people; We bless Thy holy Name that it hath pleased Thee to appease the tumults which have been lately raised up among us; most humbly beseeching Thee to grant to all of us grace, that we may henceforth obediently walk in Thy holy commandments; and, leading a quiet and peaceable life in all godliness and honesty, may continually offer unto Thee our sacrifice of praise and thanksgiving for these Thy mercies toward us; through Jesus Christ our Lord. *Amen.*

A LMIGHTY and everlasting God, who makest wars to cease unto the ends of the earth; We praise and magnify that great mercy, whereby Thou hast not only freed our borders from every enemy, and given us rest and quietness, but out of Thine abundant goodness art shedding down the same blessed tranquillity upon the nations round about us; and we humbly beseech Thee, that, being subdued by Thy truth, they may evermore dwell together in love as one family of mankind; through Jesus Christ our Lord. *Amen.*

INTERCESSIONS FOR SPECIAL OBJECTS AND PERSONS.

FOR OUR COUNTRY.

A LMIGHTY God, King of kings, and Lord of lords, from whom proceed all power and dominion in heaven and earth; Most heartily we beseech Thee to look with favour upon Thy servants, the President of the United States, the Governor of this State, and all others in authority. Imbue them with the spirit of wisdom, goodness, and truth; and so rule their hearts, and bless their endeavours, that law and order, justice and peace may everywhere prevail. Preserve us from public calamities; from pestilence and famine; from war, privy conspiracy, and rebellion; but especially from national sins and corruption. Make us strong and great in the fear of God, and in the love of righteousness; so that being blessed of Thee, we may become a blessing to all nations, to the praise of the glory of Thy grace; through Jesus Christ. *Amen.*

O MOST powerful Lord God, blessed and only Potentate, who hast granted unto our country liberty, and established our Nation in righteousness by the people's will: Guide and direct the multitudes whom Thou hast ordained in power, by Thy pure wisdom and Thy just laws ; that their counsels may be filled with knowledge and equity, and the whole estate of the Commonwealth be preserved in peace, unity, strength, and honour : And take under Thy governance and protection, Thy servants, the President, the Governor of this State, the lawgivers, the judges, the counsellors, the magistrates, and all who are entrusted with authority; so defending them from all evil and enriching them with all needed good, that the people may prosper in freedom beneath an equal law, and our Nation may magnify Thy Name in all the earth; through Jesus Christ our Lord. *Amen.*

For Deliverance from National Sins.

LORD God Almighty, defend our land, we beseech Thee, from the secret power and the open shame of great national sins. From all dishonesty and civic corruption ; from all vainglory and selfish luxury ; from all cruelty and the spirit of violence; from covetousness which is idolatry, from impurity which defiles the temple of the Holy Spirit ; and from intemperance which is the mother of many crimes and sorrows; good Lord, deliver and save us, and our children, and our children's children, in the land which Thou hast blessed with the light of pure religion; through Jesus Christ, our only Saviour and King *Amen.*

For the Church and Missions

ALMIGHTY and everlasting God, who hast revealed Thy glory, by Christ, among all nations ; Preserve the works of Thy mercy; that Thy Church, which is spread throughout the world, may persevere with steadfast faith in the confession of Thy Name; through Jesus Christ our Lord. *Amen.*

O ALMIGHTY God, who hast built Thy Church upon the foundation of the Apostles and Prophets, Jesus Christ Himself being the chief Corner Stone. Grant that by the operation of the Holy Ghost, all Christians may be so joined together in unity of Spirit, and in the bond of peace, that they may be an holy temple acceptable unto Thee.

And especially to this congregation present give the abundance of Thy grace, that with one heart they may desire the prosperity of Thy holy universal Church, and with one mouth may profess the faith once delivered to the saints. Defend them from the sins of false doctrine and the spirit of strife; let not the foot of pride come nigh to hurt them, nor the hand of the ungodly to cast them down. And grant that the course of this world may be so peaceably ordered by Thy governance, that Thy Church may joyfully serve Thee in all godly quietness: that so they may walk in the ways of truth and peace, and at last be numbered with Thy saints in glory everlasting; through Thy merits, O blessed Jesus, Thou gracious Bishop and Shepherd of our souls, who art, with the Father and the Holy Ghost, one God, world without end. *Amen.*

O THOU who hast founded a Church for Thyself, and hast promised to dwell in it for ever; Enlighten and sanctify it, we beseech Thee, by Thy Word and Spirit; endue all pastors and ministers with Thy grace, that they may with joy and assurance guard and feed Thy sheep, looking to the great Bishop and Shepherd of souls. Bless all who serve Thee in the rule of Thy Church; in the care of Thy poor; in the ministry of Thy praise; and in the teaching of the young. Strengthen them in their labours; give them courage to witness a good confession; and cause Thy Church to increase more and more, that every knee may bow before Thee, and every tongue confess that Jesus Christ is Lord. *Amen.*

O GOD, the Father of our Lord Jesus Christ, our only Saviour, the Prince of Peace; give us grace seriously to lay to heart the great dangers we are in by our unhappy divisions. Take away all hatred and prejudice, and whatsoever else may hinder us from godly union and concord, that, as there is but one body, and one Spirit, and one hope of our calling, one Lord, one faith, one baptism, one God and Father of us all, so we may be all of one heart and of one soul, united in one holy bond of truth and peace, of faith and charity, and may with one mind and one mouth glorify Thee; through Jesus Christ our Lord. *Amen.*

O LORD, who didst come to seek and to save the lost and to whom all power is given in heaven and in earth; Hear the prayers of Thy Church for those who, at Thy command, go forth to preach the Gospel to every creature Preserve them from all dangers; from perils by land and perils by water; from the deadly pestilence; from the violence of the persecutor; from doubt and impatience; from discouragement and discord, and from all the devices of the powers of darkness. While they plant and water, O Lord, send Thou the increase; gather in the multitude of the heathen; and convert in Christian lands such as neglect Thy great salvation, that Thy Name may be glorified, and Thy kingdom come, O Saviour of the world; to whom, with the Father and the Holy Ghost, be honour and glory, world without end. *Amen.*

O GOD, who hast made of one blood all nations of men for to dwell on the face of the whole earth, and didst send Thy blessed Son to preach peace to them that are far off and to them that are nigh; Grant that all men everywhere may seek after Thee and find Thee. Bring the nations into Thy fold, and add the heathen to Thine inheritance And we pray Thee shortly to accomplish the number of Thine elect, and to hasten Thy kingdom; through the same Jesus Christ our Lord. *Amen*

ETERNAL Father, who art loving unto every man, and hast given Thy Son to be the Saviour of the world; Grant that the pure light of His Gospel may overcome the darkness of idolatry in every land, and that all Thy lost children, dwelling in far countries, may be brought home to Thee. Revive the spirit of missions in Thy Church, that all Thy people may earnestly desire the conversion of mankind; and so quicken our hearts, that there may be a larger outpouring of prayer and gifts and personal service, to advance the world-wide triumph of Thy kingdom. Protect the messengers of the Gospel amid all perils, guide them through all perplexities; give them wisdom, strength, and courage to make known by word and life the grace of our Lord Jesus; prosper all that they do, in His blessed Name, to serve the bodies and the souls of men; and hasten, we beseech Thee, the promised day, when at the Name of Jesus every knee shall bow, and every tongue confess that He is Lord, to the glory of God the Father. *Amen.*

For Evangelistic Work.

INCREASE, O God, the faith and the zeal of all Thy people, that they may more earnestly desire, and more diligently seek, the salvation of their fellow-men, through the message of Thy love in Jesus Christ our Lord. Send forth a mighty call unto Thy servants to preach Thy Word, and multiply the number of those who labour in the Gospel ; granting unto them a heart of love, sincerity of speech, and the power of the Holy Ghost, that they may be able to persuade men to forsake sin and turn unto Thee. And so bless and favour the work of Thine evangelists, that multitudes may be brought from the kingdom of evil into the kingdom of Thy dear Son, our Saviour Jesus Christ. *Amen.*

For All who do Good to their Fellow–Men.

O GOD, who hast given unto Thy servants diversities of gifts by the same Spirit, and hast taught us by Thy holy apostle that all our doings without charity are nothing worth ; Be pleased to bless and prosper all who love and serve their fellow-men with a pure heart fervently, remembering the poor, healing the sick, comforting the sorrowful, teaching the ignorant, and lifting up the afflicted ; let their prayers and alms come up for a memorial before Thee; and reward them plentifully with peace; through the merits of Jesus Christ our only Saviour *Amen.*

For the Coming of God's Kingdom and Universal Peace.

O THOU King eternal, immortal, invisible, Thou only wise God our Saviour ; Hasten, we beseech Thee, the coming of Thy kingdom upon earth, and draw the whole world of mankind into willing obedience to Thy blessed reign. Overcome all the enemies of Christ, and bring low every power that is exalted against Him. Cast out all the evil things which cause wars and fightings among us, and let Thy Spirit rule the hearts of men in righteousness and love. Restore the desolations of former days; rejoice the wilderness with beauty, and make glad the city with Thy law Establish every work that is founded on truth and equity, and fulfil all the good hopes and desires of Thy people. Manifest Thy will, Almighty Father, in the brotherhood of man, and bring in universal peace; through the victory of Christ our Lord. *Amen.*

For the Young.

ETERNAL Father, who out of the mouths of babes and sucklings hast ordained strength; Reveal Thyself unto our children, we beseech Thee, and grant them an entrance into Thy heavenly kingdom; that, being born again of the Spirit and taught by the Lord Jesus, they may grow up before Thee in purity of heart and innocency of life, until they come unto the measure of the stature of the fulness of Christ *Amen.*

For Sunday-Schools.

O GOD, our Father, in whose image all the children of men are made; Most heartily we beseech Thee to bless the Sunday-schools of the Church, that the young may be instructed in Thy Word, and that Thy likeness may be renewed in their hearts, through the knowledge of Thy dear Son, our Lord Open the Holy Scripture, both to those who teach and to those who learn, that the difficulties of the letter may not hide the light of the Spirit. Make all the scholars ready to be taught and willing to obey, that they may find joy and peace in the way of Thy commandments Enrich the teachers with patient faithfulness and loving wisdom, and send out more labourers into this part of Thy vineyard, that the young and tender plants may be nourished and trained to bring forth fruit unto everlasting life Finally we beseech Thee, O most merciful Father, for all Thy little children who dwell in darkness and in the shadow of the evil that is in the world; that it may please Thee to have pity on them, and to gather them, by the kindly hand of Thy true servants, into the light of the

Christian fold, that they may sit at the feet of Jesus and learn of Him. So let Thy truth be manifest from generation to generation, and the whole family of mankind rejoice together in Thy mercy; through Jesus Christ the Saviour of the world. *Amen.*

For Schools and Colleges.

THOU only wise God, our Saviour, with whom are all the treasures of heavenly understanding, Illuminate all schools and colleges and universities with the light that cometh from above; that those who teach may be taught of Thee, and those who learn may be led by Thy Spirit; and grant that by the increase of knowledge Thy truth may be confirmed, and Thy glory manifested; through Jesus Christ, Thy Living Word. *Amen.*

O FATHER of Lights and Fountain of all knowledge; Bless, we beseech Thee, all teachers and institutions of learning, and grant that from them the light of truth may shine with growing brightness on all men, so that wisdom and knowledge may be the stability of our times, in Jesus Christ our Lord. *Amen.*

ALMIGHTY and everlasting God, whose Son came into the world to destroy the power of darkness, and make us the children of light; Illumine our minds, we beseech Thee, with the full and abiding knowledge of Christ and His Gospel. Send Thy favour upon all efforts to train the young in intelligence, virtue, and piety. Bless all schools and colleges of sound learning and Christian education, and make them instruments in Thy hand of great good to the world. Endue the officers and teachers with a true sense of their high stewardship, and enlarge the hearts of the people to a loyal support of good institutions of learning, where the precepts of the Gospel are honoured as the supreme wisdom

Enlighten the minds, purify the hearts and lives of the students, so that they may go forth a noble host, made ready and consecrated for large and fruitful work. Bless everywhere those who are striving for a Christian education amid the hindrances of poverty and friendlessness; and raise up friends, and strengthen wise agencies, to prosper their endeavours. Pour out Thy Spirit from on high, and sanctify all minds and hearts for Thine acceptable service here and Thy blessed kingdom hereafter. All which we ask in the Name of Him who is the Way, the Truth, and the Life, Jesus Christ our Lord. *Amen.*

A PRAYER FOR A SERVICE IN A SCHOOL OR COLLEGE.

O LORD our Heavenly Father, by whose Spirit man is taught knowledge, who givest wisdom to all that ask Thee; Grant Thy blessing, we beseech Thee, to all who serve Thee here, whether as teachers or learners, and help us in the work which Thou hast given us to do. Enable us to labour diligently and faithfully, not with eye-service, but in singleness of heart, remembering that without Thee we can do nothing, and that in Thy fear is the beginning of wisdom. May we set Thy holy will ever before us, and do that which is well-pleasing in Thy sight, that so our work here may count for good to others, both now and in the days to come. Open Thou our eyes to know Thy marvellous works, to search our own spirits, and to understand the wondrous things of Thy law. Of Thy great goodness pour into our hearts the excellent gift of charity, and grant that in meekness and truth and purity we may glorify Thee, the Father of lights, in the spirit of Thy dear Son, Jesus Christ our Lord. *Amen.*

FOR ALL WHO ARE IN TROUBLE.

O GOD, remember in Thy mercy the poor and needy, the widow and the fatherless, the stranger and the friendless, the sick and the dying [and any such known to ourselves, whom we name in our hearts before Thee]: relieve their needs, sanctify their sufferings, strengthen their weakness: and in due time bring them out of bondage into the glorious liberty of the sons of God. *Amen.*

ALMIGHTY and everlasting God, the Comfort of the sad, the Strength of sufferers; Let the prayers of those that cry out of any tribulation come unto Thee; that all may rejoice to find Thy mercy present with them in their afflictions; through Christ our Lord. *Amen.*

GOD of all comfort, we commend to Thy mercy all those upon whom any cross or tribulation is laid; the nations who are afflicted with famine, pestilence, or war; those of our brethren who suffer persecution for the sake of the Gospel; all such as are in danger by sea or land, and all persons oppressed with poverty, sickness, or any infirmity of body or sorrow of mind. We pray particularly for the sick and afflicted members of this church, and for those who desire to be remembered in our prayers [and for any such known to ourselves, whom we name in our hearts before Thee]. May it please Thee to show them Thy fatherly kindness, chastening them for their good: that their hearts may turn unto Thee, and receive perfect consolation, and deliverance from all their troubles, for Christ's sake. *Amen.*

BE merciful, O God, unto all who need Thy mercy, and let the Angel of Thy Presence save the afflicted: Be Thou the Strength of the weary, the Comfort of the sorrowful, the Friend of the desolate, the Light of the wandering, the Hope of the dying, the Saviour of the lost, for Jesus' sake. *Amen.*

WE remember before Thee, O Lord, our brethren who are tried with sickness: entreating Thee to increase their faith and patience, to restore them to health, if it be Thy will, and to give them a happy issue out of all their troubles. Have pity on all widows and orphans; succour all who are in danger by sea and land, all prisoners and captives, and all who are oppressed with labour and toil. Have mercy on those who are tempted, and on those who are in darkness and perplexity, and strengthen them with Thy Holy Spirit. Be present with those who are dying, and grant that they may depart in peace, fearing no evil, and live before Thee in Thy heavenly kingdom; through Christ our Lord. *Amen.*

FOR KINDRED AND FRIENDS.

O LORD, our heavenly Father, bless and keep, we pray Thee, our kindred, friends, and benefactors, and graciously watch between them and us while we are absent one from another, that in due time we may meet again to praise Thee, and hereafter dwell together in heavenly mansions ; through Christ our Lord. *Amen.*

O THOU who art the God of all the families of the earth ; We beseech Thee to bless all our friends and kindred, and to grant that we may ever be knit together in the bonds of mutual love, and, above all, that we may be members together of the mystical body of Christ. *Amen.*

O GOD, who by the grace of the Holy Ghost hast poured the gifts of love into the hearts of Thy faithful people ; Grant unto our friends and kindred, for whom we implore Thy mercy, health of body and soul; that they may love Thee with all their strength, and with perfect affection fulfil Thy pleasure , through Jesus Christ our Lord. *Amen.*

A LMIGHTY God, we commend to Thee our families and our children.   Dwell in our homes, we beseech Thee; protect our dwellings from all evil, both outwardly and inwardly, and fill them with peace and holiness.   We pray for all who are dear to us, that they may be delivered from all the dangers of this present life, and kept by Thy grace unto salvation.   And O, most loving Father, we remember with undying affection those whom death has taken, and who sleep in Jesus   United in one household of faith and love, may we live in the blessed hope, that when the day dawns and the shadows flee away, we shall meet with them and all Thy redeemed, in Thy presence, where there is fulness of joy ; through Jesus Christ our Lord.   *Amen.*

FOR A SICK PERSON.

O LORD our God, who art the Physician of our souls and of our bodies; who chastenest and again Thou healest; We beseech Thee mercifully to regard Thy servant, [N ,] for whom we pray that *his* life may be spared, and *his* strength restored.   O Thou, who didst give Thy Son to bear our sicknesses and carry our sorrows: for His sake deal compassionately with this Thy servant, and send upon *him* Thy healing power and virtue, both in *his* body and in *his* soul and spirit.   Into Thy hands we commit *him;*

unto Thy gracious mercy and protection we commend *him*, as unto a faithful and merciful Saviour. *Amen.*

MOST wise and loving Father, look down from heaven, behold, visit, and relieve this Thy servant. Look upon *him* with the eyes of Thy mercy, give *him* comfort and sure confidence in Thee, defend *him* from the danger of the enemy, and keep *him* in perpetual peace and safety ; through Jesus Christ our Lord. *Amen.*

FOR A SICK CHILD.

O ALMIGHTY God, our Father in heaven, have pity upon the young child, [N.,] now lying upon the bed of sickness. Spare the life which Thou hast given, and relieve the pains of the helpless: direct the ministry of healing for *his* recovery, and revive *his* spirit, that the frailty of the body may pass away: renew *his* strength both inwardly and outwardly, and grant unto *him* many years on earth, to serve Thee faithfully by doing good in *his* generation. Nevertheless, O Father, whatsoever Thy will may be concerning this child, we know that *he* is in Thy keeping, and we pray that *his* soul may be Thine, for ever and ever, in Jesus Christ our Lord. *Amen.*

FOR ONE WHO IS NEAR TO DEATH.

ETERNAL God, to whom belong the issues of life and death ; We implore Thy mercy for Thy servant, [N.,] whose time of departure seemeth to be near at hand. With Thee there is nothing impossible, and Thou canst raise *him* up even yet, and prolong *his* earthly pilgrimage, if it be Thy will: but if not, O God, be gracious unto *him*, and prepare *his* heart to return to Thee. Give unto *him* sincere repentance, true faith, abundant forgiveness, and a heavenly hope; suffer *him* not, in the last hour, for any pain or fear of death, to fall away from Thee; but let Thine everlasting arms be underneath *him*, and grant *him* a peaceful departure, and a happy entrance into eternal rest; through the merits and intercession of Jesus Christ our Saviour. *Amen.*

For One Restored from Sickness.

O GOD, who art the Giver of life, of health, and of safety; We bless Thy Name, that Thou hast been pleased to deliver from *his* bodily sickness Thy servant. who now desireth to return thanks unto Thee, in the presence of Thy people. Gracious art Thou, O Lord, and full of compassion to the children of men. May *his* heart be duly impressed with a sense of Thy merciful goodness, and may *he* devote the residue of *his* days to an humble, holy, and obedient walking before Thee; through Jesus Christ our Lord. *Amen.*

For One Going a Journey.

LORD God omnipotent, who reignest in the heavens and on the earth; We implore Thy guidance and protection for Thy servant, [N.,] now setting forth upon *his* journey. Against all perils be Thou *his* strong defense, and in far regions be Thou *his* faithful friend; keep *him* in health and heart; prosper the ends of *his* adventure, and make the way of *his* going and of *his* returning both safe and happy; and so direct the steps of all Thy pilgrims through this world, that we shall finally arrive in the better country, even the heavenly, with Jesus Christ our Lord. *Amen.*

For a Person, or Persons, Going to Sea.

O ETERNAL Lord God, who alone spreadest out the heavens, and rulest the raging of the sea; We commend to Thy almighty protection Thy *servant,* for whose preservation on the great deep our prayers are desired. Guard *him,* we beseech Thee, from the dangers of the sea, from sickness, from the violence of enemies, from every evil; and conduct *him* in safety to the haven where *he* would be, with a grateful sense of Thy mercies; through Jesus Christ our Lord. *Amen.*

For Our Enemies.

LORD Jesus Christ, who hast commanded us not to return evil for evil, but to pray for those who hate us;

Enable us by Thy blessed example and Thy loving Spirit, to offer a true prayer for all our enemies, [and especially for those persons known to Thee, who have wrought us harm.] If in anything we have given just cause of offense, teach us to feel, and to confess, and to amend our fault, that a way of reconciliation may be found. Let not their anger burn against us, but deliver them and us from the power of hatred, so that we may be as ready to grant forgiveness as they to ask it, and the peace of God may rule in all our hearts, both now and evermore. *Amen.*

For Benefactors.

ALMIGHTY God, by whose good Spirit the minds of men are inclined to deeds of love and kindness; We thank Thee for all the help and comfort which we have received from friends and benefactors, [and especially from those whose bounty we now remember and record.] As they have been mindful of us, so be Thou ever mindful of them: as they have freely given, so may they freely receive at Thy hands abundant mercies and blessings. Do Thou have regard unto all their necessities, and reward all their good deeds, that in this life the comfort of grateful thoughts may follow them, and in the life to come Thy love may welcome them to an everlasting habitation; through Jesus Christ our Lord. *Amen.*

For Distant Friends.

OUR heavenly Father, who hast bestowed upon us the dear comfort of earthly friends; Look down in mercy upon those whom we love, and who love us, while they are far away, [and especially upon those for whom we ask Thy favour.] Protect and keep them from all danger in body and in soul: prosper and bless them in all things good: suffer them never to be lonely, desolate, or afraid: let no shadow come between them and us to divide our hearts: but in Thine own good time may we renew sweet fellowship together on earth, and at last be united in the felicity of heaven; through Jesus Christ our Lord. *Amen.*

A Thanksgiving for a Prayer Granted.

OUR heavenly Father, who hast mercifully inclined Thine ear unto our supplications, and granted our heart's desire in [*here let the special mercy be named*] ; Let this new proof and token of Thy favour, we beseech Thee, more closely bind our hearts to Thee in grateful love ; that the blessing which Thou hast bestowed may never be turned from the good purpose of Thy giving; that the lives to which Thou hast been gracious may be consecrated to Thy glory ; and that our thankfulness may not be in word only, but in deed and in truth; through our Lord Jesus Christ. *Amen.*

BRIEF PETITIONS.

For the Spirit of Prayer.

O LORD our God, who alone foreseest and bestowest things needful for our salvation; Do Thou bestow on our souls the hearty desire of imploring Thy mercy, and graciously vouchsafe us what will be for our good ; through Jesus Christ our Lord. *Amen.*

O LORD, grant unto us an unceasing perseverance in praying unto Thee; that as Thou dost not forsake us when we are bowed down in tribulation, so Thou mayest cherish us with more abundant grace when we continually beseech Thy Majesty ; through Jesus Christ our Lord. *Amen.*

LET the prayers of Thy suppliants, O Lord, come up to the ears of Thy mercy ; and that we may obtain what we ask, make us ever to ask what pleases Thee ; through Jesus Christ our Lord. *Amen.*

O HOLY Spirit the Comforter, who, with the Father, and the Son, abidest One God in Trinity ; Descend this day into our hearts, that while Thou makest intercession for us, we may with full confidence call upon our Father. *Amen.*

For Penitence.

O LORD God, who despisest not a contrite heart, and forgettest the sin and wickedness of a sinner, in whatsoever hour he doth mourn and lament his old manner of living ; Grant unto us, we beseech Thee, true contrition of heart, that we may vehemently despise our sinful life past, and wholly be converted unto Thee, by our Saviour and Lord Jesus Christ *Amen.*

O GOD, who art rich in forgiveness ; Grant that we may always hold fast the good things which we receive from Thee, and as often as we fall into sins, may be raised up by repentance ; through Thy mercy. *Amen.*

ALMIGHTY and everlasting God, who hatest nothing that Thou hast made, and dost forgive the sins of all them that are penitent ; Create in us new and contrite hearts, that we, duly lamenting our sins, and acknowledging our wretchedness, may obtain of Thee perfect remission and forgiveness ; through Jesus Christ our Lord. *Amen.*

For Forgiveness.

HAVE compassion, O God, upon Thy servants ; seeing that our hearts are grieved for having offended against Thee, and our own consciences condemn us, and we have no refuge save only in Thy mercy, which Thou hast revealed through Jesus Christ our Lord. *Amen.*

O MERCIFUL God, the Fountain of all goodness, who knowest the thoughts of our hearts ; We confess unto Thee that we have sinned against Thee, and done evil in Thy sight. Wash us, we beseech Thee, from the stains of our past sins, and give us grace and power to put away all hurtful things ; that being delivered from the bondage of sin, we may walk in the path of Thy commandments ; through Jesus Christ our Lord. *Amen.*

LET Thy mercy come upon us, O God, in great fulness, even as our sins against Thee have been many ; and may Thy forgiving love overflow all our transgressions, that they may be covered and blotted out, and we may be purified unto newness of life; for the sake of Jesus Christ, who loved us, and died for us. *Amen.*

FORGIVE, O Lord, we beseech Thee, all that we have done amiss, all that we have spoken falsely or in anger, and all that we have thought or purposed against Thy will. Forgive our ignorant and hasty faults, our wilful and deliberate offenses, and all our sins of slothfulness and neglect. Forgive us freely; forgive us graciously; forgive us entirely; in the Name of Jesus Christ. *Amen.*

For Faith.

O ALMIGHTY and everlasting God, who not only givest every good and perfect gift, but also increasest those gifts Thou hast given; We most humbly beseech Thee to increase in us the gift of faith, that we may truly believe in Thee, and in Thy promises; and that neither by our negligence or infirmity of the flesh, nor by grievousness of temptation, nor by the subtle crafts and assaults of the devil, we be driven from faith in our Saviour and Lord Jesus Christ. *Amen.*

GRANT us, O Lord, we pray Thee, to trust in Thee with all our heart; seeing that as Thou dost always resist the proud who confide in their own strength, so Thou dost not forsake those who make their boast of Thy mercy; through Jesus Christ our Lord. *Amen.*

LORD Jesus Christ, very God and very Man, who changest not, but art holy in all Thy works; Turn away from us the unbelief of a doubtful mind, and fill our hearts with the gifts of Thy grace; that we may believe and know Thee to be very God, who by Thy mighty works art proved to be the Saviour of all. *Amen.*

For Hope.

IT is good for us to hold fast by Thee, O Lord; and do Thou so increase in us the desire of good, that the hope which joins us to Thee may not be shaken by any wavering of faith but may endure in steadfastness of love. *Amen.*

O GOD, who by Thy Word hast given unto us exceeding great and precious promises; Encourage us by Thy Spirit to a confident expectation of all good things from Thee; that we may abide and labour in the cheerfulness of a godly hope. *Amen.*

FOR LOVE.

O GOD, who hast taught us to keep all Thy heavenly commandments by loving Thee and our neighbour; Grant us the spirit of peace and grace, that Thy universal family may be devoted to Thee with their whole heart, and united to each other with a perfect charity; through Jesus Christ our Lord. *Amen.*

O GOD the Father almighty, good beyond all that is good, fair beyond all that is fair, in whom is calmness, peace, and concord; Do Thou remove the dissensions which divide us from each other, and bring us back into an unity of love, which may bear some likeness to Thy nature. And grant that, being made one in Thee, who art above all, and through all, and in all, we may be kept in the unity of Thy Spirit in the bond of peace; through that peace of Thine which maketh all things peaceful, and through the grace, mercy, and tenderness of Thine only-begotten Son. *Amen.*

O GOD of love, Giver of concord, who hast sent us a new commandment, through Thine only-begotten Son, that we should love one another, even as Thou didst love us, the unworthy and the wandering, and gavest Thy Son for our life and salvation; We pray Thee, Lord, give to us Thy servants, in all time of our life on the earth, (but especially and pre-eminently now,) a mind forgetful of past ill-will, a pure conscience and sincere thoughts, and a heart to love our brethren. *Amen.*

FOR HUMILITY AND PATIENCE.

O GOD, who resistest the proud, and givest grace to the humble; Grant to us that true humility, whereof Thine only-begotten Son hath given in Himself an example to the faithful : that by our foolish pride we may never provoke Thine indignation, but receive the gifts of Thy grace in lowliness ; through Jesus Christ our Lord. *Amen.*

OUR Father in heaven, who chastenest every son whom Thou receivest ; Grant unto us that with a meek and lowly heart we may endure Thy fatherly corrections, and submit ourselves quietly to Thy wise discipline: so that we may learn obedience by the things which we suffer, and have a place among those who through faith and patience inherit Thy promises. *Amen.*

ALMIGHTY God, who dost suffer Thy children to be sorely tried and tempted; Grant that we may bear patiently the troubles of this mortal life, neither rebelling against Thee, nor turning away from Thine instruction; so that in the end we may be made wise and humble, and obtain the blessing of those who, with patience and fortitude, wait upon the Lord. *Amen.*

For Perseverance.

O GOD, who in Thy loving-kindness dost both begin and finish all good things; Grant that as we glory in the beginnings of Thy grace, so we may rejoice in its completion; through Jesus Christ our Lord *Amen.*

O GOD, who hast willed that the gate of mercy should stand open to the faithful ; Look on us, and have mercy upon us ; that we, who by Thy grace are following the path of Thy will, may never turn aside from the ways of life ; through Jesus Christ our Lord. *Amen*

LOOK upon us and hear us, O Lord our God; and assist those endeavours to please Thee which Thou Thyself hast granted to us ; as Thou hast given the first act of will, so give the completion of the work ; grant that we may be able to finish what Thou hast granted us to wish to begin. *Amen.*

For Purity.

O GOD, whose blessed Son was manifested that He might destroy the works of the devil, and make us the sons of God and heirs of eternal life; Grant us, we beseech Thee, that having this hope we may purify ourselves, even as He is pure ; that when He shall appear again with power and great glory, we may be made like unto Him in His eternal and glorious kingdom. *Amen.*

IN Thy mercy and majesty, O Lord, behold Thy household, that they may be neither stained with vices of their own, nor held in bondage by the sins of others; but that being ever freed and cleansed from both, they may do service unto Thee; through Jesus Christ our Lord *Amen.*

For Temperance.

ALMIGHTY God, gracious Father of men and angels, who openest Thine hand and fillest all things with plenty ; Teach us to use the gifts of Thy providence soberly and temperately, that our temptations may not be too strong for us, nor our affections sensual and unholy. Grant, O Lord, that the blessings which Thou givest us may neither minister to sin nor to sickness, but to health and holiness and thanksgiving ; that in the strength of Thy provision we may faithfully and diligently serve Thee, may worthily feast at Thy Table here, and be accounted worthy to sit down at Thy Table hereafter; through Jesus Christ our Lord. *Amen.*

MOST merciful Father, who desirest not the death of a sinner, but rather that he should turn from his wicked ways and live ; Have pity, we beseech Thee, upon all miserable captives who are in bondage to drunkenness. Deliver them from the tyranny of that blind and wicked spirit, whereby their lives are confused and defiled, and they are driven into all manner of shameful deeds. Strengthen them to resist their besetting sin, and lead them into the liberty and purity of the sons of God. Direct and bless Thy servants who fight against the cruel dominion of strong drink, according to the precepts of Thy holy religion; and grant that all who minister to intemperance, and all who are entangled in its net, may be converted to a godly, righteous, and sober life· through the grace of our Lord Jesus Christ. *Amen.*

For a Heavenly Mind.

O ALMIGHTY God, who alone canst order the unruly wills and affections of sinful men; Grant unto Thy people that they may love the thing which Thou commandest, and desire that which Thou dost promise; that so, among the sundry and manifold changes of the world, our hearts may surely there be fixed, where true joys are to be found; through Jesus Christ our Lord. *Amen.*

GRANT us, O Lord, we beseech Thee, always to seek Thy kingdom and righteousness; and of whatsoever Thou seest us to stand in need, mercifully grant us an abundant portion; through Jesus Christ our Lord. *Amen.*

ALMIGHTY and eternal God, who dost bid us walk as pilgrims and strangers in this passing world, seeking that abiding city which Thou hast prepared for us in heaven; We pray Thee so to govern our hearts by Thy Holy Spirit, that we, avoiding all fleshly lusts which war against the soul, and quietly obedient to the rule which Thou hast set over us, may show forth Thy glory before the world by our good works; for Jesus Christ's sake. *Amen.*

O LORD, whose favour is life, and in whose presence there is fulness of peace and joy; Vouchsafe unto us, we beseech Thee, such an abiding sense of the reality and glory of those things which Thou hast prepared for them that love Thee, as may serve to raise us above the vanity of this present world, both in its pleasures and in its necessary trials and pains; so that under Thy guidance and help all things here shall work together for our everlasting salvation; through Jesus Christ our Lord. *Amen.*

For Guidance.

O THOU great Shepherd of Israel, who, by Thine outstretched arm, didst bring Thy people of old out of the land of Egypt and the house of bondage, guiding them safely through the wilderness to the promised land; We pray Thee to deliver us from the bondage and slavery of our sins, and so to lead us through the wilderness of this world, feeding us with bread from heaven, and with water out of the smitten rock, and upholding us amid the swellings of Jordan, that we may enter at last into that rest which remaineth for Thy faithful people. *Amen.*

JESUS, our Master, do Thou meet us while we walk in the way, and long to reach the better country ; so that following Thy light, we may keep the path of righteousness, and never wander into the darkness of this world's night, while Thou, who art the Way, the Truth, and the Life, art guiding us. *Amen.*

FOR PROTECTION.

ALMIGHTY God, who seest that we have no power of ourselves to help ourselves ; Keep us both outwardly in our bodies and inwardly in our souls, that we may be defended from all adversities which may happen to the body, and from all evil thoughts which may assault and hurt the soul ; through Jesus Christ our Lord. *Amen.*

O God, who knowest us to be set in the midst of so many and great dangers, that by reason of the frailty of our nature we cannot always stand upright ; Grant to us such strength and protection as may support us in all dangers, and carry us through all temptations ; through Jesus Christ our Lord. *Amen.*

O ALMIGHTY Lord and everlasting God, vouchsafe, we beseech Thee, to direct, sanctify, and govern, both our hearts and bodies in the ways of Thy laws, and in the works of Thy commandments; that through Thy most mighty protection, both here and ever, we may be preserved in body and soul; through our Lord and Saviour Jesus Christ. *Amen.*

INTO Thy hands we commit ourselves, O God. We say of the Lord : Thou art our refuge ; our present help in time of trouble ; our hiding-place from the wind and covert from the tempest; our God, in Thee will we trust; through Jesus Christ our Lord. *Amen.*

A Prayer for
Anything Desired According to the Will of God.

LORD, if it be Thy will, let this come to pass : Lord, if it be for Thy glory, so be it in Thy Name. Lord, if Thou seest this is well for us and useful, then grant it unto us to use for Thine honour : But if Thou knowest it to be harmful and of no profit, then take from us the longing. Lord, Thou knowest in what way it is better : Let this or that be as Thou wilt. Give unto us what Thou wilt, how much Thou wilt, and when Thou wilt. Do with us as Thou wilt, put us where Thou wilt, deal freely with us every day. We are in Thy hand : Behold, we are Thy servants. We would not live unto ourselves but unto Thee : O that we could do so worthily and perfectly ; through Jesus Christ our Lord. *Amen.*

For Grace to Live.

O GOD, who, by the example of Thy dear Son hast warned us that we should work Thy works while it is day, before the night cometh, when no man can work ; Keep us from sloth and idleness, and from the misuse of those talents which Thou hast committed to our trust Enable us to perform the several duties of our state and calling with such care and diligence that our work may never be reproved in Thy sight ; and forasmuch as the needful business of this life is apt to steal away our hearts from Thee, give us grace to remember that we have a Master in heaven, and to do everything in singleness of heart, as unto Thee and not unto men, that of Thee we may receive the reward of the inheritance which Thou hast promised in Thy Son, our Saviour Jesus Christ. *Amen.*

O GOD, by whom the meek are guided in judgment, and light riseth up in darkness for the godly ; Grant us, in all our doubts and uncertainties, the grace to ask what Thou wouldest have us to do ; that the Spirit of Wisdom may save us from all false choices, and that in Thy light we may see light, and in Thy straight path may not stumble ; through Jesus Christ our Lord. *Amen.*

FOR GRACE TO DIE.

O GOD, who holdest our souls in life, and hast appointed unto all men once to die; Grant that when our last hour cometh, and the time of our earthly sojourn is ended, we may neither be troubled nor dismayed; but being satisfied with Thy goodness and mercy, we may commend our spirits to Thy care; and firmly trusting in the merits of Thy Son, our Saviour, we may obtain a peaceful death and a happy entrance into glory. And this we beg for the sake of Him who died for us that we might live with Thee for ever. *Amen.*

ASCRIPTIONS OF PRAISE.

I.

NOW unto Him that is able to do exceeding abundantly above all that we ask or think, according to the power that worketh in us; unto Him be glory in the Church by Christ Jesus, throughout all ages, world without end. *Amen.*

II.

NOW unto Him that is able to keep you from falling, and to present you faultless before the presence of His glory with exceeding joy; to the only wise God our Saviour, be glory and majesty, dominion and power, both now and ever. *Amen.*

III.

UNTO Him that loved us, and washed us from our sins in His own blood, and hath made us kings and priests unto God and His Father; to Him be glory and dominion for ever and ever. *Amen.*

IV.

NOW unto the blessed and only Potentate, the King of kings, and Lord of lords; who only hath immortality, dwelling in the light which no man can approach unto; whom no man hath seen or can see: to Him be honour and power everlasting. *Amen.*

v.

NOW unto the God of all grace, who hath called us unto His eternal glory by Christ Jesus, be glory and dominion for ever and ever. *Amen.*

vi.

AND now to the Father, Son, and Holy Ghost, three Persons and one God, be ascribed by us, and by the whole Church, as is most due, the kingdom, the power, and the glory, for ever and ever. *Amen.*

vii.

UNTO the Father, and unto the Son, and unto the Holy Ghost, be ascribed in the Church all honour and glory, might, majesty, dominion, and blessing, now, henceforth, and for ever. *Amen.*

viii.

BLESSING, and honour, and glory, and power, be unto Him that sitteth upon the throne, and unto the Lamb for ever and ever. *Amen.*

FAMILY PRAYERS.

MORNING.

SUNDAY.

GLORY be to Thee, O God; Giver of the morning light, who hast raised our Lord Jesus from the dead, on this first day of the week, that we might rejoice in it and keep it holy, a Sabbath of the heart.

Cleanse us now, we implore Thee, from all our sin, and bathe us with the dew of Thy divine forgiveness, that we, being renewed in spirit, may enter gladly into the pure worship of this day, and serve Thee with heavenly meditation and holy music, with faithful prayer and thankful praise, with words of love and works of mercy, with joy in Thy creation and perfect peace in Thee, according to the teaching and the example of Thy Son, our living Saviour Jesus Christ. *Amen.*

AS the hart panteth after the water-brooks, O God, our souls do thirst after Thee, that we may see Thy power and Thy glory, as we have seen them in the sanctuary, and be satisfied with the goodness of Thy House. Lead us and guide us unto Thy holy hill, and bring us together with sweet converse to the place of prayer, to hear Thy Word of Truth in the spirit, to offer the sacrifices of joy with Thy people, and to make melody in our hearts with the songs of Zion. Prepare us, we beseech Thee, for a true entrance into the secret of Thy tabernacle ; and bless Thy churches everywhere this day with the clear shining of Thy Presence ; that the Holy Spirit may descend on many hearts, and multitudes may be brought from the kingdom of Satan into the kingdom of Thy dear Son Jesus Christ. *Amen.*

ALMIGHTY God, we praise Thee for the mercies which Thou hast bestowed upon us as a household, and we beseech Thee to bless all the families of earth with a Father's blessing. Look mercifully upon the solitary and the lonely, the weary and the heavy-laden, and grant them rest unto their souls. Pity and relieve the sorrows of all mankind. Shed abroad the holy influence of the Sabbath throughout our land, and keep our whole country, with those who are chosen to govern it, in the way of righteousness and peace. Finally we commend to Thy fatherly goodness all who are near and dear to us, wherever they may be to-day, praying Thee to watch over them, to provide for them, to bless them in body and soul, and at last to bring them and us into the perfect and eternal joy of heaven; through Jesus Christ our Lord. *Amen.*

¶ *Here any special prayer or brief petition, suited to the need of the household, to any particular occasion, or to the season of the year, may be added; and let all present join their voices and hearts in*

THE LORD'S PRAYER.

MONDAY.

O GOD, our Father, of whom the whole family in heaven and on earth is named; Bestow upon our household, at the beginning of this day, that grace which shall keep us in the fellowship of the Christian way : and grant unto each one of us that heavenly guidance and control, in all our labours, pleasures, and trials, which shall maintain our hearts in peace with one another and with Thee. Graciously help and prosper us in the doing of our various duties, with a willing and a cheerful mind; and defend us all, by Thine almighty power, both from inward evil and from outward harm ; so that, when the day is ended, it may not leave us in sorrow, strife, or shame, but in true unity and thankful rest, through Thy merciful favour and Thy forgiving love, in Christ Jesus our Lord. *Amen.*

ALMIGHTY God, the Fountain of all wisdom, who knowest our necessities before we ask, and our ignorance in asking; We beseech Thee to have compassion upon our infirmities; and those things which for our unworthiness we dare not, and for our blindness we cannot, ask, vouchsafe to give us in the fulness of Thy love and grace, which Thou hast made known to us; through Jesus Christ our Lord. *Amen.*

LIFT upon us the light of Thy countenance, O God, that we may rejoice and be glad in Thee; and send into our souls the purifying gift of Thy pardon, that our sins may be utterly removed from us, and we may go forth with a clean spirit, a joyful courage, and strength sufficient for our needs, to meet whatever thou hast appointed for us during this day. And grant, O most merciful Lord, that we may neither forget the precepts and the promises of Thy holy Word, nor depart in thought, or word, or deed from the obedient faith of Thy true children in Jesus Christ. *Amen.*

¶ *Here any special prayer or brief petition, suited to the need of the household, to any particular occasion, or to the season of the year, may be added; and let all present join their voices and hearts in*

THE LORD'S PRAYER

TUESDAY.

O THOU, who art the true Sun of the world, evermore rising, and never going down; who, by Thy most wholesome appearing and light dost nourish, and make joyful all things, as well that are in heaven, as also that are on earth; We beseech Thee mercifully and favourably to shine into our hearts, that the night and darkness of sin, and the mists of error on every side, being driven away, Thou brightly shining within our hearts, we may all our life long go without any stumbling or offense, and may walk as in the daytime, being pure and clean from the works of darkness, and abounding in all good works which Thou hast prepared for us to walk in. *Amen.*

ALMIGHTY God, who alone gavest us the breath of life, and alone canst keep alive in us the breathing of holy desires; We beseech Thee for Thy compassion's sake to sanctify all our thoughts and endeavours, that we may neither begin any action without a pure intention, nor continue it without Thy blessing; and grant that, having the eyes of our understanding purged to behold things invisible and unseen, we may in heart be inspired with Thy wisdom, and in work be upheld by Thy strength, and in the end be accepted of Thee, as Thy faithful servants, having done all things to Thy glory, and thereby to our endless peace. Grant this prayer, O Lord. *Amen.*

O GOD, most merciful, who healest those that are broken in heart, and turnest the sadness of the sorrowful to joy; Let Thy Fatherly goodness be upon all that Thou hast made. Especially we beseech Thee to remember in pity such as are this day destitute, homeless, or forgotten of their fellow-men. Bless the congregation of the poor. Uplift those who are cast down, mightily befriend innocent sufferers, and sanctify to them the endurance of their wrongs. Cheer with hope all discouraged and unhappy people, and by Thy heavenly grace preserve from falling those whose penury tempteth them to sin. Though they be troubled on every side, suffer them not to be distressed; though they be perplexed, save them from despair. Grant this. O Lord, for the love of Him who for our sakes became poor, Thy Son, our Saviour Jesus Christ. *Amen.*

¶ *Here any special prayer or brief petition, suited to the need of the household, to any particular occasion, or to the season of the year, may be added; and let all present join their voices and hearts in*

The Lord's Prayer.

Wednesday.

ALMIGHTY and most merciful Father, in whom we live and move and have our being, to whose tender compassion we owe our safety in days past, together with all the comforts of this present life, and the hopes of that which is to come; We praise Thee, O God, our exceeding Joy, who daily pourest Thy benefits upon us Grant, we beseech Thee, that Jesus our Lord, the Hope of glory, may be formed in us, in all humility, meekness, patience, contentedness, and absolute surrender of our souls and bodies to Thy holy will and pleasure Leave us not, nor forsake us, O Father, but conduct us safe through all changes of our condition here, in an unchangeable love to Thee, and in holy tranquillity of mind in Thy love to us, till we come to dwell with Thee, and rejoice in Thee for ever. *Amen.*

GRANT, O Lord, that this day which Thou hast given unto us in mercy, may be returned unto Thee in service : As Thou hast guarded us during the helpless hours of sleep, so do Thou guide us during the appointed hours of labour ; that all our tasks may be gladly and faithfully performed, as in Thy sight ; that our burdens may not be too heavy for us, because Thine aid and comfort are with us continually ; and that in nothing may we displease Thee, or injure one another. But if in anything we fail or come short, through ignorance or weakness, O God, let Thy fatherly wisdom correct us, and Thine infinite mercy forgive us, and Thy divine love amend our fault ; through Jesus Christ our Saviour. *Amen.*

¶ *Here any special prayer or brief petition, suited to the need of the household, to any particular occasion, or to the season of the year, may be added ; and let all present join their voices and hearts in*

THE LORD'S PRAYER.

THURSDAY.

O LORD, lift up the light of Thy countenance upon us : let Thy peace rule in our hearts ; and may it be our strength, and our song in the house of our pilgrimage. We commit ourselves to Thy care and keeping this day ; let Thy grace be mighty in us, and sufficient for us, and let it work in us both to will and to do of Thine own good pleasure. Keep us from sin ; give us the rule over our own spirits ; and keep us from speaking unadvisedly with our lips. May we live together in peace and holy love, and do Thou command Thy blessing upon us, even life for evermore. Prepare us for all the events of the day : for we know not what a day may bring forth. Give us grace to deny ourselves, to take up our cross daily, and to follow in the steps of our Lord and Master. *Amen.*

O THOU who dwellest in heaven, mercifully regard all
Thy sorrowful and afflicted children upon earth, we
beseech Thee. Draw near to them with the comfort of
Thy love, and sustain them by the right hand of Thy
power Grant us a heart to sympathize with them in
their distress, and give us both the opportunity and the
will to help those who are in any trouble, for Jesus Christ's
sake. *Amen.*

O GOD, the Protector of all that trust in Thee, without
whom nothing is strong, nothing is holy; Increase and
multiply upon us Thy mercy, that, Thou being our ruler
and guide, we may so pass through things temporal, that
we may finally lose not the things eternal. Grant this, O
Lord, most merciful, for the sake of Thy dear Son, our
Saviour. *Amen.*

¶ *Here any special prayer or brief petition, suited to the need of the
household, to any particular occasion, or to the season of the
year, may be added; and let all present join their voices and
hearts in*

The Lord's Prayer.

Friday.

WE praise Thee, O God, with the morning light, and in
the brightness of a new day we bless Thy holy Name.
For all Thou hast bestowed upon us with the gift of life,
making us in Thine own image, and granting us to share
as children in Thy knowledge and Thy love, in Thy work
and Tny joy; we thank Thee, heavenly Father. For all
good things in the world, for food and raiment, for home
and friendship, for useful tasks and pure pleasures; we
thank Thee, heavenly Father. For all spiritual blessings,
for Thy holy Word, for the Christian fellowship, for the good
example and blessed memory of Thy saints, for the secret
influence of Thy Spirit; we thank Thee, heavenly Father.
And above all we praise and bless Thee for the life and
death of Thy dear Son, our Saviour Jesus Christ. *Amen.*

O LORD, grant that our hearts may be truly cleansed, and filled with Thy Holy Spirit, and that we may arise to serve Thee, in entire confidence and submission to Thy will, ready to do and to endure whatsoever Thou hast appointed for us. Let us live for the day, not overcharged with worldly cares, but feeling that our treasure is not here, and desiring truly to be joined to Thee in Thy heavenly kingdom, and to those who are already gone to Thee. O Lord, save us from sin, and guide us with Thy Spirit, and keep us in faithful obedience to Thee; through Jesus Christ our Lord. *Amen.*

¶ *Here any special prayer or brief petition, suited to the need of the household, to any particular occasion, or to the season of the year, may be added; and let all present join their voices and hearts in*

THE LORD'S PRAYER.

SATURDAY.

ALMIGHTY God, our Father and Preserver; We give Thee thanks that of Thy goodness Thou hast watched over us the past night, and brought us to a new day: and we beseech Thee to strengthen and guard us by Thy Spirit, that we may spend it wholly in Thy service and to Thy glory, looking for all prosperity to Thy blessing, and seeking only those things which are well-pleasing in Thy sight. Enable us, O Lord, while we labour for the life that now is, ever to have regard unto that heavenly life which Thou hast promised Thy children. Defend us in soul and body from all harm. And seeing it is a small thing to have begun well, except we also persevere, take us, O Lord, into Thy good keeping this day and all our days: continue and increase Thy grace within us, until we shall be perfectly united in the glory of Thy Son. Show Thy loving-kindness unto all men and women and little children, according to the need of every living soul, especially unto those whom we love, and those who are in any kind of trouble or distress, whom we now remember silently before Thee : [*here let there be a moment of prayer in silence:*] Protect our country, and prosper Thy Church: Bless all who do good in the world, and restrain and convert all who do evil. And finally, be pleased to cast out of Thy remembrance all our past offenses, forgiving them in Thy boundless mercy and purifying our hearts, that we may lead a better life ; through Jesus Christ our Lord. *Amen.*

¶ *Here any special prayer or brief petition, suited to the need of the household, to any particular occasion, or to the season of the year, may be added; and let all present join their voices and hearts in*

THE LORD'S PRAYER.

FOR THE SICK.

O THOU who hearest prayer, we pray Thee to be very kind and merciful to Thy child ——, whose body suffers in pain and weakness, [and whose life, dear to us, is in danger.] Grant unto *him* patience and tranquillity of mind; peace, purity, and courage of soul; the strong will to live if it be Thy will; and a heart ready to trust Thee waking or sleeping. Bless all the means used for *his* recovery, and all who minister to *him* in *his* suffering [and peril] Make Thou *his* bed in *his* sickness, and comfort *him* as a mother comforteth her child. Restore *him* speedily to health, if it please Thee, but above all things grant *him* that which Thou knowest to be best for *him*, and keep *him* Thine for evermore ; through Jesus Christ our Saviour. *Amen.*

FOR THE ABSENT.

ALMIGHTY God, who art not far from any one of us ; We commend into Thy fatherly care and keeping——, to whom our hearts go out in absence. Let these our loving thoughts come up before Thee as prayers and supplications ; defend our beloved from all danger and harm, in body and in soul; enrich *him* with all blessings both for this life and for that which is to come; and grant that we may soon meet together, with joy and not with grief, to thank Thee for all Thy mercies, in Christ Jesus our Lord. *Amen.*

For Departing Friends and Travellers.

MOST merciful Father, we beseech Thee to protect and prosper —— on *his* intended journey. May the Angel of Thy Presence be with *him* wherever *he* may go, and may all *his* steps be ordered of Thee in wisdom and love ; so that *he* shall travel with Thee as *his* guardian and *his* guide, and arrive in safety at *his* desired haven. O Lord, bless *his* going-out and *his* coming-in, from this time forth and even for evermore. *Amen.*

For a Family in Time of Distress.

O GOD, most wise and loving and faithful Redeemer, Thou hast permitted us to come into this present trial, [*here the affliction may be named or silently remembered,*] in order that we may learn obedience by the things that we suffer, and turn to Thee, our Helper in the time of trouble. Grant, therefore, that there may be no bitterness in our sorrow, no despair in our submission, and no doubt of Thee in our perplexity of heart. But do Thou teach us to face our trial manfully, and cause even the dark things of life to work together for our good, and bring us speedily out of our distress, that we may praise Thee with a joyful heart, in Christ Jesus our Lord. *Amen.*

Brief Petitions.

O GOD, who hast taught us to keep all Thy heavenly commandments by loving Thee and our neighbour; Grant us the spirit of peace and grace, that we may be both devoted to Thee with our whole heart, and united to each other with a pure will; through Jesus Christ our Lord *Amen.*

HEAR our prayers, O Lord, and consider our desires Give unto us true humility, a meek and quiet spirit, a loving and a friendly, a holy and a useful manner of life ; bearing the burdens of our neighbours, denying ourselves, and studying to benefit others, and to please Thee in all things. Grant us to be righteous in performing promises, loving to our relatives, careful of our charges ; to be gentle and easy to be entreated, slow to anger, and readily prepared for every good work. *Amen.*

LOOK upon us, O Lord, and let all the darkness of our souls vanish before the beams of Thy brightness. Fill us with holy love, and open to us the treasures of Thy wisdom. All our desire is known unto Thee: therefore perfect what Thou hast begun, and what Thy Spirit has awakened us to ask in prayer. We seek Thy face: turn Thy face unto us, and show us Thy glory. Then shall our longing be satisfied, and our peace shall be perfect. *Amen.*

GRANT, Lord, that we may not, for one moment, admit willingly into our souls any thought contrary to Thy love. *Amen.*

O LORD, perfect, we beseech Thee, the faith of us who believe, and sow the good seed of faith in their hearts who as yet lack it; that we all may look steadfastly unto Thee, and run with patience the race that is set before us. Give us grace to show our faith by our works; teach us to walk by faith, having respect unto the promises: which of Thy mercy make good to us in Thine own good time, O our most gracious Lord God and Saviour. *Amen.*

ALMIGHTY God, who art the Giver of all wisdom; Enlighten our understandings with knowledge of right, and govern our wills by Thy laws, that no deceit may mislead us, nor temptation corrupt us; that we may always endeavour to do good, and to hinder evil. Amidst all the hopes and fears of this world, take not Thy Holy Spirit from us; but grant that our thoughts may be fixed on Thee, and that we may finally attain everlasting happiness, for Jesus Christ's sake. *Amen.*

O GOD, who hast commanded us to be perfect, as Thou our Father in heaven art perfect; Put into our hearts, we pray Thee, a continual desire to obey Thy holy will. Teach us day by day what Thou wouldest have us do, and give us grace and power to fulfil the same. May we never, from love of ease, decline the path which Thou pointest out, nor, for fear of shame, turn away from it. *Amen.*

O ALMIGHTY Lord, and everlasting God, vouchsafe, we beseech Thee, to direct, sanctify, and govern, both our hearts and bodies in the ways of Thy laws, and in the works of Thy commandments; that through Thy most mighty protection, both here and ever, we may be preserved in body and soul; through our Lord and Saviour Jesus Christ. *Amen.*

EVENING.

A General Prayer.

O GOD most merciful, Light eternal in the darkness shining, by whom the night of sin and the blindness of our hearts are driven away: Since Thou hast appointed the day for labour and the night for rest; grant unto us, we beseech Thee, that our bodies may repose in peace and quietness, that afterward they may be able to endure the toil which Thou hast laid upon us in Thy service: Temper our sleep that it be not disorderly, and keep us spotless both in body and in soul, that our very rest may be to Thy glory, renewing the strength of our hearts and our joy in Thee: Enlighten the eyes of our understanding that we may not sleep in death, but obtain deliverance, through faith and hope, from all fear of this misery: Defend us against all assaults of our enemies, and take us into Thy holy protection. And although we have not passed this day without greatly sinning against Thee, we beseech Thee to hide our sins with Thy mercy, as Thou coverest all things on earth with the darkness of the night, that they may be blotted out from Thy remembrance, and we may abide in Thy presence and Thy favour, both now and for evermore. Relieve and comfort, with Thy fatherly goodness, all who are afflicted or distressed in mind, body, or estate: Protect and prosper, with Thine almighty power, our country and our rulers, the whole Church of Christ on earth, our home, and all that we hold dear and sacred: Be pleased to guard and help those whom we silently remember before Thee: [*here let there be a moment of prayer in silence:*] Bless us and keep us, watch over us and save us, O God in whom we trust; through Jesus Christ our Lord. *Amen.*

Various Prayers.

ALMIGHTY God, who seest that we have no power of ourselves to help ourselves; Keep us both outwardly in our bodies and inwardly in our souls, that we may be defended from all adversities which may happen to the body, and from all evil thoughts which may assault and hurt the soul; through Jesus Christ our Lord. *Amen.*

ALMIGHTY God, the Father of our spirits; Meet with us at close of day, and grant unto us, Thy children, the peace which the world cannot give. May no unhallowed thoughts or cares disturb the quiet of this evening hour. Deliver us from the vain things which have such power over us. May we learn wisdom, receive strength, gain hope, feel the influence of things unseen, and find rest in God. *Amen.*

CONFIRM, O Lord, we pray Thee, the hearts of Thy children, and strengthen them with the power of Thy grace; that they may both be devout in prayer to Thee, and sincere in love for each other; through Jesus Christ our Lord. *Amen.*

O GOD, Father of our spirits and Giver of all good; Grant that we may live in such fellowship with Thee that we shall grow into Thy likeness, and share Thy life. Free us from fretting and pride, and beget within us a meek and modest spirit. Deliver us from the bondage and bitterness of a worldly life, and lead us out into the large and joyous liberty of Christ. May He so dwell in us that His spirit shall become our disposition, and spring up within us a well of water unto everlasting life. Lead us in a plain path along life's journey, and at last may we enter in through the gates into the City. And this we ask in Jesus' Name. *Amen.*

FATHER of our spirits, and Father of our Lord and Saviour Jesus Christ; Bind us to Thyself with cords of faith, and love that can never be broken or strained. May we feel the impulse of our divine childhood, and find rest in Thee. Feed us out of Thy Word, and may it be sweet to our souls. May prayer daily acquaint us with Thee, and make us calm and strong. Cause the light of 'Thy face to shine upon us, so that we shall ever see our path, and find the world our Father's home. Give us patience and peace under every burden. May we not be anxious and troubled over many things, but have the one thing needful and be content. O Master, let us walk with Thee ! *Amen.*

WE beseech Thee, Lord, to behold us with favour, gathered together in the peace of this roof, weak men and women subsisting under the covert of Thy patience. Be patient still; suffer us yet a while longer; — with our broken purposes of good, with our idle endeavours against evil, suffer us a while longer to endure and (if it may be) help us to do better. Bless to us our extraordinary mercies ; if the day come when these must be taken, brace us to play the man under affliction. Be with our friends, be with ourselves. Go with each of us to rest; if any awake, temper to them the dark hours of watching ; and when the day returns, return to us, our Sun and Comforter, and call us up with morning faces and with morning hearts — eager to labour — eager to be happy, if happiness shall be our portion — and if the day be marked for sorrow, strong to endure it. *Amen.*

O LORD, make us to love Thee, and each other in Thee, and to meet before Thee to dwell in Thine everlasting love. *Amen.*

O LORD, support us all day long of this troublous life, until the shadows lengthen and the evening comes, and the busy world is hushed, and the fever of life is over, and our work is done. Then in Thy mercy grant us a safe lodging, and a holy rest, and peace at the last; through Jesus Christ our Lord. *Amen.*

SEND Thy peace into our hearts, O Lord, at the evening hour, that we may be contented with Thy mercies of this day, and confident of Thy protection for this night ; and now, having forgiven others, even as Thou dost forgive us, may we have a pure comfort and a healthful rest within the shelter of this home; through Jesus Christ our Saviour. *Amen.*

LIGHTEN our darkness, we beseech Thee, O Lord; and by Thy great mercy defend us from all perils and dangers of this night; for the love of Thy only Son, our Saviour, Jesus Christ. *Amen.*

ALMIGHTY God, with whom do rest the spirits of just men made perfect; we bless and praise Thy holy Name for all Thy servants departed this life in Thy faith and fear; and especially for those most dear to us who have fallen asleep in Jesus. And we beseech Thee to give us grace so to follow their good example, that we may continue united to them in fellowship of spirit, and that finally we may be gathered together in Thy heavenly kingdom; through Jesus Christ our Lord. *Amen.*

THE CONFESSION OF SINS.

MOST holy and merciful Father; We acknowledge and confess in Thy Presence: Our sinful nature prone to evil and slothful in good; And all our shortcomings and offenses against Thee. Thou alone knowest how often we have sinned: In wandering from Thy ways; In wasting Thy gifts; In forgetting Thy love. But Thou, O Lord, have pity upon us: Who are ashamed and sorry for all wherein we have displeased Thee. Teach us to hate our errors; Cleanse us from our secret faults; And forgive our sins; For the sake of Thy dear Son our Saviour. And O most holy and loving Father; Send Thy purifying grace into our hearts, we beseech Thee; That we may henceforth live in Thy light and walk in Thy ways; According to the commandments of Jesus Christ our Lord. *Amen.*

THE LORD'S PRAYER.

OUR Father which art in heaven, Hallowed be Thy Name. Thy kingdom come. Thy will be done in earth, As it is in heaven. Give us this day our daily bread. And forgive us our debts, As we forgive our debtors. And lead us not into temptation, But deliver us from evil: For Thine is the kingdom, and the power, and the glory, for ever. Amen.

FORMS OF GRACE BEFORE MEAT.

THE Lord make us grateful for all His mercies, and add His blessing, for Christ's sake. *Amen.*

ALMIGHTY God, who providest for us, nourish our souls with the Bread of Life in Jesus Christ. *Amen.*

BLESS us, O Lord, in blessing Thee, as we receive Thy gift of daily bread. *Amen.*

THE Lord bless this food to our use, and us to His service. *Amen.*

LORD, help us to receive all good things as from Thy hand, and to use them to Thy praise. *Amen.*

HEAVENLY Father, make us thankful to Thee, and mindful of others, as we receive these blessings, in Jesus' Name. *Amen.*

FATHER in heaven, sustain our bodies with this food, our hearts with true friendship, and our souls with Thy truth, for Christ's sake. *Amen.*

LORD Jesus, be our holy Guest,
Our morning Joy, our evening Rest;
And with our daily bread impart
Thy love and peace to every heart. *Amen.*

THE PSALTER.

SELECTION 1.

PSALM 1.

1 BLESSED is the man that walketh not in the counsel of the ungodly, nor standeth in the way of sinners. nor sitteth in the seat of the scornful.

2 But his delight is in the law of the Lord. and in his law doth he meditate day and night.

3 And he shall be like a tree planted by the rivers of water, that bringeth forth his fruit in his season; his leaf also shall not wither; and whatsoever he doeth shall prosper

4 The ungodly are not so: but are like the chaff which the wind driveth away.

5 Therefore the ungodly shall not stand in the judgment: nor sinners in the congregation of the righteous.

6 For the Lord knoweth the way of the righteous: but the way of the ungodly shall perish.

PSALM 2.

7 WHY do the heathen rage: and the people imagine a vain thing?

8 The kings of the earth set themselves, and the rulers take counsel together: against the Lord, and against his Anointed, saying,

9 Let us break their bands asunder: and cast away their cords from us.

10 He that sitteth in the heavens shall laugh: the Lord shall have them in derision.

11 Then shall he speak unto them in his wrath: and vex them in his sore displeasure.

12 Yet have I set my King: upon my holy hill of Zion.

13 I will declare the decree, the Lord hath said unto me: Thou art my Son, this day have I begotten thee.

14 Ask of me, and I shall give thee the heathen for thine inheritance: and the uttermost parts of the earth for thy possession.

15 Thou shalt break them with a rod of iron: thou shalt dash them in pieces like a potter's vessel.

16 Be wise now therefore, O ye kings: be instructed, ye judges of the earth.

17 Serve the Lord with fear : and rejoice with trembling.

18 Kiss the Son, lest he be angry, and ye perish from the way: when his wrath is kindled but a little. Blessed are all they that put their trust in him.

Psalm 4.

19 HEAR me when I call, O God of my righteousness: thou hast enlarged me when I was in distress; have mercy upon me, and hear my prayer.

20 O ye sons of men, how long will ye turn my glory into shame: how long will ye love vanity, and seek after leasing ?

21 But know that the Lord hath set apart him that is godly for himself: the Lord will hear when I call unto him.

22 Stand in awe, and sin not: commune with your own heart upon your bed, and be still.

23 Offer the sacrifices of righteousness: and put your trust in the Lord.

24 There be many that say, Who will show us any good : Lord, lift thou up the light of thy countenance upon us.

25 Thou hast put gladness in my heart: more than in the time that their corn and their wine increased.

26 I will both lay me down in peace, and sleep: for thou, Lord, only makest me dwell in safety

SELECTION 2.

PSALM 5. 1-7.

1 GIVE ear to my words, O Lord : consider my meditation.

2 Hearken unto the voice of my cry, my King, and my God : for unto thee will I pray

3 My voice shalt thou hear in the morning, O Lord : in the morning will I direct my prayer unto thee, and will look up.

4 For thou art not a God that hath pleasure in wickedness: neither shall evil dwell with thee.

5 The foolish shall not stand in thy sight: thou hatest all workers of iniquity.

6 Thou shalt destroy them that speak leasing: the Lord will abhor the bloody and deceitful man.

7 But as for me, I will come into thy house in the multitude of thy mercy · and in thy fear will I worship toward thy holy temple

PSALM 8.

8 O LORD our Lord, how excellent is thy name in all the earth · who hast set thy glory above the heavens !

9 Out of the mouth of babes and sucklings hast thou ordained strength because of thine enemies : that thou mightest still the enemy and the avenger.

10 When I consider thy heavens, the work of thy fingers : the moon and the stars, which thou hast ordained ;

11 What is man, that thou art mindful of him : and the son of man, that thou visitest him ?

12 For thou hast made him a little lower than the angels : and hast crowned him with glory and honour

13 Thou madest him to have dominion over the works of thy hands · thou hast put all things under his feet ;

14 All sheep and oxen: yea, and the beasts of the field ;

15 The fowl of the air, and the fish of the sea . and whatsoever passeth through the paths of the seas.

16 O Lord our Lord: how excellent is thy name in all the earth!

PSALM 11.

17 IN the Lord put I my trust: how say ye to my soul, Flee as a bird to your mountain?

18 For, lo, the wicked bend their bow, they make ready their arrow upon the string : that they may privily shoot at the upright in heart

19 If the foundations be destroyed: what can the righteous do?

20 The Lord is in his holy temple, the Lord's throne is in heaven: his eyes behold, his eyelids try the children of men.

21 The Lord trieth the righteous: but the wicked and him that loveth violence his soul hateth.

22 Upon the wicked he shall rain snares, fire and brimstone, and a horrible tempest : this shall be the portion of their cup.

23 For the righteous Lord loveth righteousness : his countenance doth behold the upright.

SELECTION 3.

PSALM 13.

1 HOW long wilt thou forget me, O Lord: for ever? how long wilt thou hide thy face from me?

2 How long shall I take counsel in my soul, having sorrow in my heart daily : how long shall mine enemy be exalted over me?

3 Consider and hear me, O Lord my God. lighten mine eyes, lest I sleep the sleep of death,

4 Lest mine enemy say, I have prevailed against him : and those that trouble me rejoice when I am moved.

5 But I have trusted in thy mercy : my heart shall rejoice in thy salvation.

6 I will sing unto the Lord· because he hath dealt bountifully with me.

PSALM 15

7 LORD, who shall abide in thy tabernacle : who shall dwell in thy holy hill?

8 He that walketh uprightly : and worketh righteousness, and speaketh the truth in his heart.

9 He that backbiteth not with his tongue, nor doeth evil to his neighbour : nor taketh up a reproach against his neighbour

10 In whose eyes a vile person is contemned ; but he honoureth them that fear the Lord: he that sweareth to his own hurt, and changeth not.

11 He that putteth not out his money to usury, nor taketh reward against the innocent: he that doeth these things shall never be moved.

PSALM 16.

12 PRESERVE me, O God : for in thee do I put my trust.

13 O my soul, thou hast said unto the Lord: Thou art my Lord, my goodness extendeth not to thee ;

14 But to the saints that are in the earth · and to the excellent, in whom is all my delight.

15 Their sorrows shall be multiplied that hasten after another god : their drink offerings of blood will I not offer, nor take up their names into my lips

16 The Lord is the portion of mine inheritance and of my cup: thou maintainest my lot

17 The lines are fallen unto me in pleasant places: yea, I have a goodly heritage.

18 I will bless the Lord, who hath given me counsel my reins also instruct me in the night seasons.

19 I have set the Lord always before me: because he is at my right hand, I shall not be moved.

20 Therefore my heart is glad, and my glory rejoiceth : my flesh also shall rest in hope.

21 For thou wilt not leave my soul in hell : neither wilt thou suffer thine Holy One to see corruption.

22 Thou wilt show me the path of life; in thy presence is fulness of joy . at thy right hand there are pleasures for evermore.

SELECTION 4.

PSALM 17: 1-9, 15.

1 HEAR the right, O Lord, attend unto my cry: give ear unto my prayer, that goeth not out of feigned lips.

2 Let my sentence come forth from thy presence: let thine eyes behold the things that are equal.

3 Thou hast proved mine heart, thou hast visited me in the night; thou hast tried me, and shalt find nothing: I am purposed that my mouth shall not transgress.

4 Concerning the works of men, by the word of thy lips: I have kept me from the paths of the destroyer.

5 Hold up my goings in thy paths: that my footsteps slip not.

6 I have called upon thee, for thou wilt hear me, O God: incline thine ear unto me, and hear my speech.

7 Show thy marvellous loving-kindness, O thou that savest by thy right hand them which put their trust in thee: from those that rise up against them.

8 Keep me as the apple of the eye: hide me under the shadow of thy wings,

9 From the wicked that oppress me: from my deadly enemies, who compass me about.

10 As for me, I will behold thy face in righteousness: I shall be satisfied, when I awake, with thy likeness.

PSALM 18: 1-19.

11 I WILL love thee. O Lord, my strength.

12 The Lord is my rock, and my fortress, and my deliverer: my God, my strength, in whom I will trust; my buckler, and the horn of my salvation, and my high tower.

13 I will call upon the Lord, who is worthy to be praised: so shall I be saved from mine enemies.

14 The sorrows of death compassed me: and the floods of ungodly men made me afraid.

15 The sorrows of hell compassed me about: the snares of death prevented me.

16 In my distress I called upon the Lord, and cried unto my God. he heard my voice out of his temple, and my cry came before him, even into his ears.

17 Then the earth shook and trembled · the foundations also of the hills moved and were shaken, because he was wroth.

18 There went up a smoke out of his nostrils: and fire out of his mouth devoured, coals were kindled by it.

19 He bowed the heavens also, and came down: and darkness was under his feet.

20 And he rode upon a cherub, and did fly: yea, he did fly upon the wings of the wind.

21 He made darkness his secret place: his pavilion round about him were dark waters and thick clouds of the skies

22 At the brightness that was before him his thick clouds passed: hail stones and coals of fire.

23 The Lord also thundered in the heavens, and the Highest gave his voice: hail stones and coals of fire.

24 Yea, he sent out his arrows, and scattered them: and he shot out lightnings, and discomfited them.

25 Then the channels of waters were seen, and the foundations of the world were discovered at thy rebuke, O Lord: at the blast of the breath of thy nostrils.

26 He sent from above, he took me: he drew me out of many waters

27 He delivered me from my strong enemy, and from them which hated me: for they were too strong for me.

28 They prevented me in the day of my calamity: but the Lord was my stay.

29 He brought me forth also into a large place: he delivered me, because he delighted in me.

SELECTION 5.

PSALM 18. 25-35.

1 WITH the merciful thou wilt show thyself merciful: with an upright man thou wilt show thyself upright;

2 With the pure thou wilt show thyself pure: and with the froward thou wilt show thyself froward.

3 For thou wilt save the afflicted people: but wilt bring down high looks

4 For thou wilt light my candle: the Lord my God will enlighten my darkness.

5 For by thee I have run through a troop: and by my God have I leaped over a wall.

6 As for God, his way is perfect: the word of the Lord is tried: he is a buckler to all those that trust in him.

7 For who is God save the Lord: or who is a rock save our God?

8 It is God that girdeth me with strength: and maketh my way perfect.

9 He maketh my feet like hinds' feet: and setteth me upon my high places

10 He teacheth my hands to war: so that a bow of steel is broken by mine arms.

11 Thou hast also given me the shield of thy salvation: and thy right hand hath holden me up, and thy gentleness hath made me great.

PSALM 19.

12 THE heavens declare the glory of God: and the firmament showeth his handywork.

13 Day unto day uttereth speech: and night unto night showeth knowledge.

14 There is no speech nor language: where their voice is not heard

15 Their line is gone out through all the earth, and their words to the end of the world: In them hath he set a tabernacle for the sun,

16 Which is as a bridegroom coming out of his chamber: and rejoiceth as a strong man to run a race.

17 His going forth is from the end of the heaven, and his circuit unto the ends of it: and there is nothing hid from the heat thereof.

18 The law of the Lord is perfect, converting the soul: the testimony of the Lord is sure, making wise the simple

19 The statutes of the Lord are right, rejoicing the heart: the commandment of the Lord is pure, enlightening the eyes.

20 The fear of the Lord is clean, enduring for ever: the judgments of the Lord are true and righteous altogether.

21 More to be desired are they than gold, yea, than much fine gold: sweeter also than honey and the honeycomb.

22 Moreover by them is thy servant warned: and in keeping of them there is great reward.

23 Who can understand his errors: cleanse thou me from secret faults

24 Keep back thy servant also from presumptuous sins; let them not have dominion over me: then shall I be upright, and I shall be innocent from the great transgression.

25 Let the words of my mouth, and the meditation of my heart, be acceptable in thy sight : O Lord, my strength, and my redeemer

SELECTION 6.

Psalm 20.

1 THE Lord hear thee in the day of trouble: the name of the God of Jacob defend thee ;

2 Send thee help from the sanctuary : and strengthen thee out of Zion ;

3 Remember all thy offerings : and accept thy burnt sacrifice ;

4 Grant thee according to thine own heart: and fulfil all thy counsel.

5 We will rejoice in thy salvation, and in the name of our God we will set up our banners : the Lord fulfil all thy petitions.

6 Now know I that the Lord saveth his anointed: he will hear him from his holy heaven with the saving strength of his right hand

7 Some trust in chariots, and some in horses : but we will remember the name of the Lord our God.

8 They are brought down and fallen : but we are risen, and stand upright.

9 Save, Lord : let the king hear us when we call.

Psalm 23.

10 THE Lord is my shepherd . I shall not want.

11 He maketh me to lie down in green pastures: he leadeth me beside the still waters

12 He restoreth my soul: he leadeth me in the paths of righteousness for his name's sake.

13 Yea, though I walk through the valley of the shadow of death, I will fear no evil: for thou art with me; thy rod and thy staff they comfort me.

14 Thou preparest a table before me in the presence of mine enemies: thou anointest my head with oil, my cup runneth over.

15 Surely goodness and mercy shall follow me all the days of my life: and I will dwell in the house of the Lord for ever.

PSALM 24.

16 THE earth is the Lord's, and the fulness thereof: the world, and they that dwell therein.

17 For he hath founded it upon the seas: and established it upon the floods.

18 Who shall ascend into the hill of the Lord: or who shall stand in his holy place?

19 He that hath clean hands, and a pure heart. who hath not lifted up his soul unto vanity, nor sworn deceitfully.

20 He shall receive the blessing from the Lord: and righteousness from the God of his salvation.

21 This is the generation of them that seek him: that seek thy face, O Jacob.

22 Lift up your heads, O ye gates; and be ye lifted up, ye everlasting doors: and the King of glory shall come in

23 Who is this King of glory: The Lord strong and mighty, the Lord mighty in battle.

24 Lift up your heads, O ye gates; even lift them up, ye everlasting doors: and the King of glory shall come in.

25 Who is this King of glory: The Lord of hosts, he is the King of glory.

SELECTION 7.

PSALM 25.

1 UNTO thee, O Lord: do I lift up my soul.

2 O my God, I trust in thee: let me not be ashamed, let not mine enemies triumph over me.

3 Yea, let none that wait on thee be ashamed: let them be ashamed which transgress without cause.

4 Show me thy ways, O Lord: teach me thy paths.

5 Lead me in thy truth, and teach me: for thou art the God of my salvation; on thee do I wait all the day.

6 Remember, O Lord, thy tender mercies and thy loving-kindnesses: for they have been ever of old.

7 Remember not the sins of my youth, nor my transgressions: according to thy mercy remember thou me for thy goodness' sake, O Lord.

8 Good and upright is the Lord: therefore will he teach sinners in the way.

9 The meek will he guide in judgment and the meek will he teach his way.

10 All the paths of the Lord are mercy and truth: unto such as keep his covenant and his testimonies.

11 For thy name's sake, O Lord· pardon mine iniquity; for it is great

12 What man is he that feareth the Lord: him shall he teach in the way that he shall choose.

13 His soul shall dwell at ease. and his seed shall inherit the earth.

14 The secret of the Lord is with them that fear him: and he will show them his covenant.

15 Mine eyes are ever toward the Lord: for he shall pluck my feet out of the net

16 Turn thee unto me, and have mercy upon me: for I am desolate and afflicted.

17 The troubles of my heart are enlarged O bring thou me out of my distresses.

18 Look upon mine affliction and my pain: and forgive all my sins.

19 Consider mine enemies, for they are many· and they hate me with cruel hatred.

20 O keep my soul, and deliver me: let me not be ashamed; for I put my trust in thee.

21 Let integrity and uprightness preserve me: for I wait on thee.

22 Redeem Israel, O God. out of all his troubles.

SELECTION 8.

Psalm 26· 8-12.

1 LORD, I have loved the habitation of thy house: and the place where thine honour dwelleth.

2 Gather not my soul with sinners: nor my life with bloody men,

3 In whose hands is mischief. and their right hand is full of bribes

4 But as for me, I will walk in mine integrity: redeem me, and be merciful unto me

5 My foot standeth in an even place: in the congregations will I bless the Lord.

PSALM 27.

6 THE Lord is my light and my salvation; whom shall I fear: the Lord is the strength of my life; of whom shall I be afraid?

7 When the wicked, even mine enemies and my foes, came upon me to eat up my flesh : they stumbled and fell.

8 Though a host should encamp against me, my heart shall not fear: though war should rise against me, in this will I be confident.

9 One thing have I desired of the Lord, that will I seek after: that I may dwell in the house of the Lord all the days of my life, to behold the beauty of the Lord, and to inquire in his temple.

10 For in the time of trouble he shall hide me in his pavilion : in the secret of his tabernacle shall he hide me ; he shall set me up upon a rock.

11 And now shall mine head be lifted up above mine enemies round about me therefore will I offer in his tabernacle sacrifices of joy; I will sing, yea, I will sing praises unto the Lord.

12 Hear, O Lord, when I cry with my voice: have mercy also upon me, and answer me.

13 When thou saidst, Seek ye my face: my heart said unto thee, Thy face, Lord, will I seek.

14 Hide not thy face far from me; put not thy servant away in anger: thou hast been my help ; leave me not, neither forsake me, O God of my salvation.

15 When my father and my mother forsake me : then the Lord will take me up.

16 Teach me thy way, O Lord: and lead me in a plain path, because of mine enemies.

17 Deliver me not over unto the will of mine enemies : for false witnesses are risen up against me, and such as breathe out cruelty.

18 I had fainted: unless I had believed to see the goodness of the Lord in the land of the living

19 Wait on the Lord : be of good courage, and he shall strengthen thine heart; wait, I say, on the Lord.

20 BLESSED be the Lord: because he hath heard the voice of my supplications.

21 The Lord is my strength and my shield; my heart trusted in him, and I am helped : therefore my heart greatly rejoiceth; and with my song will I praise him.

22 The Lord is their strength· and he is the saving strength of his anointed.

23 Save thy people, and bless thine inheritance: feed them also, and lift them up for ever.

SELECTION 9.

PSALM 28: 6-9.

1 GIVE unto the Lord, O ye mighty : give unto the Lord glory and strength

2 Give unto the Lord the glory due unto his name: worship the Lord in the beauty of holiness.

3 The voice of the Lord is upon the waters : the God of glory thundereth; the Lord is upon many waters.

4 The voice of the Lord is powerful: the voice of the Lord is full of majesty.

5 The voice of the Lord breaketh the cedars: yea, the Lord breaketh the cedars of Lebanon.

6 He maketh them also to skip like a calf · Lebanon and Sirion like a young unicorn.

7 The voice of the Lord : divideth the flames of fire.

8 The voice of the Lord shaketh the wilderness : the Lord shaketh the wilderness of Kadesh.

9 The voice of the Lord maketh the hinds to calve, and discovereth the forests: and in his temple doth every one speak of his glory

10 The Lord sitteth upon the flood: yea, the Lord sitteth King for ever.

11 The Lord will give strength unto his people· the Lord will bless his people with peace.

PSALM 29.

12 I WILL extol thee, O Lord, for thou hast lifted me up· and hast not made my foes to rejoice over me.

13 O Lord my God, I cried unto thee. and thou hast healed me.

14 O Lord, thou hast brought up my soul from the grave · thou hast kept me alive, that I should not go down to the pit.

15 Sing unto the Lord, O ye saints of his : and give thanks at the remembrance of his holiness.

16 For his anger endureth but a moment; in his favour is life: weeping may endure for a night, but joy cometh in the morning.

17 And in my prosperity I said: I shall never be moved.

18 Lord, by thy favour thou hast made my mountain to stand strong: thou didst hide thy face, and I was troubled.

19 I cried to thee, O Lord : and unto the Lord I made supplication.

20 What profit is there in my blood, when I go down to the pit : Shall the dust praise thee? shall it declare thy truth?

21 Hear, O Lord, and have mercy upon me : Lord, be thou my helper

22 Thou hast turned for me my mourning into dancing : thou hast put off my sackcloth, and girded me with gladness;

23 To the end that my glory may sing praise to thee, and not be silent : O Lord my God, I will give thanks unto thee for ever.

SELECTION 10.

PSALM 31: 1-5, 15-16, 19-24.

1 IN thee, O Lord, do I put my trust : let me never be ashamed ; deliver me in thy righteousness.

2 Bow down thine ear to me ; deliver me speedily : be thou my strong rock, for a house of defense to save me.

3 For thou art my rock and my fortress · therefore for thy name's sake lead me, and guide me

4 Pull me out of the net that they have laid privily for me : for thou art my strength.

5 Into thine hand I commit my spirit: thou hast redeemed me, O Lord God of truth.

6 My times are in thy hand : deliver me from the hand of mine enemies, and from them that persecute me.

7 Make thy face to shine upon thy servant: save me for thy mercies' sake.

8 Oh how great is thy goodness, which thou hast laid up for them that fear thee: which thou hast wrought for them that trust in thee before the sons of men !

9 Thou shalt hide them in the secret of thy presence from the pride of man: thou shalt keep them secretly in a pavilion from the strife of tongues

10 Blessed be the Lord: for he hath showed me his marvellous kindness in a strong city.

11 For I said in my haste, I am cut off from before thine eyes: nevertheless thou heardest the voice of my supplications when I cried unto thee.

12 O love the Lord, all ye his saints : for the Lord preserveth the faithful, and plentifully rewardeth the proud doer.

13 Be of good courage, and he shall strengthen your heart : all ye that hope in the Lord.

Psalm 32.

14 BLESSED is he whose transgression is forgiven: whose sin is covered.

15 Blessed is the man unto whom the Lord imputeth not iniquity : and in whose spirit there is no guile.

16 When I kept silence : my bones waxed old through my roaring all the day long

17 For day and night thy hand was heavy upon me : my moisture is turned into the drought of summer.

18 I acknowledged my sin unto thee, and mine iniquity have I not hid : I said, I will confess my transgressions unto the Lord ; and thou forgavest the iniquity of my sin

19 For this shall every one that is godly pray unto thee in a time when thou mayest be found : surely in the floods of great waters they shall not come nigh unto him

20 Thou art my hiding place; thou shalt preserve me from trouble: thou shalt compass me about with songs of deliverance.

21 I will instruct thee and teach thee in the way which thou shalt go: I will guide thee with mine eye.

22 Be ye not as the horse, or as the mule, which have no understanding : whose mouth must be held in with bit and bridle, lest they come near unto thee.

23 Many sorrows shall be to the wicked : but he that trusteth in the Lord, mercy shall compass him about.

24 Be glad in the Lord, and rejoice, ye righteous: and shout for joy, all ye that are upright in heart.

SELECTION 11.

PSALM 33.

1 REJOICE in the Lord, O ye righteous: for praise is comely for the upright.

2 Praise the Lord with harp: sing unto him with the psaltery and an instrument of ten strings.

3 Sing unto him a new song: play skilfully with a loud noise.

4 For the word of the Lord is right: and all his works are done in truth

5 He loveth righteousness and judgment: the earth is full of the goodness of the Lord

6 By the word of the Lord were the heavens made: and all the host of them by the breath of his mouth

7 He gathereth the waters of the sea together as a heap. he layeth up the depth in storehouses.

8 Let all the earth fear the Lord: let all the inhabitants of the world stand in awe of him.

9 For he spake, and it was done: he commanded, and it stood fast.

10 The Lord bringeth the counsel of the heathen to nought: he maketh the devices of the people of none effect.

11 The counsel of the Lord standeth for ever: the thoughts of his heart to all generations.

12 Blessed is the nation whose God is the Lord · and the people whom he hath chosen for his own inheritance.

13 The Lord looketh from heaven: he beholdeth all the sons of men.

14 From the place of his habitation: he looketh upon all the inhabitants of the earth.

15 He fashioneth their hearts alike: he considereth all their works.

16 There is no king saved by the multitude of a host: a mighty man is not delivered by much strength.

17 A horse is a vain thing for safety: neither shall he deliver any by his great strength.

18 Behold, the eye of the Lord is upon them that fear him: upon them that hope in his mercy;

19 To deliver their soul from death: and to keep them alive in famine

20 Our soul waiteth for the Lord : he is our help and our shield.

21 For our heart shall rejoice in him: because we have trusted in his holy name.

22 Let thy mercy, O Lord, be upon us: according as we hope in thee.

SELECTION 12.

PSALM 34.

1 I WILL bless the Lord at all times: his praise shall continually be in my mouth.

2 My soul shall make her boast in the Lord : the humble shall hear thereof, and be glad.

3 O magnify the Lord with me : and let us exalt his name together.

4 I sought the Lord, and he heard me : and delivered me from all my fears.

5 They looked unto him, and were lightened : and their faces were not ashamed.

6 This poor man cried, and the Lord heard him : and saved him out of all his troubles.

7 The angel of the Lord encampeth round about them that fear him : and delivereth them.

8 O taste and see that the Lord is good: blessed is the man that trusteth in him.

9 O fear the Lord, ye his saints : for there is no want to them that fear him.

10 The young lions do lack, and suffer hunger: but they that seek the Lord shall not want any good thing.

11 Come, ye children, hearken unto me: I will teach you the fear of the Lord.

12 What man is he that desireth life : and loveth many days, that he may see good ?

13 Keep thy tongue from evil: and thy lips from speaking guile.

14 Depart from evil, and do good : seek peace, and pursue it.

15 The eyes of the Lord are upon the righteous : and his ears are open unto their cry.

16 The face of the Lord is against them that do evil: to cut off the remembrance of them from the earth.

17 The righteous cry, and the Lord heareth . and deliver-eth them out of all their troubles.

18 The Lord is nigh unto them that are of a broken heart : and saveth such as be of a contrite spirit.

19 Many are the afflictions of the righteous: but the Lord delivereth him out of them all.

20 He keepeth all his bones: not one of them is broken

21 Evil shall slay the wicked : and they that hate the righteous shall be desolate.

22 The Lord redeemeth the soul of his servants: and none of them that trust in him shall be desolate.

PSALM 36: 5-10.

23 THY mercy, O Lord, is in the heavens : and thy faith-fulness reacheth unto the clouds.

24 Thy righteousness is like the great mountains thy judgments are a great deep : O Lord, thou preservest man and beast.

25 How excellent is thy loving-kindness, O God : there-fore the children of men put their trust under the shadow of thy wings.

26 They shall be abundantly satisfied with the fatness of thy house : and thou shalt make them drink of the river of thy pleasures.

27 For with thee is the fountain of life: in thy light shall we see light.

28 O continue thy loving-kindness unto them that know thee: and thy righteousness to the upright in heart.

SELECTION 13.

PSALM 37: 1-9, 23-40.

1 FRET not thyself because of evil doers: neither be envious against the workers of iniquity.

2 For they shall soon be cut down like the grass : and wither as the green herb.

3 Trust in the Lord, and do good : so shalt thou dwell in the land, and verily thou shalt be fed.

4 Delight thyself also in the Lord : and he shall give thee the desires of thine heart.

5 Commit thy way unto the Lord : trust also in him; and he shall bring it to pass.

6 And he shall bring forth thy righteousness as the light: and thy judgment as the noonday.

7 Rest in the Lord, and wait patiently for him : fret not thyself because of him who prospereth in his way, because of the man who bringeth wicked devices to pass.

8 Cease from anger, and forsake wrath : fret not thyself in any wise to do evil.

9 For evil doers shall be cut off: but those that wait upon the Lord, they shall inherit the earth.

10 The steps of a good man are ordered by the Lord : and he delighteth in his way.

11 Though he fall, he shall not be utterly cast down: for the Lord upholdeth him with his hand.

12 I have been young, and now am old: yet have I not seen the righteous forsaken, nor his seed begging bread.

13 He is ever merciful, and lendeth: and his seed is blessed.

14 Depart from evil, and do good : and dwell for ever-more.

15 For the Lord loveth judgment, and forsaketh not his saints, they are preserved for ever : but the seed of the wicked shall be cut off.

16 The righteous shall inherit the land : and dwell therein for ever.

17 The mouth of the righteous speaketh wisdom: and his tongue talketh of judgment.

18 The law of his God is in his heart: none of his steps shall slide.

19 The wicked watcheth the righteous: and seeketh to slay him.

20 The Lord will not leave him in his hand: nor condemn him when he is judged.

21 Wait on the Lord, and keep his way, and he shall exalt thee to inherit the land: when the wicked are cut off, thou shalt see it.

22 I have seen the wicked in great power : and spreading himself like a green bay tree.

23 Yet he passed away, and, lo, he was not: yea, I sought him, but he could not be found.

24 Mark the perfect man, and behold the upright: for the end of that man is peace.

25 But the transgressors shall be destroyed together : the end of the wicked shall be cut off.

26 But the salvation of the righteous is of the Lord : he is their strength in the time of trouble.

27 And the Lord shall help them, and deliver them: he shall deliver them from the wicked, and save them, because they trust in him.

SELECTION 14.

PSALM 39.

1 I SAID, I will take heed to my ways, that I sin not with my tongue : I will keep my mouth with a bridle, while the wicked is before me.

2 I was dumb with silence, I held my peace, even from good : and my sorrow was stirred.

3 My heart was hot within me ; while I was musing the fire burned : then spake I with my tongue.

4 Lord, make me to know mine end, and the measure of my days, what it is : that I may know how frail I am.

5 Behold, thou hast made my days as a handbreadth ; and mine age is as nothing before thee : verily every man at his best state is altogether vanity.

6 Surely every man walketh in a vain show ; surely they are disquieted in vain : he heapeth up riches, and knoweth not who shall gather them.

7 And now, Lord, what wait I for : my hope is in thee.

8 Deliver me from all my transgressions: make me not the reproach of the foolish

9 I was dumb, I opened not my mouth : because thou didst it.

10 Remove thy stroke away from me : I am consumed by the blow of thine hand.

11 When thou with rebukes dost correct man for iniquity, thou makest his beauty to consume away like a moth : surely every man is vanity.

12 Hear my prayer, O Lord, and give ear unto my cry ; hold not thy peace at my tears: for I am a stranger with thee, and a sojourner, as all my fathers were.

13 O spare me, that I may recover strength : before I go hence, and be no more.

PSALM 40: 1-13, 16-17.

14 I WAITED patiently for the Lord: and he inclined unto me, and heard my cry.

15 He brought me up also out of a horrible pit, out of the miry clay : and set my feet upon a rock, and established my goings.

16 And he hath put a new song in my mouth, even praise unto our God: many shall see it, and fear, and shall trust in the Lord.

17 Blessed is that man that maketh the Lord his trust : and respecteth not the proud, nor such as turn aside to lies

18 Many, O Lord my God, are thy wonderful works which thou hast done : and thy thoughts which are to us-ward :

19 They cannot be reckoned up in order unto thee. if I would declare and speak of them, they are more than can be numbered.

20 Sacrifice and offering thou didst not desire ; mine ears hast thou opened: burnt offering and sin offering hast thou not required.

21 Then said I, Lo, I come : in the volume of the book it is written of me,

22 I delight to do thy will, O my God · yea, thy law is within my heart.

23 I have preached righteousness in the great congrega-tion : lo, I have not refrained my lips, O Lord, thou knowest.

24 I have not hid thy righteousness within my heart ; I have declared thy faithfulness and thy salvation: I have not concealed thy loving-kindness and thy truth from the great congregation.

25 Withhold not thou thy tender mercies from me, O Lord : let thy loving-kindness and thy truth continually preserve me

26 For innumerable evils have compassed me about, mine iniquities have taken hold upon me, so that I am not able to look up: they are more than the hairs of mine head; therefore my heart faileth me

27 Be pleased, O Lord, to deliver me : O Lord, make haste to help me.

28 Let all those that seek thee rejoice and be glad in thee. let such as love thy salvation say continually, The Lord be magnified.

29 But I am poor and needy ; yet the Lord thinketh upon me: thou art my help and my deliverer; make no tarrying, O my God.

SELECTION 15.

PSALM 42.

1 AS the hart panteth after the water brooks: so panteth my soul after thee, O God.

2 My soul thirsteth for God, for the living God: when shall I come and appear before God ?

3 My tears have been my meat day and night: while they continually say unto me, Where is thy God?

4 When I remember these things, I pour out my soul in me, for I had gone with the multitude: I went with them to the house of God, with the voice of joy and praise, with a multitude that kept holyday.

5 Why art thou cast down, O my soul ? and why art thou disquieted in me ? hope thou in God: for I shall yet praise him for the help of his countenance.

6 O my God, my soul is cast down within me. therefore will I remember thee from the land of Jordan, and of the Hermonites, from the hill Mizar.

7 Deep calleth unto deep at the noise of thy waterspouts: all thy waves and thy billows are gone over me.

8 Yet the Lord will command his loving-kindness in the daytime: and in the night his song shall be with me, and my prayer unto the God of my life.

9 I will say unto God my rock, Why hast thou forgotten me: why go I mourning because of the oppression of the enemy ?

10 As with a sword in my bones, mine enemies reproach me: while they say daily unto me, Where is thy God ?

11 Why art thou cast down, O my soul ? and why art thou disquieted within me ? hope thou in God: for I shall yet praise him, who is the health of my countenance, and my God.

PSALM 43.

12 JUDGE me, O God, and plead my cause against an ungodly nation: O deliver me from the deceitful and unjust man.

13 For thou art the God of my strength; why dost thou cast me off: why go I mourning because of the oppression of the enemy?

14 O send out thy light and thy truth; let them lead me: let them bring me unto thy holy hill, and to thy tabernacles.

15 Then will I go unto the altar of God, unto God my exceeding joy: yea, upon the harp will I praise thee, O God my God.

16 Why art thou cast down, O my soul? and why art thou disquieted within me? hope in God: for I shall yet praise him, who is the health of my countenance, and my God.

PSALM 44· 1-8.

17 WE have heard with our ears, O God, our fathers have told us· what work thou didst in their days, in the times of old.

18 How thou didst drive out the heathen with thy hand, and plantedst them: how thou didst afflict the people, and cast them out.

19 For they got not the land in possession by their own sword, neither did their own arm save them: but thy right hand, and thine arm, and the light of thy countenance, because thou hadst a favour unto them.

20 Thou art my King, O God. command deliverances for Jacob.

21 Through thee will we push down our enemies: through thy name will we tread them under that rise up against us.

22 For I will not trust in my bow: neither shall my sword save me

23 But thou hast saved us from our enemies: and hast put them to shame that hated us.

24 In God we boast all the day long: and praise thy name for ever.

SELECTION 16.

PSALM 45.

1 MY heart is inditing a good matter: I speak of the things which I have made touching the King; my tongue is the pen of a ready writer.

2 Thou art fairer than the children of men: grace is poured into thy lips; therefore God hath blessed thee for ever.

3 Gird thy sword upon thy thigh, O most Mighty: with thy glory and thy majesty.

4 And in thy majesty ride prosperously, because of truth and meekness and righteousness: and thy right hand shall teach thee terrible things

5 Thine arrows are sharp in the heart of the King's enemies: whereby the people fall under thee.

6 Thy throne, O God, is for ever and ever: the sceptre of thy kingdom is a right sceptre.

7 Thou lovest righteousness, and hatest wickedness. therefore God, thy God, hath anointed thee with the oil of gladness above thy fellows.

8 All thy garments smell of myrrh, and aloes, and cassia out of the ivory palaces, whereby they have made thee glad

9 Kings' daughters were among thy honourable women · upon thy right hand did stand the queen in gold of Ophir.

10 Hearken, O daughter, and consider, and incline thine ear : forget also thine own people, and thy father's house;

11 So shall the King greatly desire thy beauty : for he is thy Lord, and worship thou him.

12 And the daughter of Tyre shall be there with a gift: even the rich among the people shall entreat thy favour.

13 The King's daughter is all glorious within. her clothing is of wrought gold.

14 She shall be brought unto the King in raiment of needlework · the virgins her companions that follow her shall be brought unto thee.

15 With gladness and rejoicing shall they be brought: they shall enter into the King's palace

16 Instead of thy fathers shall be thy children : whom thou mayest make princes in all the earth.

17 I will make thy name to be remembered in all generations : therefore shall the people praise thee for ever and ever.

PSALM 46.

18 GOD is our refuge and strength: a very present help in trouble.

19 Therefore will not we fear, though the earth be re-

moved : and though the mountains be carried into the midst of the sea;

20 Though the waters thereof roar and be troubled: though the mountains shake with the swelling thereof.

21 There is a river, the streams whereof shall make glad the city of God : the holy place of the tabernacles of the Most High

22 God is in the midst of her, she shall not be moved : God shall help her, and that right early.

23 The heathen raged, the kingdoms were moved : he uttered his voice, the earth melted.

24 The Lord of hosts is with us: the God of Jacob is our refuge.

25 Come, behold the works of the Lord what desolations he hath made in the earth.

26 He maketh wars to cease unto the end of the earth: he breaketh the bow, and cutteth the spear in sunder . he burneth the chariot in the fire.

27 Be still, and know that I am God: I will be exalted among the heathen, I will be exalted in the earth.

28 The Lord of hosts is with us: the God of Jacob is our refuge.

SELECTION 17.

Psalm 47.

1 O CLAP your hands, all ye people : shout unto God with the voice of triumph.

2 For the Lord most high is terrible: he is a great King over all the earth.

3 He shall subdue the people under us: and the nations under our feet.

4 He shall choose our inheritance for us : the excellency of Jacob whom he loved.

5 God is gone up with a shout. the Lord with the sound of a trumpet.

6 Sing praises to God, sing praises . sing praises unto our King, sing praises.

7 For God is the King of all the earth sing ye praises with understanding.

8 God reigneth over the heathen: God sitteth upon the throne of his holiness.

9 The princes of the people are gathered together, even the people of the God of Abraham: for the shields of the earth belong unto God; he is greatly exalted.

PSALM 48.

10 GREAT is the Lord, and greatly to be praised . in the city of our God, in the mountain of his holiness.

11 Beautiful for situation, the joy of the whole earth, is mount Zion : on the sides of the north, the city of the great King.

12 God is known : in her palaces for a refuge.

13 For, lo, the kings were assembled : they passed by together.

14 They saw it, and so they marvelled: they were troubled, and hasted away.

15 Fear took hold upon them there, and pain. as of a woman in travail.

16 Thou breakest the ships of Tarshish. with an east wind.

17 As we have heard, so have we seen in the city of the Lord of hosts, in the city of our God: God will establish it for ever.

18 We have thought of thy loving-kindness, O God. in the midst of thy temple.

19 According to thy name, O God, so is thy praise unto the ends of the earth: thy right hand is full of righteousness.

20 Let mount Zion rejoice, let the daughters of Judah be glad: because of thy judgments

21 Walk about Zion, and go round about her: tell the towers thereof.

22 Mark ye well her bulwarks, consider her palaces: that ye may tell it to the generation following.

23 For this God is our God for ever and ever: he will be our guide even unto death.

SELECTION 18.

PSALM 51.

1 HAVE mercy upon me, O God, according to thy loving-kindness: according unto the multitude of thy tender mercies blot out my transgressions.

2 Wash me thoroughly from mine iniquity: and cleanse me from my sin.

3 For I acknowledge my transgressions: and my sin is ever before me.

4 Against thee, thee only, have I sinned, and done this evil in thy sight. that thou mightest be justified when thou speakest, and be clear when thou judgest.

5 Behold, I was shapen in iniquity: and in sin did my mother conceive me.

6 Behold, thou desirest truth in the inward parts: and in the hidden part thou shalt make me to know wisdom.

7 Purge me with hyssop, and I shall be clean: wash me, and I shall be whiter than snow.

8 Make me to hear joy and gladness: that the bones which thou hast broken may rejoice.

9 Hide thy face from my sins: and blot out all mine iniquities.

10 Create in me a clean heart, O God: and renew a right spirit within me

11 Cast me not away from thy presence: and take not thy Holy Spirit from me.

12 Restore unto me the joy of thy salvation: and uphold me with thy free Spirit.

13 Then will I teach transgressors thy ways: and sinners shall be converted unto thee.

14 Deliver me from bloodguiltiness, O God, thou God of my salvation: and my tongue shall sing aloud of thy righteousness.

15 O Lord, open thou my lips: and my mouth shall show forth thy praise.

16 For thou desirest not sacrifice; else would I give it: thou delightest not in burnt offering.

17 The sacrifices of God are a broken spirit: a broken and a contrite heart, O God, thou wilt not despise.

18 Do good in thy good pleasure unto Zion: build thou the walls of Jerusalem.

19 Then shalt thou be pleased with the sacrifices of righteousness, with burnt offering and whole burnt offering: then shall they offer bullocks upon thine altar.

SELECTION 19.

PSALM 53.

1 THE fool hath said in his heart, There is no God: Corrupt are they, and have done abominable iniquity; there is none that doeth good.

2 God looked down from heaven upon the children of men: to see if there were any that did understand, that did seek God.

3 Every one of them is gone back; they are altogether become filthy: there is none that doeth good, no, not one.

4 Have the workers of iniquity no knowledge: who eat up my people as they eat bread; they have not called upon God.

5 There were they in great fear, where no fear was: for God hath scattered the bones of him that encampeth against thee; thou hast put them to shame, because God hath despised them.

6 Oh that the salvation of Israel were come out of Zion: When God bringeth back the captivity of his people, Jacob shall rejoice, and Israel shall be glad.

PSALM 56: 3-4, 8-13.

7 WHAT time I am afraid: I will trust in thee.

8 In God I will praise his word, in God I have put my trust: I will not fear what flesh can do unto me.

9 Thou tellest my wanderings; put thou my tears into thy bottle: are they not in thy book?

10 When I cry unto thee, then shall mine enemies turn back: this I know; for God is for me.

11 In God will I praise his word: in the Lord will I praise his word.

12 In God have I put my trust: I will not be afraid what man can do unto me.

13 Thy vows are upon me, O God: I will render praises unto thee.

14 For thou hast delivered my soul from death; wilt not thou deliver my feet from falling: that I may walk before God in the light of the living?

PSALM 57.

15 BE merciful unto me, O God, be merciful unto me, for my soul trusteth in thee: yea, in the shadow of thy

wings will I make my refuge, until these calamities be overpast.

16 I will cry unto God most high: unto God that performeth all things for me.

17 He shall send from heaven, and save me from the reproach of him that would swallow me up: God shall send forth his mercy and his truth.

18 My soul is among lions; and I lie even among them that are set on fire: even the sons of men, whose teeth are spears and arrows, and their tongue a sharp sword.

19 Be thou exalted, O God, above the heavens · let thy glory be above all the earth.

20 They have prepared a net for my steps; my soul is bowed down: they have digged a pit before me, into the midst whereof they are fallen themselves.

21 My heart is fixed, O God, my heart is fixed: I will sing and give praise.

22 Awake up, my glory; awake, psaltery and harp: I myself will awake early.

23 I will praise thee, O Lord, among the people: I will sing unto thee among the nations.

24 For thy mercy is great unto the heavens: and thy truth unto the clouds.

25 Be thou exalted, O God, above the heavens: let thy glory be above all the earth.

SELECTION 20.

PSALM 61.

1 HEAR my cry, O God: attend unto my prayer.

2 From the end of the earth will I cry unto thee when my heart is overwhelmed: lead me to the rock that is higher than I.

3 For thou hast been a shelter for me: and a strong tower from the enemy.

4 I will abide in thy tabernacle for ever: I will trust in the covert of thy wings.

5 For thou, O God, hast heard my vows: thou hast given me the heritage of those that fear thy name.

6 Thou wilt prolong the king's life: and his years as many generations.

7 He shall abide before God for ever: O prepare mercy and truth, which may preserve him.

8 So will I sing praise unto thy name for ever: that I may daily perform my vows.

PSALM 62.

9 TRULY my soul waiteth upon God: from him cometh my salvation.

10 He only is my rock and my salvation: he is my defense; I shall not be greatly moved.

11 How long will ye imagine mischief against a man: ye shall be slain all of you; as a bowing wall shall ye be, and as a tottering fence.

12 They only consult to cast him down from his excellency: they delight in lies; they bless with their mouth, but they curse inwardly.

13 My soul, wait thou only upon God: for my expectation is from him.

14 He only is my rock and my salvation: he is my defense; I shall not be moved.

15 In God is my salvation and my glory: the rock of my strength, and my refuge, is in God.

16 Trust in him at all times, ye people: pour out your heart before him; God is a refuge for us.

17 Surely men of low degree are vanity, and men of high degree are a lie: to be laid in the balance, they are altogether lighter than vanity.

18 Trust not in oppression, and become not vain in robbery: if riches increase, set not your heart upon them.

19 God hath spoken once ; twice have I heard this· that power belongeth unto God.

20 Also unto thee, O Lord, belongeth mercy: for thou renderest to every man according to his work.

SELECTION 21.

PSALM 63.

1 O GOD, thou art my God; early will I seek thee: my soul thirsteth for thee, my flesh longeth for thee in a dry and thirsty land, where no water is;

2 To see thy power and thy glory: so as I have seen thee in the sanctuary.

3 Because thy loving-kindness is better than life: my lips shall praise thee.

4 Thus will I bless thee while I live: I will lift up my hands in thy name.

5 My soul shall be satisfied as with marrow and fatness: and my mouth shall praise thee with joyful lips:

6 When I remember thee upon my bed: and meditate on thee in the night watches.

7 Because thou hast been my help: therefore in the shadow of thy wings will I rejoice.

8 My soul followeth hard after thee: thy right hand upholdeth me.

9 But those that seek my soul, to destroy it: shall go into the lower parts of the earth.

10 They shall fall by the sword: they shall be a portion for foxes.

11 But the king shall rejoice in God; every one that sweareth by him shall glory: but the mouth of them that speak lies shall be stopped.

PSALM 65.

12 PRAISE waiteth for thee, O God, in Zion: and unto thee shall the vow be performed.

13 O thou that hearest prayer: unto thee shall all flesh come.

14 Iniquities prevail against me: as for our transgressions, thou shalt purge them away.

15 Blessed is the man whom thou choosest, and causest to approach unto thee, that he may dwell in thy courts: we shall be satisfied with the goodness of thy house, even of thy holy temple.

16 By terrible things in righteousness wilt thou answer us, O God of our salvation: who art the confidence of all the ends of the earth, and of them that are afar off upon the sea;

17 Which by his strength setteth fast the mountains: being girded with power:

18 Which stilleth the noise of the seas: the noise of their waves, and the tumult of the people.

19 They also that dwell in the uttermost parts are afraid at thy tokens: thou makest the outgoings of the morning and evening to rejoice.

20 Thou visitest the earth, and waterest it; thou greatly enrichest it with the river of God, which is full of water: thou preparest them corn, when thou hast so provided for it.

21 Thou waterest the ridges thereof abundantly; thou settlest the furrows thereof: thou makest it soft with showers; thou blessest the springing thereof.

22 Thou crownest the year with thy goodness: and thy paths drop fatness.

23 They drop upon the pastures of the wilderness: and the little hills rejoice on every side.

24 The pastures are clothed with flocks: the valleys also are covered over with corn; they shout for joy, they also sing.

SELECTION 22.

PSALM 66.

1 MAKE a joyful noise unto God· all ye lands:

2 Sing forth the honour of his name: make his praise glorious.

3 Say unto God, How terrible art thou in thy works: through the greatness of thy power shall thine enemies submit themselves unto thee.

4 All the earth shall worship thee, and shall sing unto thee: they shall sing to thy name.

5 Come and see the works of God: he is terrible in his doing toward the children of men.

6 He turned the sea into dry land: they went through the flood on foot; there did we rejoice in him.

7 He ruleth by his power for ever; his eyes behold the nations: let not the rebellious exalt themselves.

8 O bless our God, ye people: and make the voice of his praise to be heard

9 Which holdeth our soul in life: and suffereth not our feet to be moved

10 For thou, O God, hast proved us· thou hast tried us, as silver is tried. ·

11 Thou broughtest us into the net: thou laidst affliction upon our loins.

12 Thou hast caused men to ride over our heads; we went through fire and through water: but thou broughtest us out into a wealthy place.

13 I will go into thy house with burnt offerings: I will pay thee my vows,

14 Which my lips have uttered, and my mouth hath spoken: when I was in trouble.

15 I will offer unto thee burnt sacrifices of fatlings, with the incense of rams: I will offer bullocks with goats.

16 Come and hear, all ye that fear God: and I will declare what he hath done for my soul.

17 I cried unto him with my mouth: and he was extolled with my tongue.

18 If I regard iniquity in my heart: the Lord will not hear me.

19 But verily God hath heard me: he hath attended to the voice of my prayer.

20 Blessed be God, which hath not turned away my prayer: nor his mercy from me.

Psalm 67.

21 GOD be merciful unto us, and bless us: and cause his face to shine upon us,

22 That thy way may be known upon earth: thy saving health among all nations.

23 Let the people praise thee, O God: let all the people praise thee.

24 O let the nations be glad and sing for joy: for thou shalt judge the people righteously, and govern the nations upon earth.

25 Let the people praise thee, O God: let all the people praise thee.

26 Then shall the earth yield her increase: and God, even our own God, shall bless us.

27 God shall bless us: and all the ends of the earth shall fear him.

SELECTION 23.

Psalm 68: 1-19, 28-29; 31-35.

1 LET God arise, let his enemies be scattered: let them also that hate him flee before him.

2 As smoke is driven away, so drive them away: as wax melteth before the fire, so let the wicked perish at the presence of God.

3 But let the righteous be glad; let them rejoice before God : yea, let them exceedingly rejoice.

4 Sing unto God, sing praises to his name: extol him that rideth upon the heavens by his name JAH, and rejoice before him.

5 A father of the fatherless, and a judge of the widows: is God in his holy habitation.

6 God setteth the solitary in families; he bringeth out those which are bound with chains: but the rebellious dwell in a dry land.

7 O God, when thou wentest forth before thy people : when thou didst march through the wilderness;

8 The earth shook, the heavens also dropped at the presence of God: even Sinai itself was moved at the presence of God, the God of Israel.

9 Thou, O God, didst send a plentiful rain, whereby thou didst confirm thine inheritance : when it was weary.

10 Thy congregation hath dwelt therein : thou, O God, hast prepared of thy goodness for the poor.

11 The Lord gave the word: great was the company of those that published it.

12 Kings of armies did flee apace : and she that tarried at home divided the spoil.

13 Though ye have lain among the pots, yet shall ye be as the wings of a dove covered with silver: and her feathers with yellow gold.

14 When the Almighty scattered kings in it: it was white as snow in Salmon.

15 The hill of God is as the hill of Bashan : a high hill as the hill of Bashan.

16 Why leap ye, ye high hills? this is the hill which God desireth to dwell in : yea, the Lord will dwell in it for ever.

17 The chariots of God are twenty thousand, even thousands of angels: the Lord is among them, as in Sinai, in the holy place.

18 Thou hast ascended on high, thou hast led captivity captive · thou hast received gifts for men; yea, for the rebellious also, that the Lord God might dwell among them.

19 Blessed be the Lord, who daily loadeth us with benefits: even the God of our salvation.

20 Thy God hath commanded thy strength : strengthen, O God, that which thou hast wrought for us.

21 Because of thy temple at Jerusalem : shall kings bring presents unto thee.

22 Princes shall come out of Egypt : Ethiopia shall soon stretch out her hands unto God.

23 Sing unto God, ye kingdoms of the earth. O sing praises unto the Lord;

24 To him that rideth upon the heavens of heavens, which were of old : lo, he doth send out his voice, and that a mighty voice.

25 Ascribe ye strength unto God : his excellency is over Israel, and his strength is in the clouds.

26 O God, thou art terrible out of thy holy places : the God of Israel is he that giveth strength and power unto his people. Blessed be God.

SELECTION 24.

PSALM 70.

1 MAKE haste, O God, to deliver me : make haste to help me, O Lord.

2 Let them be ashamed and confounded that seek after my soul : let them be turned backward, and put to confusion, that desire my hurt.

3 Let them be turned back for a reward of their shame : that say, Aha, aha.

4 Let all those that seek thee rejoice and be glad in thee : and let such as love thy salvation say continually, Let God be magnified.

5 But I am poor and needy; make haste unto me, O God : thou art my help and my deliverer; O Lord, make no tarrying.

PSALM 71: 1-5, 8-9, 12, 14-24.

6 IN thee, O Lord, do I put my trust : let me never be put to confusion.

7 Deliver me in thy righteousness, and cause me to escape : incline thine ear unto me, and save me.

8 Be thou my strong habitation, whereunto I may continually resort : thou hast given commandment to save me ; for thou art my rock and my fortress.

9 Deliver me, O my God, out of the hand of the wicked : out of the hand of the unrighteous and cruel man.

10 For thou art my hope, O Lord God : thou art my trust from my youth.

11 Let my mouth be filled with thy praise : and with thy honour all the day.

12 Cast me not off in the time of old age : forsake me not when my strength faileth.

13 O God, be not far from me : O my God, make haste for my help.

14 But I will hope continually : and will yet praise thee more and more.

15 My mouth shall show forth thy righteousness and thy salvation all the day : for I know not the numbers thereof.

16 I will go in the strength of the Lord God · I will make mention of thy righteousness, even of thine only.

17 O God, thou hast taught me from my youth : and hitherto have I declared thy wondrous works.

18 Now also when I am old and gray-headed, O God, forsake me not : until I have showed thy strength unto this generation, and thy power to every one that is to come.

19 Thy righteousness also, O God, is very high, who hast done great things : O God, who is like unto thee !

20 Thou, which hast showed me great and sore troubles, shalt quicken me again : and shalt bring me up again from the depths of the earth.

21 Thou shalt increase my greatness : and comfort me on every side.

22 I will also praise thee with the psaltery, even thy truth, O my God : unto thee will I sing with the harp, O thou Holy One of Israel.

23 My lips shall greatly rejoice when I sing unto thee : and my soul, which thou hast redeemed.

24 My tongue also shall talk of thy righteousness all the day long : for they are confounded, for they are brought unto shame, that seek my hurt.

SELECTION 25.

PSALM 72.

1 GIVE the king thy judgments, O God : and thy right-eousness unto the king's son.

2 He shall judge thy people with righteousness : and thy poor with judgment.

3 The mountains shall bring peace to the people : and the little hills, by righteousness.

4 He shall judge the poor of the people : he shall save the children of the needy, and shall break in pieces the oppressor.

5 They shall fear thee as long as the sun and moon endure : throughout all generations.

6 He shall come down like rain upon the mown grass : as showers that water the earth.

7 In his days shall the righteous flourish : and abundance of peace so long as the moon endureth.

8 He shall have dominion also from sea to sea : and from the river unto the ends of the earth.

9 They that dwell in the wilderness shall bow before him : and his enemies shall lick the dust.

10 The kings of Tarshish and of the isles shall bring presents: the kings of Sheba and Seba shall offer gifts.

11 Yea, all kings shall fall down before him . all nations shall serve him.

12 For he shall deliver the needy when he crieth: the poor also, and him that hath no helper.

13 He shall spare the poor and needy . and shall save the souls of the needy.

14 He shall redeem their soul from deceit and violence : and precious shall their blood be in his sight.

15 And he shall live, and to him shall be given of the gold of Sheba . prayer also shall be made for him continually ; and daily shall he be praised.

16 There shall be a handful of corn in the earth upon the top of the mountains ; the fruit thereof shall shake like Lebanon : and they of the city shall flourish like grass of the earth.

17 His name shall endure for ever , his name shall be continued as long as the sun: and men shall be blessed in him ; all nations shall call him blessed.

18 Blessed be the Lord God, the God of Israel : who only doeth wondrous things

19 And blessed be his glorious name for ever . and let the whole earth be filled with his glory. Amen, and Amen.

SELECTION 26.

PSALM 73: 1-26.

1 TRULY God is good to Israel: even to such as are of a clean heart.

2 But as for me, my feet were almost gone· my steps had well nigh slipped.

3 For I was envious at the foolish: when I saw the prosperity of the wicked.

4 For there are no bands in their death: but their strength is firm.

5 They are not in trouble as other men : neither are they plagued like other men

6 Therefore pride compasseth' them about as a chain : violence covereth them as a garment.

7 Their eyes stand out with fatness : they have more than heart could wish.

8 They are corrupt, and speak wickedly concerning oppression : they speak loftily.

9 They set their mouth against the heavens : and their tongue walketh through the earth.

10 Therefore his people return hither : and waters of a full cup are wrung out to them.

11 And they say, How doth God know: and is there knowledge in the Most High ?

12 Behold, these are the ungodly, who prosper in the world : they increase in riches.

13 Verily I have cleansed my heart in vain : and washed my hands in innocency.

14 For all the day long have I been plagued: and chastened every morning.

15 If I say, I will speak thus: behold, I should offend against the generation of thy children.

16 When I thought to know this. it was too painful for me ;

17 Until I went into the sanctuary of God: then understood I their end.

18 Surely thou didst set them in slippery places : thou castedst them down into destruction.

19 How are they brought into desolation, as in a moment: they are utterly consumed with terrors.

20 As a dream when one awaketh: so, O Lord, when thou awakest, thou shalt despise their image.

21 Thus my heart was grieved. and I was pricked in my reins.

22 So foolish was I, and ignorant : I was as a beast before thee.

23 Nevertheless I am continually with thee : thou hast holden me by my right hand

24 Thou shalt guide me with thy counsel. and afterward receive me to glory.

25 Whom have I in heaven but thee: and there is none upon earth that I desire besides thee.

26 My flesh and my heart faileth: but God is the strength of my heart, and my portion for ever.

SELECTION 27.

PSALM 77.

1 I CRIED unto God with my voice, even unto God with my voice : and he gave ear unto me.

2 In the day of my trouble I sought the Lord: my sore ran in the night, and ceased not ; my soul refused to be comforted.

3 I remembered God, and was troubled: I complained, and my spirit was overwhelmed.

4 Thou holdest mine eyes waking. I am so troubled that I cannot speak.

5 I have considered the days of old : the years of ancient times

6 I call to remembrance my song in the night · I commune with mine own heart; and my spirit made diligent search.

7 Will the Lord cast off for ever : and will he be favourable no more ?

8 Is his mercy clean gone for ever: doth his promise fail for evermore ?

9 Hath God forgotten to be gracious: hath he in anger shut up his tender mercies ?

10 And I said, This is my infirmity : but I will remember the years of the right hand of the Most High.

11 I will remember the works of the Lord : surely I will remember thy wonders of old

12 I will meditate also of all thy work · and talk of thy doings.

13 Thy way, O God, is in the sanctuary: who is so great a God as our God?

14 Thou art the God that doest wonders: thou hast declared thy strength among the people.

15 Thou hast with thine arm redeemed thy people: the sons of Jacob and Joseph.

16 The waters saw thee, O God, the waters saw thee; they were afraid: the depths also were troubled.

17 The clouds poured out water, the skies sent out a sound: thine arrows also went abroad.

18 The voice of thy thunder was in the heaven: the lightnings lightened the world; the earth trembled and shook.

19 Thy way is in the sea, and thy path in the great waters: and thy footsteps are not known.

20 Thou leddest thy people like a flock: by the hand of Moses and Aaron.

SELECTION 28.

PSALM 80.

1 GIVE ear, O Shepherd of Israel, thou that leadest Joseph like a flock: thou that dwellest between the cherubim, shine forth.

2 Before Ephraim and Benjamin and Manasseh: stir up thy strength, and come and save us.

3 Turn us again, O God: and cause thy face to shine: and we shall be saved.

4 O Lord God of hosts: how long wilt thou be angry against the prayer of thy people?

5 Thou feedest them with the bread of tears: and givest them tears to drink in great measure.

6 Thou makest us a strife unto our neighbours: and our enemies laugh among themselves.

7 Turn us again, O God of hosts, and cause thy face to shine: and we shall be saved.

8 Thou hast brought a vine out of Egypt: thou hast cast out the heathen, and planted it.

9 Thou preparedst room before it: and didst cause it to take deep root, and it filled the land.

10 The hills were covered with the shadow of it: and the boughs thereof were like the goodly cedars.

11 She sent out her boughs unto the sea · and her branches unto the river.

12 Why hast thou then broken down her hedges: so that all they which pass by the way do pluck her ?

13 The boar out of the wood doth waste it: and the wild beast of the field doth devour it.

14 Return, we beseech thee, O God of hosts : look down from heaven, and behold, and visit this vine ;

15 And the vineyard which thy right hand hath planted: and the branch that thou madest strong for thyself.

16 It is burned with fire, it is cut down : they perish at the rebuke of thy countenance

17 Let thy hand be upon the man of thy right hand : upon the son of man whom thou madest strong for thyself.

18 So will not we go back from thee: quicken us, and we will call upon thy name.

19 Turn us again, O Lord God of hosts : cause thy face to shine; and we shall be saved.

SELECTION 29.

Psalm 84.

1 HOW amiable are thy tabernacles : O Lord of hosts!

2 My soul longeth, yea, even fainteth for the courts of the Lord: my heart and my flesh crieth out for the living God

3 Yea, the sparrow hath found a house, and the swallow a nest for herself, where she may lay her young . even thine altars, O Lord of hosts, my King, and my God.

4 Blessed are they that dwell in thy house · they will be still praising thee.

5 Blessed is the man whose strength is in thee · in whose heart are the ways of them.

6 Who passing through the valley of Baca make it a well : the rain also filleth the pools.

7 They go from strength to strength : every one of them in Zion appeareth before God.

8 O Lord God of hosts, hear my prayer: give ear, O God of Jacob.

9 Behold, O God our shield : and look upon the face of thine anointed.

10 For a day in thy courts is better than a thousand : I

had rather be a doorkeeper in the house of my God, than to dwell in the tents of wickedness.

11 For the Lord God is a sun and shield: the Lord will give grace and glory ; no good thing will he withhold from them that walk uprightly.

12 O Lord of hosts: blessed is the man that trusteth in thee.

PSALM 85.

13 LORD, thou hast been favourable unto thy land : thou hast brought back the captivity of Jacob.

14 Thou hast forgiven the iniquity of thy people : thou hast covered all their sin.

15 Thou hast taken away all thy wrath: thou hast turned thyself from the fierceness of thine anger.

16 Turn us, O God of our salvation: and cause thine anger toward us to cease.

17 Wilt thou be angry with us for ever: wilt thou draw out thine anger to all generations ?

18 Wilt thou not revive us again : that thy people may rejoice in thee ?

19 Show us thy mercy, O Lord: and grant us thy salvation.

20 I will hear what God the Lord will speak : for he will speak peace unto his people, and to his saints, but let them not turn again to folly.

21 Surely his salvation is nigh them that fear him: that glory may dwell in our land.

22 Mercy and truth are met together: righteousness and peace have kissed each other.

23 Truth shall spring out of the earth: and righteousness shall look down from heaven.

24 Yea, the Lord shall give that which is good: and our land shall yield her increase.

25 Righteousness shall go before him: and shall set us in the way of his steps.

SELECTION 30.

PSALM 86.

1 BOW down thine ear, O Lord, hear me: for I am poor and needy.

2 Preserve my soul; for I am holy: O thou my God, save thy servant that trusteth in thee.

3 Be merciful unto me, O Lord: for I cry unto thee daily.

4 Rejoice the soul of thy servant: for unto thee, O Lord, do I lift up my soul.

5 For thou, Lord, art good, and ready to forgive: and plenteous in mercy unto all them that call upon thee.

6 Give ear, O Lord, unto my prayer: and attend to the voice of my supplications.

7 In the day of my trouble I will call upon thee: for thou wilt answer me.

8 Among the gods there is none like unto thee, O Lord: neither are there any works like unto thy works.

9 All nations whom thou hast made shall come and worship before thee, O Lord: and shall glorify thy name.

10 For thou art great, and doest wondrous things: thou art God alone.

11 Teach me thy ways, O Lord; I will walk in thy truth: unite my heart to fear thy name.

12 I will praise thee, O Lord my God, with all my heart: and I will glorify thy name for evermore.

13 For great is thy mercy toward me: and thou hast delivered my soul from the lowest hell.

14 O God, the proud are risen against me: and the assemblies of violent men have sought after my soul; and have not set thee before them.

15 But thou, O Lord, art a God full of compassion· and gracious, longsuffering, and plenteous in mercy and truth

16 O turn unto me, and have mercy upon me: give thy strength unto thy servant, and save the son of thine handmaid

17 Show me a token for good: that they which hate me may see it, and be ashamed: because thou, Lord, hast holpen me, and comforted me.

PSALM 87.

18 HIS foundation: is in the holy mountains

19 The Lord loveth the gates of Zion: more than all the dwellings of Jacob.

20 Glorious things are spoken of thee: O city of God.

21 I will make mention of Rahab and Babylon to them

that know me: behold Philistia, and Tyre, with Ethiopia; this man was born there.

22 And of Zion it shall be said, This and that man was born in her: and the Highest himself shall establish her.

23 The Lord shall count, when he writeth up the people: that this man was born there.

24 As well the singers as the players on instruments shall be there: all my springs are in thee.

SELECTION 31.

PSALM 89: 1-37.

1 I WILL sing of the mercies of the Lord for ever: with my mouth will I make known thy faithfulness to all generations.

2 For I have said, Mercy shall be built up for ever. thy faithfulness shalt thou establish in the very heavens.

3 I have made a covenant with my chosen: I have sworn unto David my servant,

4 Thy seed will I establish for ever: and build up thy throne to all generations

5 And the heavens shall praise thy wonders, O Lord: thy faithfulness also in the congregation of the saints.

6 For who in the heaven can be compared unto the Lord: who among the sons of the mighty can be likened unto the Lord ?

7 God is greatly to be feared in the assembly of the saints: and to be had in reverence of all them that are about him.

8 O Lord God of hosts, who is a strong Lord like unto thee: or to thy faithfulness round about thee ?

9 Thou rulest the raging of the sea: when the waves thereof arise, thou stillest them.

10 Thou hast broken Rahab in pieces, as one that is slain: thou hast scattered thine enemies with thy strong arm

11 The heavens are thine, the earth also is thine: as for the world and the fulness thereof, thou hast founded them.

12 The north and the south thou hast created them: Tabor and Hermon shall rejoice in thy name.

13 Thou hast a mighty arm: strong is thy hand, and high is thy right hand.

14 Justice and judgment are the habitation of thy throne: mercy and truth shall go before thy face.

15 Blessed is the people that know the joyful sound: they shall walk, O Lord, in the light of thy countenance.

16 In thy name shall they rejoice all the day: and in thy righteousness shall they be exalted.

17 For thou art the glory of their strength: and in thy favour our horn shall be exalted.

18 For the Lord is our defense: and the Holy One of Israel is our King.

19 Then thou spakest in vision to thy Holy One, and saidst, I have laid help upon one that is mighty: I have exalted one chosen out of the people.

20 I have found David my servant: with my holy oil have I anointed him:

21 With whom my hand shall be established: mine arm also shall strengthen him.

22 The enemy shall not exact upon him: nor the son of wickedness afflict him.

23 And I will beat down his foes before his face: and plague them that hate him.

24 But my faithfulness and my mercy shall be with him: and in my name shall his horn be exalted.

25 I will set his hand also in the sea: and his right hand in the rivers

26 He shall cry unto me, Thou art my Father: my God, and the Rock of my salvation.

27 Also I will make him my firstborn: higher than the kings of the earth.

28 My mercy will I keep for him for evermore: and my covenant shall stand fast with him.

29 His seed also will I make to endure forever: and his throne as the days of heaven.

30 If his children forsake my law: and walk not in my judgments;

31 If they break my statutes: and keep not my commandments;

32 Then will I visit their transgression with the rod: and their iniquity with stripes.

33 Nevertheless my loving-kindness will I not utterly take from him: nor suffer my faithfulness to fail.

34 My covenant will I not break: nor alter the thing that is gone out of my lips.

35 Once have I sworn by my holiness: that I will not lie unto David

36 His seed shall endure for ever: and his throne as the sun before me

37 It shall be established for ever as the moon: and as a faithful witness in heaven.

SELECTION 32.

PSALM 90.

1 LORD, thou hast been our dwelling-place: in all generations.

2 Before the mountains were brought forth, or ever thou hadst formed the earth and the world: even from everlasting to everlasting, thou art God.

3 Thou turnest man to destruction: and sayest, Return, ye children of men.

4 For a thousand years in thy sight are but as yesterday when it is past. and as a watch in the night.

5 Thou carriest them away as with a flood; they are as a sleep: in the morning they are like grass which groweth up.

6 In the morning it flourisheth, and groweth up: in the evening it is cut down, and withereth.

7 For we are consumed by thine anger: and by thy wrath are we troubled.

8 Thou hast set our iniquities before thee: our secret sins in the light of thy countenance.

9 For all our days are passed away in thy wrath: we spend our years as a tale that is told

10 The days of our years are threescore years and ten; and if by reason of strength they be fourscore years: yet is their strength labour and sorrow; for it is soon cut off, and we fly away.

11 Who knoweth the power of thine anger: even according to thy fear, so is thy wrath.

12 So teach us to number our days: that we may apply our hearts unto wisdom.

13 Return, O Lord, how long: and let it repent thee concerning thy servants.

14 O satisfy us early with thy mercy: that we may rejoice and be glad all our days.

15 Make us glad according to the days wherein thou hast afflicted us: and the years wherein we have seen evil.

16 Let thy work appear unto thy servants: and thy glory unto their children.

17 And let the beauty of the Lord our God be upon us: and establish thou the work of our hands upon us; yea, the work of our hands establish thou it.

SELECTION 33.

PSALM 91.

1 HE that dwelleth in the secret place of the Most High: shall abide under the shadow of the Almighty.

2 I will say of the Lord, He is my refuge and my fortress: my God; in him will I trust.

3 Surely he shall deliver thee from the snare of the fowler: and from the noisome pestilence.

4 He shall cover thee with his feathers, and under his wings shalt thou trust: his truth shall be thy shield and buckler.

5 Thou shalt not be afraid for the terror by night: nor for the arrow that flieth by day ;

6 Nor for the pestilence that walketh in darkness: nor for the destruction that wasteth at noonday.

7 A thousand shall fall at thy side, and ten thousand at thy right hand : but it shall not come nigh thee.

8 Only with thine eyes shalt thou behold : and see the reward of the wicked.

9 Because thou hast made the Lord, which is my refuge: even the Most High, thy habitation ;

10 There shall no evil befall thee: neither shall any plague come nigh thy dwelling.

11 For he shall give his angels charge over thee : to keep thee in all thy ways.

12 They shall bear thee up in their hands : lest thou dash thy foot against a stone.

13 Thou shalt tread upon the lion and adder . the young lion and the dragon shalt thou trample under feet

14 Because he hath set his love upon me, therefore will

I deliver him: I will set him on high, because he hath known my name.

15 He shall call upon me, and I will answer him: I will be with him in trouble; I will deliver him, and honour him.

16 With long life will I satisfy him: and show him my salvation.

SELECTION 34.

PSALM 92.

1 IT is a good thing to give thanks unto the Lord: and to sing praises unto thy name, O Most High:

2 To show forth thy loving-kindness in the morning: and thy faithfulness every night,

3 Upon an instrument of ten strings, and upon the psaltery: upon the harp with a solemn sound.

4 For thou, Lord, hast made me glad through thy work: I will triumph in the works of thy hands

5 O Lord, how great are thy works: and thy thoughts are very deep.

6 A brutish man knoweth not: neither doth a fool understand this.

7 When the wicked spring as the grass, and when all the workers of iniquity do flourish: it is that they shall be destroyed for ever:

8 But thou, Lord: art most high for evermore.

9 For, lo, thine enemies, O Lord, for, lo, thine enemies shall perish: all the workers of iniquity shall be scattered

10 But my horn shalt thou exalt like the horn of a unicorn: I shall be anointed with fresh oil.

11 Mine eye also shall see my desire on mine enemies: and mine ears shall hear my desire of the wicked that rise up against me.

12 The righteous shall flourish like the palm tree: he shall grow like a cedar in Lebanon.

13 Those that be planted in the house of the Lord: shall flourish in the courts of our God.

14 They shall still bring forth fruit in old age: they shall be fat and flourishing;

15 To show that the Lord is upright: he is my rock, and there is no unrighteousness in him

PSALM 93.

16 THE Lord reigneth, he is clothed with majesty; the Lord is clothed with strength, wherewith he hath girded himself: the world also is stablished, that it cannot be moved.

17 Thy throne is established of old: thou art from everlasting.

18 The floods have lifted up, O Lord, the floods have lifted up their voice: the floods lift up their waves.

19 The Lord on high is mightier than the noise of many waters: yea, than the mighty waves of the sea.

20 Thy testimonies are very sure: holiness becometh thine house, O Lord, for ever.

SELECTION 35.

PSALM 95.

1 O COME, let us sing unto the Lord: let us make a joyful noise to the Rock of our salvation.

2 Let us come before his presence with thanksgiving: and make a joyful noise unto him with psalms.

3 For the Lord is a great God: and a great King above all gods.

4 In his hand are the deep places of the earth: the strength of the hills is his also.

5 The sea is his, and he made it: and his hands formed the dry land.

6 O come, let us worship and bow down: let us kneel before the Lord our maker.

7 For he is our God; and we are the people of his pasture, and the sheep of his hand: To day if ye will hear his voice,

8 Harden not your heart, as in the provocation: and as in the day of temptation in the wilderness:

9 When your fathers tempted me: proved me, and saw my work.

10 Forty years long was I grieved with this generation, and said: It is a people that do err in their heart, and they have not known my ways:

11 Unto whom I sware in my wrath: that they should not enter into my rest.

PSALM 96.

12 O SING unto the Lord a new song: sing unto the Lord, all the earth.

13 Sing unto the Lord, bless his name: show forth his salvation from day to day.

14 Declare his glory among the heathen: his wonders among all people.

15 For the Lord is great, and greatly to be praised: he is to be feared above all gods.

16 For all the gods of the nations are idols: but the Lord made the heavens.

17 Honour and majesty are before him: strength and beauty are in his sanctuary.

18 Give unto the Lord, O ye kindreds of the people: give unto the Lord glory and strength.

19 Give unto the Lord the glory due unto his name: bring an offering, and come into his courts.

20 O worship the Lord in the beauty of holiness: fear before him, all the earth.

21 Say among the heathen that the Lord reigneth: the world also shall be established that it shall not be moved; he shall judge the people righteously.

22 Let the heavens rejoice, and let the earth be glad: let the sea roar, and the fulness thereof.

23 Let the field be joyful, and all that is therein: then shall all the trees of the wood rejoice

24 Before the Lord; for he cometh, for he cometh to judge the earth: he shall judge the world with righteousness, and the people with his truth.

SELECTION 36.

PSALM 97.

1 THE Lord reigneth; let the earth rejoice: let the multitude of isles be glad thereof.

2 Clouds and darkness are round about him: righteousness and judgment are the habitation of his throne.

3 A fire goeth before him. and burneth up his enemies round about.

4 His lightnings enlightened the world: the earth saw, and trembled.

5 The hills melted like wax at the presence of the Lord: at the presence of the Lord of the whole earth.

6 The heavens declare his righteousness: and all the people see his glory.

7 Confounded be all they that serve graven images, that boast themselves of idols : worship him, all ye gods.

8 Zion heard, and was glad: and the daughters of Judah rejoiced because of thy judgments, O Lord.

9 For thou, Lord, art high above all the earth: thou art exalted far above all gods.

10 Ye that love the Lord, hate evil: he preserveth the souls of his saints ; he delivereth them out of the hand of the wicked.

11 Light is sown for the righteous: and gladness for the upright in heart.

12 Rejoice in the Lord, ye righteous: and give thanks at the remembrance of his holiness.

Psalm 98.

13 O SING unto the Lord a new song ; for he hath done marvellous things: his right hand, and his holy arm, hath gotten him the victory.

14 The Lord hath made known his salvation: his righteousness hath he openly showed in the sight of the heathen.

15 He hath remembered his mercy and his truth toward the house of Israel : all the ends of the earth have seen the salvation of our God.

16 Make a joyful noise unto the Lord, all the earth : make a loud noise, and rejoice, and sing praise.

17 Sing unto the Lord with the harp: with the harp, and the voice of a psalm.

18 With trumpets and sound of cornet: make a joyful noise before the Lord, the King.

19 Let the sea roar, and the fulness thereof: the world, and they that dwell therein.

20 Let the floods clap their hands: let the hills be joyful together

21 Before the Lord ; for he cometh to judge the earth. with righteousness shall he judge the world, and the people with equity

PSALM 99.

22 THE Lord reigneth; let the people tremble . he sitteth between the cherubim; let the earth be moved

23 The Lord is great in Zion : and he is high above all the people

24 Let them praise thy great and terrible name : for it is holy.

25 The king's strength also loveth judgment : thou dost establish equity, thou executest judgment and righteousness in Jacob.

26 Exalt ye the Lord our God, and worship at his footstool : for he is holy.

27 Moses and Aaron among his priests, and Samuel among them that call upon his name : they called upon the Lord, and he answered them.

28 He spake unto them in the cloudy pillar: they kept his testimonies, and the ordinance that he gave them.

29 Thou answeredst them, O Lord our God : thou wast a God that forgavest them, though thou tookest vengeance of their inventions

30 Exalt the Lord our God, and worship at his holy hill : for the Lord our God is holy.

SELECTION 37.

PSALM 100.

1 MAKE a joyful noise unto the Lord: all ye lands.

2 Serve the Lord with gladness : come before his presence with singing.

3 Know ye that the Lord he is God · it is he that hath made us, and not we ourselves ; we are his people, and the sheep of his pasture.

4 Enter into his gates with thanksgiving, and into his courts with praise : be thankful unto him, and bless his name.

5 For the Lord is good, his mercy is everlasting : and his truth endureth to all generations.

PSALM 103.

6 BLESS the Lord, O my soul: and all that is within me, bless his holy name.

7 Bless the Lord, O my soul: and forget not all his benefits:

8 Who forgiveth all thine iniquities: who healeth all thy diseases;

9 Who redeemeth thy life from destruction: who crowneth thee with loving-kindness and tender mercies;

10 Who satisfieth thy mouth with good things: so that thy youth is renewed like the eagle's.

11 The Lord executeth righteousness and judgment: for all that are oppressed.

12 He made known his ways unto Moses: his acts unto the children of Israel.

13 The Lord is merciful and gracious: slow to anger, and plenteous in mercy.

14 He will not always chide: neither will he keep his anger for ever.

15 He hath not dealt with us after our sins: nor rewarded us according to our iniquities.

16 For as the heaven is high above the earth: so great is his mercy toward them that fear him

17 As far as the east is from the west: so far hath he removed our transgressions from us.

18 Like as a father pitieth his children: so the Lord pitieth them that fear him.

19 For he knoweth our frame: he remembereth that we are dust.

20 As for man, his days are as grass: as a flower of the field, so he flourisheth

21 For the wind passeth over it, and it is gone: and the place thereof shall know it no more.

22 But the mercy of the Lord is from everlasting to everlasting upon them that fear him: and his righteousness unto children's children;

23 To such as keep his covenant: and to those that remember his commandments to do them.

24 The Lord hath prepared his throne in the heavens: and his kingdom ruleth over all.

25 Bless the Lord, ye his angels, that excel in strength: that do his commandments, hearkening unto the voice of his word.

26 Bless ye the Lord, all ye his hosts: ye ministers of his, that do his pleasure.

27 Bless the Lord, all his works in all places of his dominion: bless the Lord, O my soul.

SELECTION 38.

PSALM 104.

1 BLESS the Lord, O my soul: O Lord my God, thou art very great; thou art clothed with honour and majesty;

2 Who coverest thyself with light as with a garment: who stretchest out the heavens like a curtain ;

3 Who layeth the beams of his chambers in the waters: who maketh the clouds his chariot; who walketh upon the wings of the wind ;

4 Who maketh his angels spirits: his ministers a flaming fire ;

5 Who laid the foundations of the earth: that it should not be removed for ever.

6 Thou coveredst it with the deep as with a garment: the waters stood above the mountains.

7 At thy rebuke they fled: at the voice of thy thunder they hasted away.

8 They go up by the mountains: they go down by the valleys unto the place which thou hast founded for them.

9 Thou hast set a bound that they may not pass over: that they turn not again to cover the earth.

10 He sendeth the springs into the valleys: which run among the hills.

11 They give drink to every beast of the field: the wild asses quench their thirst.

12 By them shall the fowls of the heaven have their habitation: which sing among the branches.

13 He watereth the hills from his chambers: the earth is satisfied with the fruit of thy works.

14 He causeth the grass to grow for the cattle, and herb for the service of man: that he may bring forth food out of the earth;

15 And wine that maketh glad the heart of man · and oil to make his face to shine, and bread which strengtheneth man's heart.

16 The trees of the Lord are full of sap: the cedars of Lebanon, which he hath planted ;

17 Where the birds make their nests: as for the stork, the fir trees are her house.

18 The high hills are a refuge for the wild goats: and the rocks for the conies.

19 He appointed the moon for seasons: the sun knoweth his going down

20 Thou makest darkness, and it is night: wherein all the beasts of the forest do creep forth.

21 The young lions roar after their prey: and seek their meat from God.

22 The sun ariseth, they gather themselves together: and lay them down in their dens.

23 Man goeth forth unto his work and to his labour: until the evening.

24 O Lord, how manifold are thy works. in wisdom hast thou made them all; the earth is full of thy riches.

25 So is this great and wide sea: wherein are things creeping innumerable, both small and great beasts.

26 There go the ships ; there is that leviathan: whom thou hast made to play therein.

27 These wait all upon thee: that thou mayst give them their meat in due season.

28 That thou givest them they gather: thou openest thine hand, they are filled with good

29 Thou hidest thy face, they are troubled: thou takest away their breath, they die, and return to their dust

30 Thou sendest forth thy spirit, they are created: and thou renewest the face of the earth.

31 The glory of the Lord shall endure for ever: the Lord shall rejoice in his works

32 He looketh on the earth, and it trembleth: he toucheth the hills, and they smoke.

33 I will sing unto the Lord as long as I live: I will sing praise to my God while I have my being.

34 My meditation of him shall be sweet: I will be glad in the Lord

35 Let the sinners be consumed out of the earth, and let the wicked be no more: Bless thou the Lord, O my soul. Praise ye the Lord.

SELECTION 39.

PSALM 107: 1-22.

1 O GIVE thanks unto the Lord, for he is good: for his mercy endureth for ever.

2 Let the redeemed of the Lord say so, whom he hath redeemed: from the hand of the enemy;

3 And gathered them out of the lands, from the east, and from the west: from the north, and from the south.

4 They wandered in the wilderness in a solitary way: they found no city to dwell in.

5 Hungry and thirsty: their soul fainted in them.

6 Then they cried unto the Lord in their trouble: and he delivered them out of their distresses.

7 And he led them forth by the right way: that they might go to a city of habitation.

8 Oh that men would praise the Lord for his goodness: and for his wonderful works to the children of men!

9 For he satisfieth the longing soul: and filleth the hungry soul with goodness

10 Such as sit in darkness and in the shadow of death: being bound in affliction and iron;

11 Because they rebelled against the words of God: and contemned the counsel of the Most High:

12 Therefore he brought down their heart with labour: they fell down, and there was none to help.

13 Then they cried unto the Lord in their trouble: and he saved them out of their distresses

14 He brought them out of darkness and the shadow of death: and brake their bands in sunder.

15 Oh that men would praise the Lord for his goodness: and for his wonderful works to the children of men!

16 For he hath broken the gates of brass: and cut the bars of iron in sunder

17 Fools, because of their transgression: and because of their iniquities, are afflicted.

18 Their soul abhorreth all manner of meat: and they draw near unto the gates of death.

19 Then they cry unto the Lord in their trouble: and he saveth them out of their distresses

20 He sent his word, and healed them and delivered them from their destructions

21 Oh that men would praise the Lord for his goodness: and for his wonderful works to the children of men!

22 And let them sacrifice the sacrifices of thanksgiving: and declare his works with rejoicing

SELECTION 40.

Psalm 107: 23-40.

1 THEY that go down to the sea in ships: that do business in great waters ;

2 These see the works of the Lord: and his wonders in the deep.

3 For he commandeth, and raiseth the stormy wind: which lifteth up the waves thereof.

4 They mount up to the heaven, they go down again to the depths: their soul is melted because of trouble.

5 They reel to and fro, and stagger like a drunken man. and are at their wit's end

6 Then they cry unto the Lord in their trouble: and he bringeth them out of their distresses

7 He maketh the storm a calm: so that the waves thereof are still.

8 Then are they glad because they be quiet: so he bringeth them unto their desired haven

9 Oh that men would praise the Lord for his goodness: and for his wonderful works to the children of men!

10 Let them exalt him also in the congregation of the people: and praise him in the assembly of the elders.

11 He turneth rivers into a wilderness: and the watersprings into dry ground ;

12 A fruitful land into barrenness: for the wickedness of them that dwell therein

13 He turneth the wilderness into a standing water · and dry ground into watersprings

14 And there he maketh the hungry to dwell: that they may prepare a city for habitation;

15 And sow the fields, and plant vineyards: which may yield fruits of increase.

16 He blesseth them also, so that they are multiplied greatly: and suffereth not their cattle to decrease.

17 Again, they are minished and brought low: through oppression, affliction, and sorrow.

18 He poureth contempt upon princes: and causeth them to wander in the wilderness, where there is no way.

19 Yet setteth he the poor on high from affliction: and maketh him families like a flock.

20 The righteous shall see it, and rejoice: and all iniquity shall stop her mouth.

21 Whoso is wise, and will observe these things: even they shall understand the loving-kindness of the Lord.

SELECTION 41.

PSALM 110.

1 THE Lord said unto my Lord: Sit thou at my right hand, until I make thine enemies thy footstool.

2 The Lord shall send the rod of thy strength out of Zion: rule thou in the midst of thine enemies.

3 Thy people shall be willing in the day of thy power, in the beauties of holiness from the womb of the morning: thou hast the dew of thy youth.

4 The Lord hath sworn, and will not repent: Thou art a priest for ever after the order of Melchizedek.

5 The Lord at thy right hand: shall strike through kings in the day of his wrath.

6 He shall judge among the heathen: he shall fill the places with the dead bodies; he shall wound the heads over many countries.

7 He shall drink of the brook in the way: therefore shall he lift up the head.

PSALM 111.

8 PRAISE ye the Lord. I will praise the Lord with my whole heart: in the assembly of the upright, and in the congregation.

9 The works of the Lord are great: sought out of all them that have pleasure therein.

10 His work is honourable and glorious: and his righteousness endureth forever.

11 He hath made his wonderful works to be remembered: the Lord is gracious and full of compassion.

12 He hath given meat unto them that fear him : he will ever be mindful of his covenant.

13 He hath showed his people the power of his works: that he may give them the heritage of the heathen.

14 The works of his hands are verity and judgment : all his commandments are sure.

15 They stand fast for ever and ever: and are done in truth and uprightness.

16 He sent redemption unto his people: he hath commanded his covenant for ever; holy and reverend is his name.

17 The fear of the Lord is the beginning of wisdom : a good understanding have all they that do his commandments , his praise endureth for ever.

Psalm 112.

18 PRAISE ye the Lord   Blessed is the man that feareth the Lord : that delighteth greatly in his commandments

19 His seed shall be mighty upon earth : the generation of the upright shall be blessed.

20 Wealth and riches shall be in his house: and his righteousness endureth for ever

21 Unto the upright there ariseth light in the darkness : he is gracious, and full of compassion, and righteous

22 A good man showeth favour, and lendeth : he will guide his affairs with discretion.

23 Surely he shall not be moved for ever : the righteous shall be in everlasting remembrance.

24 He shall not be afraid of evil tidings: his heart is fixed, trusting in the Lord.

25 His heart is established, he shall not be afraid: until he see his desire upon his enemies.

26 He hath dispersed, he hath given to the poor: his righteousness endureth for ever ; his horn shall be exalted with honour.

27 The wicked shall see it, and be grieved : he shall gnash with his teeth, and melt away ; the desire of the wicked shall perish

SELECTION 42.

Psalm 113. 1-6.

1 PRAISE ye the Lord   Praise, O ye servants of the Lord: praise the name of the Lord

2 Blessed be the name of the Lord : from this time forth and for evermore.

3 From the rising of the sun unto the going down of the same the Lord's name is to be praised.

4 The Lord is high above all nations : and his glory above the heavens.

5 Who is like unto the Lord our God : who dwelleth on high,

6 Who humbleth himself to behold the things: that are in heaven, and in the earth!

Psalm 115.

7 NOT unto us, O Lord, not unto us, but unto thy name give glory : for thy mercy, and for thy truth's sake.

8 Wherefore should the heathen say : Where is now their God ?

9 But our God is in the heavens : he hath done whatsoever he hath pleased.

10 Their idols are silver and gold: the work of men's hands.

11 They have mouths, but they speak not eyes have they, but they see not.

12 They have ears, but they hear not: noses have they, but they smell not :

13 They have hands, but they handle not: feet have they, but they walk not; neither speak they through their throat.

14 They that make them are like unto them : so is every one that trusteth in them.

15 O Israel, trust thou in the Lord · he is their help and their shield.

16 O house of Aaron, trust in the Lord: he is their help and their shield

17 Ye that fear the Lord, trust in the Lord : he is their help and their shield.

18 The Lord hath been mindful of us ; he will bless us : he will bless the house of Israel ; he will bless the house of Aaron.

19 He will bless them that fear the Lord: both small and great.

20 The Lord shall increase you more and more: you and your children.

21 Ye are blessed of the Lord: which made heaven and earth.

22 The heaven, even the heavens, are the Lord's: but the earth hath he given to the children of men.

23 The dead praise not the Lord: neither any that go down into silence.

24 But we will bless the Lord: from this time forth and for evermore. Praise the Lord.

SELECTION 43.

Psalm 116.

1 I LOVE the Lord: because he hath heard my voice and my supplications.

2 Because he hath inclined his ear unto me: therefore will I call upon him as long as I live.

3 The sorrows of death compassed me, and the pains of hell gat hold upon me: I found trouble and sorrow.

4 Then called I upon the name of the Lord: O Lord, I beseech thee, deliver my soul.

5 Gracious is the Lord, and righteous: yea, our God is merciful.

6 The Lord preserveth the simple: I was brought low, and he helped me.

7 Return unto thy rest, O my soul: for the Lord hath dealt bountifully with thee.

8 For thou hast delivered my soul from death: mine eyes from tears, and my feet from falling.

9 I will walk before the Lord: in the land of the living.

10 I believed, therefore have I spoken: I was greatly afflicted·

11 I said in my haste: All men are liars.

12 What shall I render unto the Lord: for all his benefits toward me ?

13 I will take the cup of salvation: and call upon the name of the Lord.

14 I will pay my vows unto the Lord: now in the presence of all his people.

15 Precious in the sight of the Lord: is the death of his saints

16 O Lord, truly I am thy servant: I am thy servant, and the son of thine handmaid, thou hast loosed my bonds.

17 I will offer to thee the sacrifice of thanksgiving: and will call upon the name of the Lord.

18 I will pay my vows unto the Lord : now in the presence of all his people,

19 In the courts of the Lord's house, in the midst of thee, O Jerusalem: Praise ye the Lord.

Psalm 117.

20 O PRAISE the Lord, all ye nations: praise him, all ye people

21 For his merciful kindness is great toward us: and the truth of the Lord endureth for ever.   Praise ye the Lord.

SELECTION 44.

Psalm 118.

1 O GIVE thanks unto the Lord; for he is good: because his mercy endureth for ever.

2 Let Israel now say: that his mercy endureth for ever.

3 Let the house of Aaron now say: that his mercy endureth for ever.

4 Let them now that fear the Lord say: that his mercy endureth for ever.

5 I called upon the Lord in distress : the Lord answered me, and set me in a large place.

6 The Lord is on my side, I will not fear: what can man do unto me ?

7 The Lord taketh my part with them that help me : therefore shall I see my desire upon them that hate me.

8 It is better to trust in the Lord : than to put confidence in man.

9 It is better to trust in the Lord: than to put confidence in princes.

10 All nations compassed me about: but in the name of the Lord will I destroy them.

11 They compassed me about; yea, they compassed me about : but in the name of the Lord I will destroy them.

12 They compassed me about like bees; they are quenched as the fire of thorns: for in the name of the Lord I will destroy them.

13 Thou hast thrust sore at me that I might fall : but the Lord helped me.

14 The Lord is my strength and song: and is become my salvation.

15 The voice of rejoicing and salvation is in the tabernacles of the righteous: the right hand of the Lord doeth valiantly.

16 The right hand of the Lord is exalted: the right hand of the Lord doeth valiantly.

17 I shall not die, but live: and declare the works of the Lord.

18 The Lord hath chastened me sore: but he hath not given me over unto death.

19 Open to me the gates of righteousness: I will go into them, and I will praise the Lord:

20 This gate of the Lord. into which the righteous shall enter.

21 I will praise thee. for thou hast heard me, and art become my salvation.

22 The stone which the builders refused: is become the head stone of the corner.

23 This is the Lord's doing: it is marvellous in our eyes

24 This is the day which the Lord hath made: we will rejoice and be glad in it.

25 Save now, I beseech thee, O Lord. O Lord, I beseech thee, send now prosperity

26 Blessed be he that cometh in the name of the Lord: we have blessed you out of the house of the Lord.

27 God is the Lord, which hath showed us light: bind the sacrifice with cords, even unto the horns of the altar.

28 Thou art my God, and I will praise thee: thou art my God, I will exalt thee.

29 O give thanks unto the Lord ; for he is good: for his mercy endureth for ever.

SELECTION 45.

PSALM 119: 1-24.

1 BLESSED are the undefiled in the way: who walk in the law of the Lord

2 Blessed are they that keep his testimonies. and that seek him with the whole heart.

3 They also do no iniquity: they walk in his ways

4 Thou hast commanded us: to keep thy precepts diligently.

5 O that my ways were directed: to keep thy statutes!

6 Then shall I not be ashamed: when I have respect unto all thy commandments.

7 I will praise thee with uprightness of heart: when I shall have learned thy righteous judgments.

8 I will keep thy statutes: O forsake me not utterly.

9 Wherewithal shall a young man cleanse his way: by taking heed thereto according to thy word.

10 With my whole heart have I sought thee: O let me not wander from thy commandments.

11 Thy word have I hid in mine heart: that I might not sin against thee.

12 Blessed art thou, O Lord: teach me thy statutes.

13 With my lips have I declared: all the judgments of thy mouth.

14 I have rejoiced in the way of thy testimonies: as much as in all riches.

15 I will meditate in thy precepts: and have respect unto thy ways.

16 I will delight myself in thy statutes: I will not forget thy word.

17 Deal bountifully with thy servant: that I may live, and keep thy word.

18 Open thou mine eyes: that I may behold wondrous things out of thy law.

19 I am a stranger in the earth: hide not thy commandments from me.

20 My soul breaketh for the longing: that it hath unto thy judgments at all times.

21 Thou hast rebuked the proud that are cursed: which do err from thy commandments.

21 Remove from me reproach and contempt: for I have kept thy testimonies.

23 Princes also did sit and speak against me: but thy servant did meditate in thy statutes.

24 Thy testimonies also are my delight: and my counsellors.

SELECTION 46.

PSALM 119: 33–48, 89-96.

1 TEACH me, O Lord, the way of thy statutes: and I shall keep it unto the end.

2 Give me understanding, and I shall keep thy law: yea, I shall observe it with my whole heart.

3 Make me to go in the path of thy commandments: for therein do I delight.

4 Incline my heart unto thy testimonies: and not to covetousness.

5 Turn away mine eyes from beholding vanity: and quicken thou me in thy way.

6 Stablish thy word unto thy servant: who is devoted to thy fear.

7 Turn away my reproach which I fear: for thy judgments are good.

8 Behold, I have longed after thy precepts: quicken me in thy righteousness.

9 Let thy mercies come also unto me, O Lord: even thy salvation, according to thy word.

10 So shall I have wherewith to answer him that reproacheth me: for I trust in thy word.

11 And take not the word of truth utterly out of my mouth: for I have hoped in thy judgments.

12 So shall I keep thy law: continually for ever and ever.

13 And I will walk at liberty: for I seek thy precepts.

14 I will speak of thy testimonies also before kings: and will not be ashamed.

15 And I will delight myself in thy commandments: which I have loved.

16 My hands also will I lift up unto thy commandments, which I have loved: and I will meditate in thy statutes.

17 For ever, O Lord: thy word is settled in heaven.

18 Thy faithfulness is unto all generations: thou hast established the earth, and it abideth.

19 They continue this day according to thine ordinances: for all are thy servants.

20 Unless thy law had been my delights: I should then have perished in mine affliction.

21 I will never forget thy precepts: for with them thou hast quickened me.

22 I am thine, save me: for I have sought thy precepts.

23 The wicked have waited for me to destroy me: but I will consider thy testimonies.

24 I have seen an end of all perfection: but thy commandment is exceeding broad

SELECTION 47.

PSALM 119. 97–120.

1 O HOW love I thy law: it is my meditation all the day.

2 Thou through thy commandments hast made me wiser than mine enemies: for they are ever with me.

3 I have more understanding than all my teachers: for thy testimonies are my meditation.

4 I understand more than the ancients: because I keep thy precepts.

5 I have refrained my feet from every evil way: that I might keep thy word.

6 I have not departed from thy judgments: for thou hast taught me.

7 How sweet are thy words unto my taste: yea, sweeter than honey to my mouth.

8 Through thy precepts I get understanding: therefore I hate every false way

9 Thy word is a lamp unto my feet: and a light unto my path.

10 I have sworn, and I will perform it: that I will keep thy righteous judgments.

11 I am afflicted very much: quicken me, O Lord, according unto thy word.

12 Accept, I beseech thee, the free-will offerings of my mouth, O Lord: and teach me thy judgments.

13 My soul is continually in my hand: yet do I not forget thy law.

14 The wicked have laid a snare for me: yet I erred not from thy precepts.

15 Thy testimonies have I taken as a heritage for ever: for they are the rejoicing of my heart.

16 I have inclined mine heart to perform thy statutes always: even unto the end.

17 I hate vain thoughts: but thy law do I love.

18 Thou art my hiding place and my shield. I hope in thy word.

19 Depart from me, ye evil doers: for I will keep the commandments of my God.

20 Uphold me according unto thy word, that I may live: and let me not be ashamed of my hope.

21 Hold thou me up, and I shall be safe: and I will have respect unto thy statutes continually.

22 Thou hast trodden down all them that err from thy statutes: for their deceit is falsehood.

23 Thou puttest away all the wicked of the earth like dross: therefore I love thy testimonies.

24 My flesh trembleth for fear of thee: and I am afraid of thy judgments.

SELECTION 48.

Psalm 121.

1 I WILL lift up mine eyes unto the hills: from whence cometh my help.

2 My help cometh from the Lord: which made heaven and earth.

3 He will not suffer thy foot to be moved: he that keepeth thee will not slumber.

4 Behold, he that keepeth Israel: shall neither slumber nor sleep.

5 The Lord is thy keeper: the Lord is thy shade upon thy right hand.

6 The sun shall not smite thee by day: nor the moon by night.

7 The Lord shall preserve thee from all evil: he shall preserve thy soul.

8 The Lord shall preserve thy going out and thy coming in: from this time forth, and even for evermore.

Psalm 122.

9 I WAS glad when they said unto me: Let us go into the house of the Lord.

10 Our feet shall stand within thy gates: O Jerusalem.

11 Jerusalem is builded as a city: that is compact together:

12 Whither the tribes go up, the tribes of the Lord: unto the testimony of Israel, to give thanks unto the name of the Lord.

13 For there are set thrones of judgment: the thrones of the house of David.

14 Pray for the peace of Jerusalem: they shall prosper that love thee.

15 Peace be within thy walls: and prosperity within thy palaces.

16 For my brethren and companions' sakes: I will now say, Peace be within thee.

17 Because of the house of the Lord our God: I will seek thy good.

PSALM 123.

18 UNTO thee lift I up mine eyes: O thou that dwellest in the heavens.

19 Behold, as the eyes of servants look unto the hand of their masters, and as the eyes of a maiden unto the hand of her mistress: so our eyes wait upon the Lord our God, until that he have mercy upon us.

20 Have mercy upon us, O Lord, have mercy upon us: for we are exceedingly filled with contempt.

21 Our soul is exceedingly filled with the scorning of those that are at ease: and with the contempt of the proud.

SELECTION 49.

PSALM 124.

1 IF it had not been the Lord who was on our side: now may Israel say ;

2 If it had not been the Lord who was on our side: when men rose up against us:

3 Then they had swallowed us up quick: when their wrath was kindled against us

4 Then the waters had overwhelmed us: the stream had gone over our soul:

5 Then the proud waters : had gone over our soul.

6 Blessed be the Lord: who hath not given us as a prey to their teeth.

7 Our soul is escaped as a bird out of the snare of the fowlers: the snare is broken, and we are escaped.

8 Our help is in the name of the Lord: who made heaven and earth.

9 THEY that trust in the Lord shall be as mount Zion: which cannot be removed, but abideth for ever.

10 As the mountains are round about Jerusalem: so the Lord is round about his people from henceforth even for ever.

11 For the rod of the wicked shall not rest upon the lot of the righteous: lest the righteous put forth their hands unto iniquity.

12 Do good, O Lord, unto those that be good: and to them that are upright in their hearts.

13 As for such as turn aside unto their crooked ways, the Lord shall lead them forth with the workers of iniquity: but peace shall be upon Israel.

14 WHEN the Lord turned again the captivity of Zion we were like them that dream.

15 Then was our mouth filled with laughter, and our tongue with singing: then said they among the heathen, The Lord hath done great things for them.

16 The Lord hath done great things for us: whereof we are glad.

17 Turn again our captivity, O Lord: as the streams in the south.

18 They that sow in tears: shall reap in joy.

19 He that goeth forth and weepeth, bearing precious seed: shall doubtless come again with rejoicing, bringing his sheaves with him.

20 EXCEPT the Lord build the house, they labour in vain that build it: except the Lord keep the city, the watchman waketh but in vain.

21 It is vain for you to rise up early, to sit up late, to eat the bread of sorrows: for so he giveth his beloved sleep.

22 Lo, children are a heritage of the Lord: and the fruit of the womb is his reward.

23 As arrows are in the hand of a mighty man: so are children of the youth.

24 Happy is the man that hath his quiver full of them: they shall not be ashamed, but they shall speak with the enemies in the gate.

SELECTION 50.

PSALM 130.

1 OUT of the depths have I cried : unto thee, O Lord.

2 Lord, hear my voice : let thine ears be attentive to the voice of my supplications.

3 If thou, Lord, shouldest mark iniquities : O Lord, who shall stand ?

4 But there is forgiveness with thee : that thou mayest be feared.

5 I wait for the Lord, my soul doth wait : and in his word do I hope.

6 My soul waiteth for the Lord more than they that watch for the morning : I say, more than they that watch for the morning.

7 Let Israel hope in the Lord : for with the Lord there is mercy, and with him is plenteous redemption.

8 And he shall redeem Israel : from all his iniquities.

PSALM 131.

9 LORD, my heart is not haughty, nor mine eyes lofty : neither do I exercise myself in great matters, or in things too high for me.

10 Surely I have behaved and quieted myself, as a child that is weaned of his mother : my soul is even as a weaned child.

11 Let Israel hope in the Lord : from henceforth and for ever.

PSALM 132.

12 LORD, remember David : and all his afflictions:

13 How he sware unto the Lord : and vowed unto the mighty God of Jacob;

14 Surely I will not come into the tabernacle of my house : nor go up into my bed ;

15 I will not give sleep to mine eyes : or slumber to mine eyelids,

16 Until I find out a place for the Lord: a habitation for the mighty God of Jacob.

17 Lo, we heard of it at Ephratah: we found it in the fields of the wood.

18 We will go into his tabernacles: we will worship at his footstool.

19 Arise, O Lord, into thy rest: thou, and the ark of thy strength.

20 Let thy priests be clothed with righteousness: and let thy saints shout for joy.

21 For thy servant David's sake: turn not away the face of thine anointed.

22 The Lord hath sworn in truth unto David; he will not turn from it: Of the fruit of thy body will I set upon thy throne.

23. If thy children will keep my covenant and my testimony that I shall teach them: their children shall also sit upon thy throne for evermore.

24 For the Lord hath chosen Zion: he hath desired it for his habitation.

25 This is my rest for ever: here will I dwell; for I have desired it.

26 I will abundantly bless her provision: I will satisfy her poor with bread.

27 I will also clothe her priests with salvation: and her saints shall shout aloud for joy.

28 There will I make the horn of David to bud: I have ordained a lamp for mine anointed.

29 His enemies will I clothe with shame: but upon himself shall his crown flourish.

SELECTION 51.

PSALM 133.

1 BEHOLD, how good and how pleasant it is: for brethren to dwell together in unity!

2 It is like the precious ointment upon the head, that ran down upon the beard: even Aaron's beard, that went down to the skirts of his garments ;

3 As the dew of Hermon, and as the dew that descended upon the mountains of Zion: for there the Lord commanded the blessing, even life for evermore.

PSALM 134.

4 BEHOLD, bless ye the Lord, all ye servants of the Lord: which by night stand in the house of the Lord.

5 Lift up your hands in the sanctuary: and bless the Lord.

6 The Lord that made heaven and earth: bless thee out of Zion.

PSALM 135.

7 PRAISE ye the Lord. Praise ye the name of the Lord: praise him, O ye servants of the Lord.

8 Ye that stand in the house of the Lord: in the courts of the house of our God,

9 Praise the Lord; for the Lord is good: sing praises unto his name; for it is pleasant.

10 For the Lord hath chosen Jacob unto himself: and Israel for his peculiar treasure.

11 For I know that the Lord is great: and that our Lord is above all gods.

12 Whatsoever the Lord pleased, that did he in heaven, and in earth: in the seas, and all deep places.

13 He causeth the vapors to ascend from the ends of the earth: he maketh lightnings for the rain; he bringeth the wind out of his treasuries.

14 Who smote the firstborn of Egypt: both of man and beast.

15 Who sent tokens and wonders into the midst of thee, O Egypt: upon Pharaoh, and upon all his servants.

16 Who smote great nations: and slew mighty kings;

17 Sihon king of the Amorites, and Og king of Bashan: and all the kingdoms of Canaan:

18 And gave their land for a heritage: a heritage unto Israel his people.

19 Thy name, O Lord, endureth for ever: and thy memorial, O Lord, throughout all generations.

20 For the Lord will judge his people. and he will repent himself concerning his servants.

21 The idols of the heathen are silver and gold: the work of men's hands.

22 They have mouths, but they speak not: eyes have they, but they see not;

23 They have ears but they hear not: neither is there any breath in their mouths.

24 They that make them are like unto them: so is every one that trusteth in them.

25 Bless the Lord, O house of Israel: bless the Lord, O house of Aaron:

26 Bless the Lord, O house of Levi: ye that fear the Lord, bless the Lord.

27 Blessed be the Lord out of Zion: which dwelleth at Jerusalem. Praise ye the Lord

SELECTION 52.

PSALM 136: 1-9, 23-26.

1 O GIVE thanks unto the Lord; for he is good: for his mercy endureth for ever.

2 O give thanks unto the God of gods: for his mercy endureth for ever.

3 O give thanks to the Lord of lords: for his mercy endureth for ever.

4 To him who alone doeth great wonders: for his mercy endureth for ever.

5 To him that by wisdom made the heavens: for his mercy endureth for ever.

6 To him that stretched out the earth above the waters: for his mercy endureth for ever.

7 To him that made great lights: for his mercy endureth for ever:

8 The sun to rule by day: for his mercy endureth for ever:

9 The moon and stars to rule by night: for his mercy endureth for ever.

10 Who remembered us in our low estate: for his mercy endureth for ever.

11 And hath redeemed us from our enemies: for his mercy endureth for ever.

12 Who giveth food to all flesh: for his mercy endureth for ever.

13 O give thanks unto the God of heaven: for his mercy endureth for ever.

PSALM 137: 1-6.

14 BY the rivers of Babylon, there we sat down: yea, we wept, when we remembered Zion.

15 We hanged our harps upon the willows: in the midst thereof.

16 For there they that carried us away captive required of us a song: and they that wasted us required of us mirth, saying, Sing us one of the songs of Zion.

17 How shall we sing the Lord's song: in a strange land?

18 If I forget thee, O Jerusalem: let my right hand forget her cunning.

19 If I do not remember thee, let my tongue cleave to the roof of my mouth: if I prefer not Jerusalem above my chief joy.

Psalm 138.

20 I WILL praise thee with my whole heart. before the gods will I sing praise unto thee.

21 I will worship toward thy holy temple, and praise thy name for thy loving-kindness and for thy truth: for thou hast magnified thy word above all thy name.

22 In the day when I cried thou answeredst me: and strengthenedst me with strength in my soul

23 All the kings of the earth shall praise thee, O Lord: when they hear the words of thy mouth.

24 Yea, they shall sing in the ways of the Lord: for great is the glory of the Lord.

25 Though the Lord be high, yet hath he respect unto the lowly: but the proud he knoweth afar off.

26 Though I walk in the midst of trouble, thou wilt revive me: thou shalt stretch forth thine hand against the wrath of mine enemies, and thy right hand shall save me.

27 The Lord will perfect that which concerneth me: thy mercy, O Lord, endureth for ever ; forsake not the works of thine own hands.

SELECTION 53.

Psalm 139: 1-12, 14-24.

1 O LORD: thou hast searched me, and known me.

2 Thou knowest my downsitting and mine uprising. thou understandest my thought afar off.

3 Thou compassest my path and my lying down: and art acquainted with all my ways.

4 For there is not a word in my tongue: but, lo, O Lord, thou knowest it altogether

5 Thou hast beset me behind and before: and laid thine hand upon me.

6 Such knowledge is too wonderful for me: it is high, I cannot attain unto it.

7 Whither shall I go from thy Spirit: or whither shall I flee from thy presence ?

8 If I ascend up into heaven, thou art there : if I make my bed in hell, behold, thou art there.

9 If I take the wings of the morning : and dwell in the uttermost parts of the sea ;

10 Even there shall thy hand lead me : and thy right hand shall hold me.

11 If I say, Surely the darkness shall cover me : even the night shall be light about me.

12 Yea, the darkness hideth not from thee ; but the night shineth as the day : the darkness and the light are both alike to thee.

13 I will praise thee ; for I am fearfully and wonderfully made: marvellous are thy works; and that my soul knoweth right well.

14 My substance was not hid from thee, when I was made in secret: and curiously wrought in the lowest parts of the earth.

15 Thine eyes did see my substance, yet being unperfect: and in thy book all my members were written, which in continuance were fashioned, when as yet there was none of them.

16 How precious also are thy thoughts unto me, O God: how great is the sum of them !

17 If I should count them, they are more in number than the sand: when I awake, I am still with thee.

18 Surely thou wilt slay the wicked, O God: depart from me therefore, ye bloody men.

19 For they speak against thee wickedly: and thine enemies take thy name in vain.

20 Do not I hate them, O Lord, that hate thee: and am not I grieved with those that rise up against thee ?

21 I hate them with perfect hatred: I count them mine enemies.

22 Search me, O God, and know my heart: try me, and know my thoughts:

23 And see if there be any wicked way in me: and lead me in the way everlasting.

SELECTION 54.

PSALM 141: 1-3.

1 LORD, I cry unto thee: make haste unto me; give unto my voice, when I cry unto thee.

2 Let my prayer be set forth before thee as incense: and the lifting up of my hands as the evening sacrifice.

3 Set a watch, O Lord, before my mouth: keep the door of my lips.

PSALM 142.

4 I CRIED unto the Lord with my voice: with my voice unto the Lord did I make my supplication.

5 I poured out my complaint before him: I showed before him my trouble.

6 When my spirit was overwhelmed within me, then thou knewest my path: In the way wherein I walked have they privily laid a snare for me.

7 I looked on my right hand, and beheld, but there was no man that would know me: refuge failed me; no man cared for my soul.

8 I cried unto thee, O Lord: I said, Thou art my refuge and my portion in the land of the living.

9 Attend unto my cry; for I am brought very low: deliver me from my persecutors; for they are stronger than I.

10 Bring my soul out of prison, that I may praise thy name: the righteous shall compass me about; for thou shalt deal bountifully with me.

PSALM 143: 1-11.

11 HEAR my prayer, O Lord, give ear to my supplications: in thy faithfulness answer me, and in thy righteousness.

12 And enter not into judgment with thy servant: for in thy sight shall no man living be justified.

13 For the enemy hath persecuted my soul: he hath smitten my life down to the ground: he hath made me to dwell in darkness, as those that have been long dead.

14 Therefore is my spirit overwhelmed within me: my heart within me is desolate.

15 I remember the days of old; I meditate on all thy works: I muse on the work of thy hands

16 I stretch forth my hands unto thee: my soul thirsteth after thee, as a thirsty land.

17 Hear me speedily, O Lord; my spirit faileth : hide not thy face from me, lest I be like unto them that go down into the pit.

18 Cause me to hear thy loving-kindness in the morning; for in thee do I trust: cause me to know the way wherein I should walk; for I lift up my soul unto thee.

19 Deliver me, O Lord, from mine enemies : I flee unto thee to hide me.

20 Teach me to do thy will; for thou art my God: thy Spirit is good; lead me into the land of uprightness.

21 Quicken me, O Lord, for thy name's sake: for thy righteousness' sake bring my soul out of trouble.

SELECTION 55.

Psalm 144.

1 BLESSED be the Lord my strength: which teacheth my hands to war, and my fingers to fight;

2 My goodness, and my fortress; my high tower, and my deliverer: my shield, and he in whom I trust; who subdueth my people under me.

3 Lord, what is man, that thou takest knowledge of him: or the son of man, that thou makest account of him !

4 Man is like to vanity: his days are as a shadow that passeth away.

5 Bow thy heavens, O Lord, and come down: touch the mountains, and they shall smoke.

6 Cast forth lightning, and scatter them: shoot out thine arrows, and destroy them.

7 Send thine hand from above: rid me, and deliver me out of great waters, from the hand of strange children;

8 Whose mouth speaketh vanity: and their right hand is a right hand of falsehood.

9 I will sing a new song unto thee, O God: upon a psaltery and an instrument of ten strings will I sing praises unto thee.

10 It is he that giveth salvation unto kings: who delivereth David his servant from the hurtful sword.

11 Rid me, and deliver me from the hand of strange children: whose mouth speaketh vanity, and their right hand is a right hand of falsehood:

12 That our sons may be as plants grown up in their youth: that our daughters may be as corner stones, polished after the similitude of a palace:

13 That our garners may be full, affording all manner of store: that our sheep may bring forth thousands and ten thousands in our streets:

14 That our oxen may be strong to labour; that there be no breaking in, nor going out: that there be no complaining in our streets.

15 Happy is that people, that is in such a case: yea, happy is that people, whose God is the Lord.

PSALM 146.

16 PRAISE ye the Lord: Praise the Lord, O my soul.

17 While I live will I praise the Lord: I will sing praises unto my God while I have any being.

18 Put not your trust in princes: nor in the son of man, in whom there is no help.

19 His breath goeth forth, he returneth to his earth: in that very day his thoughts perish.

20 Happy is he that hath the God of Jacob for his help: whose hope is in the Lord his God:

21 Which made heaven, and earth, the sea, and all that therein is: which keepeth truth for ever;

22 Which executeth judgment for the oppressed: which giveth food to the hungry. The Lord looseth the prisoners;

23 The Lord openeth the eyes of the blind; the Lord raiseth them that are bowed down: the Lord loveth the righteous;

24 The Lord preserveth the strangers; he relieveth the fatherless and widow: but the way of the wicked he turneth upside down

25 The Lord shall reign for ever: even thy God, O Zion, unto all generations. Praise ye the Lord.

SELECTION 56.

PSALM 145.

1 I WILL extol thee, my God, O King: and I will bless thy name for ever and ever.

2 Every day will I bless thee: and I will praise thy name for ever and ever.

3 Great is the Lord, and greatly to be praised: and his greatness is unsearchable.

4 One generation shall praise thy works to another: and shall declare thy mighty acts.

5 I will speak of the glorious honour of thy majesty: and of thy wondrous works.

6 And men shall speak of the might of thy terrible acts: and I will declare thy greatness.

7 They shall abundantly utter the memory of thy great goodness: and shall sing of thy righteousness.

8 The Lord is gracious, and full of compassion: slow to anger, and of great mercy.

9 The Lord is good to all: and his tender mercies are over all his works.

10 All thy works shall praise thee, O Lord: and thy saints shall bless thee.

11 They shall speak of the glory of thy kingdom: and talk of thy power;

12 To make known to the sons of men his mighty acts: and the glorious majesty of his kingdom.

13 Thy kingdom is an everlasting kingdom: and thy dominion endureth throughout all generations.

14 The Lord upholdeth all that fall: and raiseth up all those that be bowed down.

15 The eyes of all wait upon thee: and thou givest them their meat in due season.

16 Thou openest thine hand: and satisfiest the desire of every living thing.

17 The Lord is righteous in all his ways: and holy in all his works.

18 The Lord is nigh unto all them that call upon him: to all that call upon him in truth.

19 He will fulfil the desire of them that fear him: he also will hear their cry, and will save them.

20 The Lord preserveth all them that love him: but all the wicked will he destroy.

21 My mouth shall speak the praise of the Lord: and let all flesh bless his holy name for ever and ever.

SELECTION 57.

PSALM 147.

1 PRAISE ye the Lord; for it is good to sing praises unto our God: for it is pleasant; and praise is comely.

2 The Lord doth build up Jerusalem: he gathereth together the outcasts of Israel.

3 He healeth the broken in heart: and bindeth up their wounds.

4 He telleth the number of the stars: he calleth them all by their names.

5 Great is our Lord, and of great power: his understanding is infinite.

6 The Lord lifteth up the meek: he casteth the wicked down to the ground.

7 Sing unto the Lord with thanksgiving: sing praise upon the harp unto our God:

8 Who covereth the heaven with clouds, who prepareth rain for the earth: who maketh grass to grow upon the mountains.

9 He giveth to the beast his food: and to the young ravens which cry.

10 He delighteth not in the strength of the horse: he taketh not pleasure in the legs of a man.

11 The Lord taketh pleasure in them that fear him: in those that hope in his mercy.

12 Praise the Lord, O Jerusalem: praise thy God, O Zion.

13 For he hath strengthened the bars of thy gates: he hath blessed thy children within thee.

14 He maketh peace in thy borders: and filleth thee with the finest of the wheat.

15 He sendeth forth his commandment upon earth: his word runneth very swiftly.

16 He giveth snow like wool: he scattereth the hoar frost like ashes.

17 He casteth forth his ice like morsels: who can stand before his cold?

18 He sendeth out his word, and melteth them: he causeth his wind to blow, and the waters flow.

19 He showeth his word unto Jacob: his statutes and his judgments unto Israel.

20 He hath not dealt so with any nation: and as for his judgments, they have not known them. Praise ye the Lord.

SELECTION 58.

Psalm 148.

1 PRAISE ye the Lord. Praise ye the Lord from the heavens : praise him in the heights.

2 Praise ye him, all his angels: praise ye him, all his hosts.

3 Praise ye him, sun and moon: praise him, all ye stars of light.

4 Praise him, ye heavens of heavens: and ye waters that be above the heavens.

5 Let them praise the name of the Lord: for he commanded, and they were created.

6 He hath also stablished them for ever and ever: he hath made a decree which shall not pass.

7 Praise the Lord from the earth : ye dragons, and all deeps:

8 Fire, and hail; snow, and vapour: stormy wind fulfilling his word:

9 Mountains, and all hills: fruitful trees, and all cedars:

10 Beasts, and all cattle: creeping things, and flying fowl:

11 Kings of the earth, and all people: princes, and all judges of the earth:

12 Both young men, and maidens: old men, and children:

13 Let them praise the name of the Lord; for his name alone is excellent: his glory is above the earth and heaven.

14 He also exalteth the horn of his people, the praise of all his saints: even of the children of Israel, a people near unto him. Praise ye the Lord.

Psalm 149.

15 PRAISE ye the Lord. Sing unto the Lord a new song: and his praise in the congregation of saints.

16 Let Israel rejoice in him that made him: let the children of Zion be joyful in their King.

17 Let them praise his name in the dance: let them sing praises unto him with the timbrel and harp.

18 For the Lord taketh pleasure in his people: he will beautify the meek with salvation.

19 Let the saints be joyful in glory: let them sing aloud upon their beds.

20 Let the high praises of God be in their mouth: and a two-edged sword in their hand ;

21 To execute vengeance upon the heathen: and punishments upon the people ;

22 To bind their kings with chains : and their nobles with fetters of iron ;

23 To execute upon them the judgment written: this honour have all his saints.   Praise ye the Lord.

Psalm 150.

24 PRAISE ye the Lord.   Praise God in his sanctuary: praise him in the firmament of his power.

25 Praise him for his mighty acts: praise him according to his excellent greatness.

26 Praise him with the sound of the trumpet: praise him with the psaltery and harp.

27 Praise him with the timbrel and dance: praise him with stringed instruments and organs.

28 Praise him upon the loud cymbals: praise him upon the high sounding cymbals.

29 Let everything that hath breath praise the Lord: Praise ye the Lord.

SELECTION 59.

(For Good Friday.)

Psalm 22: 1-8; 11-31.

1 MY God, my God, why hast thou forsaken me : why art thou so far from helping me, and from the words of my roaring ?

2 O my God, I cry in the daytime, but thou hearest not: and in the night season, and am not silent.

3 But thou art holy: O thou that inhabitest the praises of Israel.

4 Our fathers trusted in thee: they trusted, and thou didst deliver them.

5 They cried unto thee, and were delivered they trusted in thee, and were not confounded.

6 But I am a worm, and no man: a reproach of men, and despised of the people.

7 All they that see me laugh me to scorn: they shoot out the lip, they shake the head, saying,

8 He trusted on the Lord that he would deliver him. let him deliver him, seeing he delighted in him.

9 Be not far from me; for trouble is near. for there is none to help.

10 Many bulls have compassed me: strong bulls of Bashan have beset me round.

11 They gaped upon me with their mouths: as a ravening and a roaring lion

12 I am poured out like water, and all my bones are out of joint: my heart is like wax ; it is melted in the midst of my bowels.

13 My strength is dried up like a potsherd , and my tongue cleaveth to my jaws : and thou hast brought me into the dust of death.

14 For dogs have compassed me ; the assembly of the wicked have inclosed me : they pierced my hands and my feet

15 I may tell all my bones: they look and stare upon me

16 They part my garments among them : and cast lots upon my vesture.

17 But be not thou far from me, O Lord O my strength, haste thee to help me.

18 Deliver my soul from the sword. my darling from the power of the dog.

19 Save me from the lion's mouth: for thou hast heard me from the horns of the unicorns.

20 I will declare thy name unto my brethren: in the midst of the congregation will I praise thee

21 Ye that fear the Lord, praise him: all ye the seed of Jacob, glorify him; and fear him, all ye the seed of Israel.

22 For he hath not despised nor abhorred the affliction of

the afflicted: neither hath he hid his face from him; but when he cried unto him, he heard.

23 My praise shall be of thee in the great congregation. I will pay my vows before them that fear him.

24 The meek shall eat and be satisfied; they shall praise the Lord that seek him : your heart shall live for ever.

25 All the ends of the world shall remember and turn unto the Lord: and all the kindreds of the nations shall worship before thee.

26 For the kingdom is the Lord's: and he is the governor among the nations.

27 All they that be fat upon earth shall eat and worship ; all they that go down to the dust shall bow before him : and none can keep alive his own soul.

28 A seed shall serve him: it shall be accounted to the Lord for a generation.

29 They shall come, and shall declare his righteousness . unto a people that shall be born, that he hath done this.

SELECTION 60.

(For Good Friday.)

PSALM 69: 1-21; 29-36.

1 SAVE me, O God: for the waters are come in unto my soul.

2 I sink in deep mire, where there is no standing: I am come into deep waters, where the floods overflow me.

3 I am weary of my crying; my throat is dried: mine eyes fail while I wait for my God.

4 They that hate me without a cause are more than the hairs of mine head: they that would destroy me, being mine enemies wrongfully, are mighty ; then I restored that which I took not away.

5 O God, thou knowest my foolishness: and my sins are not hid from thee.

6 Let not them that wait on thee, O Lord God of hosts, be ashamed for my sake: let not those that seek thee be confounded for my sake, O God of Israel.

7 Because for thy sake I have borne reproach: shame hath covered my face.

8 I am become a stranger unto my brethren: and an alien unto my mother's children.

9 For the zeal of thine house hath eaten me up: and the reproaches of them that reproached thee are fallen upon me.

10 When I wept, and chastened my soul with fasting: that was to my reproach.

11 I made sackcloth also my garment: and I became a proverb to them.

12 They that sit in the gate speak against me: and I was the song of the drunkards

13 But as for me, my prayer is unto thee, O Lord, in an acceptable time: O God, in the multitude of thy mercy hear me, in the truth of thy salvation.

14 Deliver me out of the mire, and let me not sink: let me be delivered from them that hate me, and out of the deep waters.

15 Let not the waterflood overflow me, neither let the deep swallow me up: and let not the pit shut her mouth upon me.

16 Hear me, O Lord; for thy loving-kindness is good: turn unto me according to the multitude of thy tender mercies.

17 And hide not thy face from thy servant: for I am in trouble; hear me speedily.

18 Draw nigh unto my soul, and redeem it: deliver me because of mine enemies.

19 Thou hast known my reproach, and my shame, and my dishonour: mine adversaries are all before thee.

20 Reproach hath broken my heart; and I am full of heaviness: and I looked for some to take pity, but there was none ; and for comforters, but I found none.

21 They gave me also gall for my meat: and in my thirst they gave me vinegar to drink.

22 But I am poor and sorrowful: let thy salvation, O God, set me up on high.

23 I will praise the name of God with a song: and will magnify him with thanksgiving.

24 This also shall please the Lord: better than an ox or bullock that hath horns and hoofs.

25 The humble shall see this, and be glad: and your heart shall live that seek God.

26 For the Lord heareth the poor: and despiseth not his prisoners.

27 Let the heaven and earth praise him: the seas, and every thing that moveth therein.

28 For God will save Zion, and will build the cities of Judah: that they may dwell there, and have it in possession.

29 The seed also of his servants shall inherit it: and they that love his name shall dwell therein.

GLORY be to the Father, and to the Son: and to the Holy Ghost.

As it was in the beginning, is now, and ever shall be: world without end. Amen.

ANCIENT HYMNS AND CANTICLES.

¶ *One of the first three Canticles may, if so desired, be sung at the beginning of Morning Service as the* OPENING HYMN.

I.

VENITE, EXULTEMUS DOMINO

O COME, let us sing unto the Lord · let us heartily rejoice in the strength of our salvation.

Let us come before His Presence with thanksgiving: and show ourselves glad in Him with psalms.

For the Lord is a great God: and a great King above all gods.

In His hand are all the corners of the earth: and the strength of the hills is His also

The sea is His, and He made it: and His hands prepared the dry land

O come, let us worship and fall down: and kneel before the Lord our Maker

For He is the Lord our God: and we are the people of His pasture, and the sheep of His hand.

O worship the Lord in the beauty of holiness: let the whole earth stand in awe of Him.

For He cometh, for He cometh to judge the earth and with righteousness to judge the world, and the people with His truth.

Glory be to the Father, and to the Son: and to the Holy Ghost,

As it was in the beginning, is now, and ever shall be. world without end. Amen.

II.

JUBILATE DEO

O BE joyful in the Lord, all ye lands: serve the Lord with gladness, and come before His Presence with a song.

Be ye sure that the Lord He is God; it is He that hath made us, and not we ourselves: we are His people, and the sheep of His pasture.

O go your way into His gates with thanksgiving, and into His courts with praise: be thankful unto Him, and speak good of His Name

For the Lord is gracious, His mercy is everlasting: and His truth endureth from generation to generation

Glory be to the Father, and to the Son: and to the Holy Ghost;

As it was in the beginning, is now, and ever shall be: world without end.   Amen.

III.

LÆTATUS SUM

I WAS glad when they said unto me: Let us go into the house of the Lord.

Our feet shall stand within thy gates: O Jerusalem.

Jerusalem is builded as a city: that is compact together:

Whither the tribes go up, the tribes of the Lord: unto the testimony of Israel, to give thanks unto the Name of the Lord.

For there are set thrones of judgment: the thrones of the house of David.

Pray for the peace of Jerusalem: they shall prosper that love thee.

Peace be within thy walls: and prosperity within thy palaces.

For my brethren and companions' sakes: I will now say, Peace be within thee.

Because of the house of the Lord our God: I will seek thy good.

Glory be to the Father, and to the Son: and to the Holy Ghost;

As it was in the beginning, is now, and ever shall be: world without end.   Amen.

IV.

Te Deum Laudamus.

WE praise Thee, O God: we acknowledge Thee to be the Lord.

All the earth doth worship Thee : the Father everlasting.

To Thee all Angels cry aloud: the Heavens, and all the Powers therein;

To Thee Cherubim and Seraphim: continually do cry,

Holy, Holy, Holy: Lord God of Sabaoth;

Heaven and earth are full of the Majesty: of Thy glory.

The glorious company of the Apostles: praise Thee.

The goodly fellowship of the Prophets: praise Thee.

The noble army of Martyrs: praise Thee.

The holy Church throughout all the world: doth acknowledge Thee;

The Father: of an infinite Majesty ;

Thine adorable, true: and only Son ;

Also the Holy Ghost: the Comforter.

Thou art the King of Glory: O Christ.

Thou art the everlasting Son: of the Father.

When Thou tookest upon Thee to deliver man : Thou didst humble Thyself to be born of a Virgin.

When Thou hadst overcome the sharpness of death: Thou didst open the Kingdom of Heaven to all believers.

Thou sittest at the right hand of God: in the glory of the Father.

We believe that Thou shalt come: to be our Judge.

We therefore pray Thee, help Thy servants: whom Thou hast redeemed with Thy precious blood.

Make them to be numbered with Thy Saints: in glory everlasting.

O Lord, save Thy people: and bless Thine heritage.

Govern them: and lift them up for ever.

Day by day: we magnify Thee;

And we worship Thy Name: ever, world without end.

Vouchsafe, O Lord: to keep us this day without sin.

O Lord, have mercy upon us: have mercy upon us.

O Lord let Thy mercy be upon us: as our trust is in Thee.

O Lord, in Thee have I trusted: let me never be confounded.

V.

Gloria in Excelsis.

GLORY be to God on high: and on earth peace, good will towards men.

We praise Thee, we bless Thee, we worship Thee: we glorify Thee, we give thanks to Thee for Thy great glory.

O Lord God, heavenly King: God the Father Almighty.

O Lord, the only-begotten Son, Jesus Christ: O Lord God, Lamb of God, Son of the Father,

That takest away the sins of the world: have mercy upon us.

Thou that takest away the sins of the world: receive our prayer.

Thou that sittest at the right hand of God the Father: have mercy upon us.

For Thou only art holy: Thou only art the Lord.

Thou only, O Christ, with the Holy Ghost: art most high in the glory of God the Father.   Amen.

VI.

Benedicite, Omnia Opera Domini.

O ALL ye Works of the Lord, bless ye the Lord: praise Him, and magnify Him for ever.

O ye Angels of the Lord, bless ye the Lord: praise Him, and magnify Him for ever.

O ye Heavens, bless ye the Lord : praise Him, and magnify Him for ever.

O ye Waters that be above the firmament, bless ye the Lord: praise Him, and magnify Him for ever.

O all ye Powers of the Lord, bless ye the Lord: praise Him, and magnify Him for ever.

O ye Sun and Moon, bless ye the Lord: praise Him, and magnify Him for ever.

O ye Stars of heaven, bless ye the Lord: praise Him, and magnify Him for ever.

O ye Showers and Dew, bless ye the Lord: praise Him, and magnify Him for ever.

O ye Winds of God, bless ye the Lord: praise Him, and magnify Him for ever.

O ye Fire and Heat, bless ye the Lord: praise Him, and magnify Him for ever.

O ye Winter and Summer, bless ye the Lord· praise Him, and magnify Him for ever.

O ye Dews and Frosts, bless ye the Lord: praise Him, and magnify Him for ever.

O ye Frost and Cold, bless ye the Lord : praise Him, and magnify Him for ever.

O ye Ice and Snow, bless ye the Lord: praise Him, and magnify Him for ever.

O ye Nights and Days, bless ye the Lord. praise Him, and magnify Him for ever.

O ye Light and Darkness, bless ye the Lord: praise Him, and magnify Him for ever.

O ye Lightnings and Clouds, bless ye the Lord: praise Him, and magnify Him for ever.

O let the Earth bless the Lord: yea, let it praise Him, and magnify Him for ever.

O ye Mountains and Hills, bless ye the Lord: praise Him, and magnify Him for ever.

O all ye Green Things upon the earth, bless ye the Lord: praise Him, and magnify Him for ever.

O ye Wells, bless ye the Lord : praise Him, and magnify Him for ever.

O ye Seas and Floods, bless ye the Lord: praise Him, and magnify Him for ever.

O ye Whales, and all that move in the waters, bless ye the Lord . praise Him, and magnify Him for ever.

O all ye Fowls of the air, bless ye the Lord : praise Him, and magnify Him for ever.

O all ye Beasts and Cattle, bless ye the Lord : praise Him, and magnify Him for ever.

O ye Children of Men, bless ye the Lord. praise Him, and magnify Him for ever.

O let Israel bless the Lord: praise Him, and magnify Him for ever.

O ye Priests of the Lord, bless ye the Lord: praise Him, and magnify Him for ever.

O ye Servants of the Lord, bless ye the Lord: praise Him, and magnify Him for ever.

O ye Spirits and Souls of the Righteous, bless ye the Lord: praise Him, and magnify Him for ever.

O ye holy and humble Men of heart, bless ye the Lord: praise Him, and magnify Him for ever.

Glory be to the Father, and to the Son: and to the Holy Ghost;

As it was in the beginning, is now, and ever shall be: world without end. Amen.

VII.

MAGNIFICAT.

MY soul doth magnify the Lord: and my spirit hath rejoiced in God my Saviour.

For He hath regarded: the lowliness of His handmaiden.

For behold, from henceforth: all generations shall call me blessed.

For He that is mighty hath magnified me: and holy is His Name.

And His mercy is on them that fear Him: throughout all generations.

He hath showed strength with His arm: He hath scattered the proud in the imagination of their hearts.

He hath put down the mighty from their seat: and hath exalted the humble and meek.

He hath filled the hungry with good things: and the rich He hath sent empty away.

He remembering His mercy hath holpen His servant Israel: as He promised to our forefathers, Abraham and his seed, for ever.

Glory be to the Father, and to the Son: and to the Holy Ghost;

As it was in the beginning, is now, and ever shall be: world without end. Amen.

VIII.

BENEDICTUS.

BLESSED be the Lord God of Israel: for He hath visited and redeemed His people;

And hath raised up a mighty salvation for us : in the house of His servant David ;

As He spake by the mouth of His holy Prophets: which have been since the world began;

That we should be saved from our enemies : and from the hand of all that hate us.

To perform the mercy promised to our forefathers: and to remember His holy covenant;

To perform the oath which He sware to our forefather Abraham : that He would give us ;

That we being delivered out of the hand of our enemies: might serve Him without fear ;

In holiness and righteousness before Him: all the days of our life.

And thou, child, shalt be called the prophet of the Highest: for thou shalt go before the face of the Lord to prepare His ways;

To give knowledge of salvation unto His people: for the remission of their sins,

Through the tender mercy of our God: whereby the dayspring from on high hath visited us ;

To give light to them that sit in darkness, and in the shadow of death: and to guide our feet into the way of peace.

Glory be to the Father, and to the Son: and to the Holy Ghost;

As it was in the beginning, is now, and ever shall be : world without end.   Amen.

IX.

Nunc Dimittis.

LORD, now lettest thou Thy servant depart in peace: according to Thy word.

For mine eyes have seen: Thy salvation,

Which Thou hast prepared: before the face of all people ;

To be a light to lighten the Gentiles : and to be the glory of Thy people Israel.

Glory be to the Father, and to the Son: and to the Holy Ghost ;

As it was in the beginning, is now, and ever shall be: world without end.   Amen.

X.

CANTATE DOMINO.

O SING unto the Lord a new song: for He hath done marvellous things.

With His own right hand, and with His holy arm: hath He gotten Himself the victory.

The Lord declared His salvation: His righteousness hath He openly showed in the sight of the heathen.

He hath remembered His mercy and truth toward the house of Israel: and all the ends of the world have seen the salvation of our God.

Show yourselves joyful unto the Lord, all ye lands: sing, rejoice, and give thanks.

Praise the Lord upon the harp: sing to the harp with a psalm of thanksgiving.

With trumpets also and shawms: O show yourselves joyful before the Lord, the King.

Let the sea make a noise, and all that therein is: the round world, and they that dwell therein.

Let the floods clap their hands, and let the hills be joyful together before the Lord: for He cometh to judge the earth.

With righteousness shall He judge the world: and the people with equity.

Glory be to the Father, and to the Son: and to the Holy Ghost;

As it was in the beginning, is now, and ever shall be: world without end.   Amen.

XI.

BONUM EST CONFITERI.

IT is a good thing to give thanks unto the Lord: and to sing praises unto Thy Name, O Most Highest;

To tell of Thy loving-kindness early in the morning: and of Thy truth in the night season;

Upon an instrument of ten strings, and upon the lute: upon a loud intsrument, and upon the harp.

For Thou, Lord, hast made me glad through Thy works:

and I will rejoice in giving praise for the operations of Thy hands.

Glory be to the Father, and to the Son : and to the Holy Ghost;

As it was in the beginning, is now, and ever shall be: world without end.   Amen.

XII.

BENEDIC, ANIMA MEA.

PRAISE the Lord, O my soul: and all that is within me, praise His holy Name.

Praise the Lord, O my soul: and forget not all His benefits :

Who forgiveth all thy sin: and healeth all thine infirmities ;

Who saveth thy life from destruction: and crowneth thee with mercy and loving-kindness.

O praise the Lord, ye angels of His, ye that excel in strength: ye that fulfil His commandment, and hearken unto the voice of His word.

O praise the Lord, all ye His hosts : ye servants of His that do His pleasure.

O speak good of the Lord, all ye works of His, in all places of His dominion: praise thou the Lord, O my soul.

Glory be to the Father, and to the Son : and to the Holy Ghost;

As it was in the beginning, is now, and ever shall be. world without end.   Amen.

XIII.

DEUS MISEREATUR.

GOD be merciful unto us, and bless us : and show us the light of His countenance, and be merciful unto us ;

That Thy way may be known upon earth: Thy saving health among all nations.

Let the people praise Thee, O God: yea, let all the people praise Thee.

O let the nations rejoice and be glad: for Thou shalt

judge the folk righteously, and govern the nations upon earth.

Let the people praise Thee, O God: yea, let all the people praise Thee.

Then shall the earth bring forth her increase: and God, even our own God, shall give us His blessing.

God shall bless us : and all the ends of the world shall fear Him.

Glory be to the Father, and to the Son: and to the Holy Ghost ;

As it was in the beginning, is now, and ever shall be: world without end.   Amen.

Printed in the USA
CPSIA information can be obtained
at www.ICGtesting.com
CBHW080103290624
10867CB00009B/379